To Ron & Sherry —

Norman Rockwell

This Year in Jerusalem

This Year in Jerusalem

MORDECAI RICHLER

Alfred A. Knopf Canada

PUBLISHED BY ALFRED A. KNOPF CANADA

Copyright © 1994 by Mordecai Richler Productions Limited

All rights reserved under International and Pan-American Copyright Conventions. Published in Canada in 1994 by Alfred A. Knopf Canada, Toronto, and simultaneously in the United States by Alfred A. Knopf Inc., New York. Distributed by Random House of Canada Limited, Toronto.

First Edition

Canadian Cataloguing in Publication Data
Richler, Mordecai, 1931–
This year in Jerusalem

ISBN 0-394-28055-5

1. Richler, Mordecai, 1931– – Biography. 2. Richler, Mordecai, 1931– – Journeys – Israel. 3. Jewish-Arab relations – 1949–. 4. Israel – History. 5. Novelists, Canadian (English) – 20th century – Biography.★ 6. Jews – Quebec (Province) – Montreal – Biography. I. Title.

PS8535.I382Z53   1994   C813'.54   C94-931199-5
PR9199.3.R53Z474   1994

Printed and bound in the United States of America

FOR EZRA LIFSHITZ,
SOL AND FAYGE COHEN,
MY COUSIN BENJY,
AND THE OTHERS WHO
MADE ALIYAH

For two thousand years our people dreamed. For two thousand years Jews remembered Zion and prayed for deliverance. In song, in prose, in their hearts and thoughts, Jews kept alive the dream of the Return to Zion — and the dream kept them alive. For two thousand years Jews piously hoped that the Return would take place "quickly in our time."

It has happened and is happening in *our* time. Ours will be the time written of, sung about, talked about as long as the Jewish people will live. Ours will be the generation of the Third Temple.

How fortunate we all are! How happy we all are!... We call upon all Jewish youth in America, but upon the members of Habonim first and foremost. Let us rise and accept the challenge of history! Ours is the chosen generation! We dare to believe that a new code of ethics will blaze forth from Zion, a new life based on the principles of equality and social justice, the code of the prophets themselves.

The new Eretz Israel calls upon us. Let us go and rebuild Zion. Our help, our support, our selves are needed.

Let us arise and build!

Resolution published by
Habonim's National Executive Committee,
November 1947

I would much rather see reasonable agreement with the Arabs on the basis of living together in peace than the creation of a Jewish state... my awareness of the essential nature of Judaism resists the idea of a Jewish state with borders, an army and a measure of temporal power, no matter how modest. I am afraid of the inner damage Judaism will suffer — especially from the development of a narrow nationalism within our own ranks.

Albert Einstein, 1938

This Year in Jerusalem

⬦ *One* ⬦

*I*N 1944, I WAS AWARE OF THREE YOUTH GROUPS committed to the compelling idea of an independent Jewish state: Hashomer Hatza'ir (The Young Guard), Young Judaea, and Habonim (The Builders).

Hashomer Hatza'ir was resolutely Marxist. According to intriguing reports I had heard, it was the custom, on their kibbutzim already established in Palestine, for boys and girls under the age of eighteen to shower together. Hashomer Hatza'ir members in Montreal included a boy I shall call Shloime Schneiderman, a high-school classmate of mine. In 1944, when we were still in the eighth grade, Shloime enjoyed a brief celebrity after his photograph appeared on the front page of the Montreal *Herald*. Following a two-cent rise in the price of chocolate bars, he had been a leader in a demonstration, holding high a placard that read: DOWN WITH THE 7¢ CHOCOLATE BAR. Hashomer Hatza'ir members wore uniforms at their meetings: blue shirts and neckerchiefs. "*They* had real court martials," wrote Marion Magid in a memoir about her days in Habonim in the Bronx in the early fifties, "group analysis, the girls were not allowed to wear lipstick."[1] Whereas, in my experience, the sweetly scented girls who belonged to Young Judaea favored pearls and cashmere twinsets. They lived on leafy streets in the suburb of Outremont, in detached cottages that had heated bathroom towel racks, basement playrooms, and a plaque hanging on the wall behind the wet bar testifying to the number of trees their parents had paid to have planted in Eretz Yisrael, the land of Israel.

I joined Habonim — the youth group of a Zionist political party, rooted in socialist doctrine — shortly after my bar mitzvah, during my first year at Baron Byng High School. I had been recruited by a Room 41 classmate whom I shall call Jerry Greenfeld.

Jerry seemed blessed. Only a few months older than I was, he already had to shave every day. Rubbing his jaw as he shot out of school late in the afternoon, bound for an hour or two of snooker at the Mount Royal Billiards Academy, he would wink and say, "Four o'clock shadow," and I would burn with envy. School days he usually wore a sharkskin windbreaker with JERRY embossed in gold letters across his broad back and a hockey-team crest over his heart. Jerry appeared effortlessly gifted in all those pursuits in which I longed, unavailingly, to shine. He had fought in the Golden Gloves for the YMHA, eliminated in a semifinal bout against an Irish boy out of Griffintown only because, he explained, the referee was an obvious anti-Semite. He was a high scorer on our school basketball team. He also pitched for a baseball team that actually wore uniforms — the North End Maccabees, sponsored by a local scrap dealer. At the occasional late-afternoon "tea dance" in our school gym, Jerry, his manner breezy, could entice pretty girls in grade ten, maybe three years older than he was, to jitterbug with him. His mother had died when he was six years old and his father didn't care what time he came home. Saturday nights he would strut down St. Urbain Street, wearing a one-button roll jacket, and trousers rakishly pegged, if not quite zoot. If he condescended to stop at the corner of Fairmount Street, immediately outside Wilensky's store, where we used to hang out, he might grant us a peek at the condom he kept in his wallet. "Just in case," he'd say.

One day Jerry approached me in the schoolyard and asked, "Can you help me out this Saturday aft?"

"Sure. How?"

"You own a baseball mitt?"

"Sure."

Starting that Saturday afternoon, Jerry allowed me to catch for him in the lane behind our cold-water flat as he worked on his fastball, low and just nibbling the outside of the plate, which he assumed would one day attract the attention of Labish "Lefty" Mandelcorn. Labish had survived a season playing left field for a Class C team in the Carolinas, and had a photograph of himself and several other players chatting with Connie Mack. If not for his asthma, he would have made the majors. Never without his pencil, its end chewed out, a spiral notebook, and his wrinkled brown bag of sunflower seeds, he now claimed to be a local scout for the Brooklyn Dodgers, parent team of our Montreal Royals of the Triple A International League. It was on his recommendation, he said, that two indigenous French Canadian infielders, Roland Gladu and Stan Bréard, had been signed by the Royals. But I had my suspicions. He often dropped the name "Branch," and I had read in Dink Carroll's column in the Montreal *Gazette* that everybody, even Leo Durocher, called the Dodgers' general manager "Mr. Rickey."

Following one Saturday afternoon workout, Jerry bounced a mock punch off my shoulder, as was his habit now, and asked, "What are you doing tonight?"

"Eff-all."

"Let's go to supper at Dinty Moore's."

That was not a neighborhood delicatessen but a real restaurant. Downtown. Beyond the pale. "Are you kidding?" I asked.

Jerry paid for our corned beef and cabbage, and apple pie and ice cream, with American dollars. Real money. He left the waitress a big tip and told her she was a looker. And then, swearing me to secrecy, he revealed that his father had been married once before, and that he had a stepbrother who was flying a P-38 with the U.S. Fifth Air Force in the Pacific *right now*, and already had five Japs to his credit. Gary sent Jerry a few bucks from time to time, and when the war was over he was going to fetch him and the two of them would settle in Palestine.

"Why does it have to be such a secret? Gary, I mean."

"Hey, I've already blabbed too much. Why don't you come to Habonim with me on Friday night? If you like it, maybe you'll join."

So Jerry, chewing on a matchstick, picked me up after supper on Friday and then we went to collect two other *chaverim* (comrades), whom I shall call Hershey Bloom and Myer Plotnik. Hershey, six foot even then, was a member of our high-school student council executive, an admirer of John Gunther's books and of movies with social content (*Watch on the Rhine, The Corn Is Green*), an awfully serious boy with puffy red cheeks and a weakness for chocolate éclairs, his big belly bulging out of his trousers. His father had died of a heart attack at the age of thirty-seven and Hershey was convinced that he was destined to do the same, which added to his aura of importance in our eyes. "It's in my genes," he often said.

Myer, with his tight curly black hair and quick laughter and bouncy carefree walk, radiated good will and was popular with the girls, who warmed to his nonthreatening nature. His father was a barber whose favorite routine depended on having a new customer in his chair, the man's face swaddled in hot wet towels. Then Mr. Plotnik would sharpen his straight razor on the strop and ask, "Hey, you ever seen *Sweeney Todd?*"

"Who?"

Gleefully lathering the man's face, he would tell him about it. "You know, that play about the *meshuggener* barber who used to slit men's throats. Some people say it was based on a true life story. Anyways...."

Mr. Plotnik's specialty for teenagers was the pompadour, and for an additional twenty-five cents he would also squeeze out unwanted blackheads with a special tool.

Slouching toward Habonim meetings with Jerry, Hershey, and Myer, the four of us puffing on Sweet Caps, became a Friday night ritual that continued unbroken through almost four years of high school, by which time Jerry had to quit Habonim in disgrace. Our rambling, three-story meeting house was in the heart of Montreal's old working-class Jewish quarter, on Jeanne Mance Street, which we used to mispronounce Jean Mance, provoking exasperated laughter from French Canadians.

Habonim, I discovered, had been founded in Eastern Europe in 1898. Near the turn of the century, socialists from the Pale of Settlement, *shtetl* progeny, and the Zionists — whose modern founder, Theodor Herzl, had sprung from the bourgeoisie of the Austro-Hungarian Empire — were at political loggerheads. The socialists, especially the Marxists with their international bias, were convinced that Judaism was a dying faith, a reactionary relic bound to expire with capitalism. The Zionists, determined nationalists, were dedicated to a revival of a Jewish state in Palestine, the Old Testament their deed, evidence of a God-given freehold.

In 1898, this philosophical incompatibility was resolved for some by Nachman Syrkin, a Russian-born graduate student in Berlin who advocated an ideological mixed marriage of a sort.

The special destiny of the Jews, he argued, could only be fulfilled in a collectivist country. "The wheels of the Jewish republic will not turn without the strong arms of the Jewish worker,"
he wrote. "The Jewish state must necessarily be socialist."[2]
Before the year was out, dozens of socialist groups calling themselves Poale Zion (The Workers of Zion) began to sprout in
Eastern Europe. In 1901, Syrkin published a broadside in which
he encouraged Jews to do battle with two heresies: the assimi-
lationism of the Marxists and the capitalist convictions of the
largely conservative Zionist movement. In 1903, David Ben-
Gurion, only seventeen years old and still answering to the
name of David Gruen, joined Poale Zion in Plonsk, Poland.
Three years later he settled in the Yishuv, as the Zionist communities in Palestine were known before the establishment of
the state of Israel.

There were Habonim chapters active in both England and
South Africa as early as 1928. The North American genesis can
be traced to the opening of a primitive summer camp by Poale
Zion in 1932: Camp Kvutza in Accord, New York. It was there
that the idea of introducing children between the ages of ten
and sixteen to scouting was first discussed. "The English word
'scouting' did not sit well with many members," wrote Jacob
Katzman. "It raised the image of the American Boy Scouts,
whom many of us saw as a jingoistic, strutting band of not-so-
innocent youth. In the labor movement, there had been allega-
tions that the Boy Scouts had been scabs in some places."[3] So,
rather than "scouting," the Hebrew word *tzofiut* — which, as it
happens, translates as "scouting" — was accepted. Then, after
debates spun out over two years, it was allowed that "self-fulfill-
ment through *aliyah*" (the ascent to Eretz Yisrael) need not be
the sole objective of a member of Habonim. Those *chaverim*
who did not immigrate by the age of twenty would not be ban-
ished from the movement. Instead, we would participate in "the

struggle of the working class against capitalism, fascism and oppression, and for the establishment of socialism" in America.

MOST OF the boys and girls in our Habonim chapters had been
raised, like me, in homes where the *pushke*, the blue-and-white
coin-collection box for the Jewish National Fund to buy land in
Eretz Yisrael, squatted on the kitchen table. It also waited next
to the cash register in just about every neighborhood store, including Mr. Palucci's shoeshine and hat-blocking parlor on Park
Avenue, but not at Debrofsky's Dry Goods on the Main, which
featured a tinted photograph of Stalin in the window, surrounded by garlands of faded red crêpe paper. All but a few of
the *chaverim* had attended a parochial primary school, either the
Folkschule or the Talmud Torah, before graduating to Baron
Byng or, if they lived in Outremont, to Strathcona Academy.
I had been to the Talmud Torah, where we studied modern
Hebrew in the morning and managed the obligatory English
and French curriculum in the afternoon. The other *chaverim*
had, for the most part, sprung from secular or only fitfully observant homes that honored Jewish cultural traditions and cherished
Yiddish literature, but were scornful of "religious mumbo-
jumbo." I, however, belonged to a Hasidic family and, after
parochial-school classes were out, had to carry on, two afternoons a week, to the Young Israel Synagogue, to study Talmud
with Mr. Yalofsky.

"The rich man is asked, 'Why did you not occupy yourself
with Torah?' If he answers that he was rich and worried about
his possessions, it is said to him, 'Were you more wealthy than
Rabbi Eleazer ben Charsom, of whom it is related that his father bequeathed to him a thousand cities and a corresponding
fleet of a thousand ships; yet every day he slung a bag of flour

over his shoulder and went from city to city and from province to province in order to learn Torah?'"[4]

I had to endure a good deal of needling from schoolmates because I wasn't allowed to switch the lights on or off, answer the phone, or listen to the radio on the Sabbath.

"Tell your father, you turkey you, that there were no radios — no Charlie McCarthy or Fibber McGee and Molly — when the laws were handed down at Sinai."

My maternal grandfather, Rabbi Yudel Rosenberg, was a celebrated Hasidic scholar, as well as a writer of playful short stories, the author of more than twenty books (some in Yiddish, others in Hebrew), published first in Warsaw and then in either New York or Montreal. Born in the Polish *shtetl* of Skaryszew in 1859, he was sufficiently proficient in Russian by 1891 to acquire an official rabbi's license from the government. He practiced in Lublin, Warsaw, and Lodz before immigrating to Canada in 1913, settling in Toronto and then, six years later, moving on to Montreal, where he preached until his death in 1935.

Rabbi Rosenberg's major scholarly work was his multi-volume translation from Aramaic into Hebrew of the *Zohar*, or *Book of Splendor*, the source of kabbalistic thought. But, arguably, he made a far more imaginative contribution with his book of stories about the Maharal of Prague, Rabbi Judah Löw, and the Golem. According to legend, the Golem was a monster of amazing strength who was brought to life in desperate times to defend the Jews from their gentile enemies. Before the Maharal of Prague created the Golem, others were supposed to have been made by the prophet Jeremiah and Rabbi Ben Sira, circa 170 B.C. Only a man of exemplary piety, a master of kabbalistic secrets, could construct a Golem, bringing him to life by slipping the Holy One's secret name into his mouth, the letters in the correct order, and laying him to rest by reversing the letters. My grandfather's book *Sefer Nifla'ot ha-Maharal im ha-Golem*, published in Warsaw in 1909, honored a traditional kabbalistic ploy by purporting to be the work of somebody else — in this case, the author of an old manuscript that had been discovered in the fictional "Royal Library of Metz."

It is a presumption of kabbalistic lore that the air about us is rampant with the tormented souls of the departed, which are constantly being goaded by evil spirits, and find their only respite by taking refuge in human beings. Anybody possessed by a *dybbuk* (an evil spirit) suffers abominations, becoming a multiple personality and speaking in alien voices until cleansed by a rabbi skilled in kabbalistic rituals. My grandfather, I was told, had been summoned more than once to exorcise a *dybbuk*.

In a more lighthearted mood, he wrote *Sefer Heshen ha-Mishpat shel ha-Kohen ha-Gadol*, which was published in Poland in 1913. This story, a variation on the theme of Arthur Conan Doyle's "The Jew's Breastplate," had the Maharal of Prague travel to London to crack the case of the theft from a museum of the original breastplate of the high priest, which was embedded with a precious stone for each of the twelve tribes.

My grandfather also believed that desecration of the Sabbath enabled Satan to denounce the children of Israel before God. In 1924, he published a pamphlet, *A Brivele fun di Zisse Mame Shabbes Malke zu Ihre Zihn un Tekhter fun Idishn Folk (A Letter from the Sweet Mother Sabbath Queen to Her Sons and Daughters of the Jewish People)*, in which he chastised Montreal Jewry for its transgressions against Sabbath observance. The *Brivele* explained why the latest diaspora had lasted longer than earlier ones and, furthermore, why Jews suffered more than other people: it was because too many of us had, by dint of dishonoring the Sabbath, lost the protection of the Shekhinah, the Divine Presence.

A rabbinical legend says that before the Romans burned the Second Temple, all the patriarchs ascended to heaven and begged the Holy One to spare Jerusalem. He would not oblige them, but He did promise that his Divine Presence, which had constantly hovered over the Temple, would go forth with them into exile in the form of an angel with white wings as wide as the world.

My grandfather's pamphlet concluded that the failure of so many to observe the Sabbath laws had also delayed the coming of the Messiah:

> Do not listen to the sinful and poisonous speeches of the Reform "rabbis" who have the selfsame sinful souls as the prophets of Baal in olden times who brought on the destruction of the First Temple, or the selfsame sinful souls of the Hellenistic leaders who brought upon the Jewish people the destruction of the Second Temple.

A sly appendix to the *Brivele* took pity on "women who are entitled to the name *Yiddishe tekhter* (Jewish daughters)." It advised them how to circumvent an irritating Sabbath injunction against the use of perambulators (baby *keridges*), which had been adjudged a form of carrying and were therefore forbidden by halakhic (rabbinical) decree. If, wrote my grandfather, a perambulator was modified so that it stood at least forty-two inches above ground, it would no longer violate the law, for it was written that beyond a certain height the rule of "Sabbath boundaries" did not apply. This adjustment, he ventured, would cost no more than twenty or thirty cents.

◦ *Two* ◦

M R. YALOFSKY WOULD BLUSH AND ZIP THROUGH
those rare juicy passages in the Talmud that made us
giggle.

"The wicked man is asked, 'Why did you not occupy yourself with Torah?' If he answers that he was good-looking and
troubled by his passions, he is asked, 'Were you more handsome
than Joseph?' It is related of Joseph the righteous that Potiphar's
wife tempted him every day. The dresses she put on for his sake
in the morning she did not wear in the evening, and vice versa.
Though she threatened him with imprisonment, with bodily
disfigurement and with blinding, though she tried to bribe him
with large sums of money, he refused to yield."[1]

Mr. Yalofsky was a devout Jew — unlike most of our
Hebrew teachers at the Talmud Torah, who had to pay lip service to religious practices in deference to "certain families out of
the Stone Age." But our Hebrew teachers were staunch Zionists.
One of them, Mr. Weingarten, had come to us in 1941 all the
way out of Russian-occupied Poland, through Siberian exile,
a hike into Manchuria, then Japan, and by timely freighter to

Vancouver. At recess, we ridiculed his broken, heavily accented English.

In arts and crafts class, we built a huge relief map representing a chunk of the Galilee, claiming it for our people:

> *El yivneh ha-Galil,*
> *An'u nivneh ha-Galil.* . . .

> God will rebuild Galilee,
> We shall rebuild Galilee,
> We are off to Galilee,
> We will rebuild Galilee. . . .

We erected a balsa-wood watchtower and instant stockade, establishing a kibbutz, populating it with Plasticine *chalutzim* (pioneers) and livestock made of pipe cleaners.

The swamps were being drained, we were told, and the desert reclaimed to yield melons, grapefruit, oranges, figs, dates, and tomatoes. We were taught about our heroes, and none loomed larger than the champion of Tel Hai, Joseph Trumpeldor, in whose memory that settlement set the statue of a lion.

Trumpeldor, who lost his left arm during a perilous mission in the Russo-Japanese War, rose to become one of the few Jewish officers in the army of the Czar. He made *aliyah* in 1912, and worked for a time at Degania, on Lake Kinneret, Israel's first kibbutz. In the Great War he fought again, this time for the British at Gallipoli, leading the Zion Mule Corps — 650 Jewish muleteers and 750 mules.[2] This corps was the precursor of the Jewish Legion, made up of East End Londoners, American and Canadian volunteers, and members of the Yishuv, who had enlisted in three battalions of the Royal Fusiliers (the 38th, 39th, and 40th) and joined General Allenby's campaign to wrest Palestine from the Turks. Trumpeldor did not serve in the

Legion but left for Russia during the revolution, and put together a group of young Jews pledged to make *aliyah*. He was back in Palestine in 1920, at a time when the Arabs, reacting to increased Jewish immigration, were attacking such settlements as Tel Hai in the Galilee. During the raid on Tel Hai, he was shot in the stomach. He ordered a comrade to stuff his protruding intestines back into his belly and bind the wound. Then he carried on directing the defense of the settlement. Trumpeldor died on a stretcher on his way to neighboring Kfar Giladi. His last words, according to legend, were "It is good to die for our country."

Many an afternoon when my parents and elder brother were out, I would crawl on the floor all the way from the kitchen to the front door, propelling myself with my good arm, shoving my Red Ryder air rifle ahead of me, even as I dodged Arab bullets. Eventually the trail of blood from my abdominal wound would attract the attention of one of the many gorgeous nurses who revered me, but I would wave her off, saying, "It's nothing, just a flesh wound. Look after the other *chaverim* first."

FOR FRIDAY evening meetings of Habonim, Jerry and I would start out from St. Urbain Street, where we lived, and pick up Hershey and Myer. Then the four of us would take a shortcut through a back lane that ended exactly where my paternal grandfather's house stood, at the corner of Jeanne Mance. On long hot summer nights, my grandfather often sat on his front porch after supper, stroking his salt-and-pepper goatee as he read *Der Kanader Adler*, the long-since-defunct Yiddish daily newspaper.

When Canada declared war on Germany on September 10, 1939, Shmariyahu Richler had four sons of military age. The most reticent of them, my uncle Israel, didn't wait to be conscripted into the "Zombies," regiments eligible for service within Canada only, but volunteered for active duty overseas. This shocked my rigidly Orthodox grandfather, who feared his son would be obliged to desecrate the Sabbath and eat non-kosher food. Uncle Israel, a self-taught mechanic, had enlisted in the Army Ordnance Corps; the wags in our neighborhood, recognizing many an old YMHA buddy sporting the same shoulder flash, had already dubbed it "the Jewish commandos."

During the early years of the war, when I was still welcome in my grandfather's house, I used to gather there with some of the other grandchildren after sunset on Saturday nights for the *havdala* ceremony ending the Sabbath. My grandfather would pronounce the blessing over the spice-box, shaking it, allowing each of us to inhale its fragrance, and then he would hand the youngest among us the *havdala* candle, light it, and say, "Be praised, Lord our God, Ruler of the Universe, who creates the lights and fires." Finally he would laugh and pinch our cheeks and present each of us with a quarter, which my father, the firstborn of his fourteen children, dubbed our weekly "*Shabbes* graft."

Later, my grandfather pointedly ignored my passing by and I in turn never acknowledged his presence on the balcony. Shmariyahu Richler was an obdurate man, hot-tempered, who had removed his belt more than once in the past to punish me for a minor infraction of the laws. Since then he had learned that, hardly a year after my bar mitzvah, I no longer put on phylacteries to say the morning prayers, or even attended Sabbath services. I had become an *apikoros*, an unbeliever. It is written in the Mishnah, the codified rendering of Jewish law, that "All Israelites have a share in the future world [except] he who says there is no resurrection, he who says the Law has not been given by God, and an *apikoros*."[3]

Our family name was actually Reichler. An immigration officer in Halifax had misspelled it on my grandfather's entry papers and, rather than risk trouble in the new land, he had let it pass. I had been consulting *The Baseball Encyclopedia* for years before I discovered that its editor, Joseph L. Reichler, and I were related. Late one afternoon in 1985, we arranged to celebrate that fact by meeting for drinks at the Algonquin Hotel, in the company of other New York Reichlers. Joe's family, like ours, had emerged from the Galician *shtetl* of Rawa Ruska, but not all of the Reichlers got out in time. "In the Galician ghettos the police were confronted by vast epidemics," wrote Raul Hilberg in *The Destruction of the European Jews*. "In the ghetto of Rawa Ruska, the Jewish population had concealed its sick in holes in the hope of saving them from deportation. Before the Rawa Ruska Aktion was over [in 1942], the SS and Police had dragged 3,000 sick and dying Jews out of their hiding places."[4] Several hundred of Rawa Ruska's Jews were herded into a barn that was surrounded by machine-gunners and then set on fire. When some of them broke out, fleeing the inferno, they were gunned down for sport.

UNCLE ISRAEL came home safely from the war in Europe.

In the exhilarating months following the end of the war, sprawled on the floor of our Habonim meeting room, we would gather round our group leader, Ezra Lifshitz, then an engineering student at McGill and, since 1952, a member of Kibbutz Urim in the Negev. In those days, Ezra was already fluent in modern Hebrew. His father, Pinchas Lifshitz, who had been my fourth-grade Hebrew teacher, spoke the language at home with his children. If Mr. Lifshitz had been a crabby disciplinarian, at least in the classroom, Ezra proved the sunniest and most warmhearted of young men, and a natural athlete as well. He was a terror on the volleyball court and a graceful swimmer. Friday nights he tutored us in Zionist mythology. It was from Ezra that we learned that Theodor Herzl (1860–1904) had been the worst sort, a typical Viennese assimilationist, a dandy, the scribbler of supercilious *feuilletons*, until — in his capacity as the Paris correspondent for the *Neue Freie Presse* — he had stood in the courtyard of the Ecole Militaire on January 5, 1895, and witnessed the badge and buttons being cut from the uniform of Alfred Dreyfus. Outside, the crowd chanted, "Death to Dreyfus! Death to the Jews!"

We were told that at the first Zionist Congress, convened at the Municipal Casino in Basel on the morning of August 29, 1897, Herzl had insisted that all the delegates wear formal dress, black tie and tails, if only to demonstrate to the *goyim* that not every Jew a generation or two out of the *shtetl* — like most of our own fathers, for that matter — was necessarily a peddler, tailor, or scrap-metal dealer.

Ezra did not leave for the *hakhsharah* (training camp) in Smithville, Ontario, until 1950. But others from Winnipeg and Brooklyn — older *chaverim*, some of whom we actually knew — were already in Europe. They were smuggling "illegals," dazed survivors of the Holocaust, out of the Displaced Persons' camps — including one dubbed "Kibbutz Buchenwald" — on to Italian ports, into dangerously overcrowded tubs, to run the British blockade. If successful, they would disembark their emaciated passengers onto the beaches of Tel Aviv and Haifa, where they would scramble away, disappearing into the night with those who had been sent down to shelter them.

In *Builders and Dreamers*, a Habonim anthology, David Glassman described how, in 1947, he had become involved with an arms-purchasing mission in New York, acting for Haganah, the Jewish defense corps. Glassman had been recruited because of his drafting experience. His project was to help produce a small light machine gun, the Dror, and to ship the blueprints and tools necessary for its manufacture to Palestine. "When I arrived in Palestine," he wrote, "I was involved in [the Dror's] production. The gun never became fully operational in the Israeli Defense Force because it was too complicated to work easily in the desert. Eventually it was replaced by the Uzi. "Our mission also handled transporting arms and munitions to Palestine. One time, we secured twenty tons of dynamite at an army surplus sale in Denver. We said we planned to use it for blasting mines. We didn't say where those mines were."[5]

Although there were never more than three thousand members of Habonim in North America, they played a disproportionately large role in the smuggling of immigrants into Palestine, and later in the War of Independence. Another Habonim alumnus, Joe Boxenbaum, related how, a day after he was discharged from the U.S. Army, he met with Ze'ev Shind, head of Mossad operations in the United States, and became involved in acquiring ships for illegal immigration. Resorting to various subterfuges, Boxenbaum and Shind purchased two Corvette-class vessels that would be called the *Wedgewood* and *Haganah*. But these U.S. surplus ships were in need of repairs before they could be declared seaworthy again and were consequently shunted in secrecy — Boxenbaum thought — from one dry-dock to another. However, when they finally set sail from Staten Island, the captain of the tugboat escorting them out hollered, "Here goes the Jewish Navy!"[6]

◇ *Three* ◇

RABBI YUDEL ROSENBERG'S FOLLOWERS CALLED HIM the Skaryszewer Illuy, the Genius of Skaryszewer. My maternal grandfather was a Ba'al Shem, a Master of the Holy Name. He believed in devils: Lilith, demon of the night, who tried to kill all newborn children; Azazel, scapegoat-god of the wilderness; and, of course, Satan. *Kesilim* (poltergeists) also figured in his nomenclature. He died when I was only four years old, and so my memories of him are few, fragmentary, and possibly even unreliable. I remember or was told that he kept a canary. I saw him smoke in bed. Once he sat me on his lap at his desk and drew a horse and then a rider in the saddle. The rider was clearly of the *shtetl* rather than the range: he wore a *shtreimel* (a saucer-shaped fur hat) and an ankle-length black satin coat.

In the early thirties, Rabbi A.Y. Kook, then Chief Rabbi of Palestine, sent for my grandfather. Rabbi Rosenberg bought a property in the Old City of Jerusalem; according to my mother, he was going to take our family with him when he moved to Eretz Yisrael, possibly in 1937. So I might have made *aliyah* long before I had even heard of Habonim. In those days I still grudgingly wore my *tallit katan*, a sleeveless undershirt the four corners of which ended in *tzitzit*, tassels of twined cord, as was written in Deuteronomy 22:12: "You shall make for yourself twisted cords [*gedilim*] on the four corners of your wrap [*kesuth*] with which you cover yourself." Hasidic kids of my acquaintance wore their *tzitziot* outside their shirts to declare their piety, but I thrust mine deep inside my trousers lest my Talmud Torah schoolmates make fun of me.

Habonim was my liberation. The *chaverim* were not obliged to pronounce the *hamotzi* blessing and eat a small chunk of bread with salt before settling into a meal. Instead, before digging in at the long plank table that stood on sawhorses in our own Camp Kvutza, in the Laurentians, we belted out a song in praise of toil, the lyrics by Chaim Nachman Bialik, the father of modern Hebrew poetry:

> *Mi yatzilenu me-ra'av?*
> *Mi yaachilenu lechem rav?* . . .

> Oh, who can save us hunger's dread?
> Who always gave us ample bread,
> And milk to drink when we are fed?

> Whom shall we praise, whom shall we bless?
> To work and toil our thankfulness.[1]

Late at night, imitating the closing, invariably moonlit scene featured in almost every rhapsodic documentary about life on a kibbutz we had ever endured, we formed a circle, linking arms, and spun into one hora after another.

I expected that once we had graduated from university, Jerry, Hershey, Myer, and I would make *aliyah* together, becoming elite desert fighters like Gary Cooper, Ray Milland, and Robert Preston in *Beau Geste*. Meanwhile, in the absence of

Arab marauders, before retiring to our tent for the night I would climb the highest hill, searching for fishy-looking French Canadians.

One day a *shaliach*, an emissary-*cum*-recruiter sent into the Diaspora from the Yishuv, hurried through Montreal. A chain-smoker given to moist coughing fits, a gaunt, round-shouldered man with pale watery blue eyes, he addressed us in a monotone, a voice beyond anger, his accent thick. In response to a timorous question about the terrorist activities of the Irgun Zvai Leumi, who had been known to place bombs in the markets of Arab towns and to fire on Arab buses, he smiled and said, "I understand that you had coffee rationing here during the war and that it was difficult for your fathers to get new tires for their Cadillacs."

Somebody else leaped up and assured the *shaliach* that he, for one, intended to make *aliyah* before the year was out.

The *shaliach* replied, "It's not the Catskills. Boys your age are sitting in prison in Latrun. They hang resistance fighters."

He told us about refugees who had survived Dachau or Treblinka only to run afoul of the British blockade and drown without sight of Eretz Yisrael, or — if they were lucky — to be interned in Cyprus. "Of course, to such human dregs barbed wire is — how to say it in English? — *haimish*?"

"Homelike?"

"Precisely."

He explained that the troops the British Labour government had posted to Palestine were drawn from the *lumpenproletariat*, imperialism's bully boys, schooled in violence in Ireland and the farther reaches of the rapacious empire. England, he said, was our enemy.

Though mesmerized by the *shaliach*, and eager for his approval, we began to shift uneasily in our chairs, avoiding each other's eyes. He had tripped up. He had failed to grasp that if we had been raised on fealty to Zion, we had also been nurtured by *The Boy's Own Annual, Ivanhoe, Tom Brown's Schooldays*, the novels of G. A. Henty, "Gunga Din," and school productions of the operettas of Gilbert and Sullivan:

He is an English-man!
For he himself has said it,
And it's greatly to his credit,
That he is an English-man!
That he is an English-man![2]

Only yesterday we had cheered each newsreel appearance of Churchill, or of King George VI as he moved through London's blitzed East End, offering comfort to Cockneys. We had celebrated the heroism of British troops at Tobruk and El Alamein. And we had, in fact, been delighted by the surprising postwar electoral triumph of the British Labour Party. Prime Minister Clement Attlee was our socialist brother. In the Spanish Civil War, the No. 1 Company of the British Battalion of the International Brigades was known as the "Major Attlee Company."

We were reassured by the knowledge that the most flamboyant of Labour's ideologues, Harold Laski, was a Jew and a Zionist sympathizer. We did not know that a colleague of his at the London School of Economics — and future Chancellor of the Exchequer — Hugh Dalton, had dismissed him as an "under-sized Semite" who suffered from "yideology."[3] Neither were we aware that Beatrice Webb had already written, "Why is it that everyone who has had dealings with Jewry ends by being prejudiced against the Jew," or that she and her husband, Sidney, were resolutely opposed to the Holy Land being turned over "to the representatives of those who had crucified Jesus of Nazareth and have continued, down all the ages, to deny that He is the Son of God!"[4]

During Labour's years on the opposition benches, and as late as 1944, the party had unequivocally favored the establishment of a Jewish national home in Palestine with unlimited immigration. But since being burdened with the responsibilities of office, Attlee had had second thoughts. Replying to a plea from President Truman to admit a hundred thousand survivors of the extermination camps into Palestine immediately, Attlee wrote to the president's representative on September 16, 1945, "One must remember that within these camps were people from almost every race in Europe and there appears to have been very little difference in the amount of torture and treatment they had to undergo. Now if our offices had placed the Jews in a special racial category at the head of the queue, my strong view is that the effect of this would have been disastrous for the Jews."[5]

Labour's Foreign Secretary, Ernest Bevin, had his own idea for the salvation of those Jews who had not been consumed by the Holocaust. "They have gone through, it is true, the most terrible massacres and persecutions," he said, "but on the other hand they have got through it and a number have survived. Now succour and help should be brought to assist them to resettle in Germany and to help them to get over the fears and nerves that arise from such treatment."[6]

The *shaliach* went on to say that Ben-Gurion, reacting to a British Labour government stricture that limited Jewish immigration to Palestine to fifteen hundred a month, had been driven to form an alliance with the Irgun, whom some, he said, "regarded as a bunch of Jewish fascists. *Oy vay iz mir*, kikes who shoot back! What is this world coming to?"

HAGANAH'S ALLIANCE of convenience with the more radical Irgun, led by Menachem Begin, had already come apart when a

British military court sentenced three members of the Irgun to death for their role in the successful attack on the ostensibly impregnable prison in Acre, a Crusader keep, on May 4, 1947. The attack had freed 251 prisoners — 131 Arabs and 120 Jews. Begin promptly had two British sergeants kidnapped, and promised that if his men were executed he would respond in kind.

By dint of belonging to Habonim, we were connected, through Poale Zion, to Ben-Gurion's Mapai Party, Haganah, and a Yishuv policy of moderation. But the truth is, in those eventful days we secretly admired Menachem Begin. He, not Ben-Gurion, was our gutsy street-fighter, our James Cagney. When a seventeen-year-old Irgun fighter, Binyamin Kimche, was caught carrying arms and sentenced to fifteen years in prison and eighteen lashes, Begin was heard from: "If you whip us, we shall whip you."[7] The warning was dismissed as braggadocio and Kimche was whipped. So Begin had a British major and three noncommissioned officers kidnapped and subjected to eighteen lashes before they were released. Then he issued a communiqué: "If the oppressors dare in the future to abuse the bodies and the human and national honour of Jewish youths, we shall no longer reply with the whip. We shall reply with fire."[8] The second Irgun youngster caught with Kimche was not whipped, and the British flogged no more Jews or Arabs for the rest of the Mandate. But in the case of the three Irgun fighters involved in the raid in Acre, the British would not bend. The three men were hanged on July 29, 1947, and two days later the bodies of the hanged sergeants were found. A mine had been placed below their corpses, and the party that came out to cut them down was injured in the explosion. There were anti-Jewish riots in London, Liverpool, Manchester, and Glasgow. But what warmed the hearts of many of us in Habonim was a "Letter to the Terrorists of Palestine," published as a full-page advertisement in *The New York Times*, and signed by Ben Hecht, co-chairman of the American League for a Free Palestine:

> *My Brave Friends,*
>   *You may not believe what I write you, for there is a lot of fertilizer in the air at the moment.*
>   *But, on my word as an old reporter, what I write is true.*
>   *The Jews of America are for you. You are their champions. You are the grin they wear. You are the feather in their hats.*
>   In the past fifteen hundred years every nation of Europe has taken a crack at the Jews.
>   This time the British are at bat.
>   You are the first answer that makes sense — to the New World.
>   Every time you blow up a British arsenal, or wreck a British jail, or send a British railroad train sky high, or rob a British bank or let go with your guns and bombs at the British betrayers and invaders of your homeland, the Jews of America make a little holiday in their hearts. . . . [9]

On impulse, I went down to the Black Watch Armory on Bleury Street one afternoon. Claiming to be eighteen years old, I enlisted in the Reserve Army. It appealed to my sense of irony to have the Black Watch train me to fight the British — the British, who were now beyond the pale, so far as I was concerned.

Wednesday nights I turned up in uniform at the armory, where I learned to field-strip and reassemble a machine gun and drink beer out of a bottle. In order to prove his manhood, Isaac Babel, riding with the Red Cavalry, had to wring a goose's neck. All that my new battalion mates required of me, in the sleazy bar we frequented after an evening in the armory, was that, following their example, I should fart resoundingly at the table. They were a good, hard-working bunch: middle-aged men, mostly, who worked in the Angus 'machine shops or at Pratt-Whitney or on one construction site or another. One evening, Gord, the battalion clown, who had been raised on a farm in the Eastern Townships, explained how his father had avoided military service in the Great War. "Mister Man," he said, "before going in for his medical, he injected milk into his cock, and they turned him down because they thought the drip meant he had the syph or something for sure."

Another evening, Gord told us that his brother-in-law, who had worked in a bobbin mill in the Townships, had died two days earlier, aged forty-three. "He was driving my sister to St. Louis, where we got cousins, and he and Sally put up at one of them roadside little hotels on the way, and a burglar came in through the window after they went to sleep and Reg saw him, shot bolt upright in bed, and died of a heart attack on the spot."

"Why, that's terrible, Gord."

"Aw," Gord said, "Reg always did have a yellow streak down his back."

The men relished their evening out, striding downtown in their uniforms, hoping, even as I did, that girls would mistake them for veterans who had been to hell and back again.

SUNDAY MORNINGS I joined my other *chaverim* in an increasingly urgent fund-raising drive. Fanning out through our neighborhood, we rang doorbells, shaking collection boxes under sleepy faces, demanding money. Jerry Greenfeld outperformed everybody in our group. Not only did he make the most effective doorstop pitch, often turned up a notch by simulated anger, but no matter how insistent or rude he was, the

mothers who answered the door unfailingly warmed to him —
emptying their change purses, asking him to wait a minute
while they hurried back into their kitchens, returning with a
knish, or a slice of honey cake wrapped in a napkin. Jerry was
also custodian of our nickels, dimes, quarters, and an occasional
dollar bill, which after three Sundays came to more than two
hundred dollars. But when we asked him to bring the money
down to our next Friday night meeting, he arrived late and out
of breath, wild-eyed, saying that he had run the four blocks
from his home. "Something terrible has happened," he said.
"Some bastard climbed in through my bedroom window, went
through my bureau drawers, found our money tucked under
my baseball uniform, and made off with it."

"Oh yeah!" said Hershey, flushing.

"Do you think it's too late to call the police?" asked Jerry.

"How did anybody know where the money was?"

"I'm supposed to know that?"

"Yeah."

"Oh," said Jerry, "I know what you're thinking. Shit. Some
friends you are. Some fucking *chaverim* you guys turned out. If
that's what you're thinking, you can go to fucking hell, every
one of you!" And grabbing the nearest folding chair, he
slammed it against the wall and charged out of our meeting
house. Within a week he had quit grade 10 and was driving a
car for Veterans' Taxi. His job lasted only three months. Then
late one night I ran into him at Ben's Delicatessen on Metcalfe
Street. The girl he had with him was a giggly, scrawny French
Canadian from the North Shore who had worked as a maid for
the Rosenbaums in Outremont, tricked out in a white dress,
black apron, and matching cap, trained to answer the phone,
"You have reached the residence of Julius Rosenbaum, KC."
Chantel, now a waitress at Aux Délices, seemed to be enamored
of Jerry, turning to me more than once to exclaim, "Isn't he

something else!" Or, as he began to fondle her knee, batting her eyelashes in mock horror and crying out, "Hubba hubba!" But between these outbursts, verging on hysteria, she was gloomy, absorbed in peeling the label off a Heinz ketchup bottle. Finally, she excused herself to make a phone call. Jerry winked. He bounced a mock punch off my shoulder and assured me that she was a terrific lay. Then his smile lapsed. "It was my father," he said. "He knew exactly where I kept the money, and he messed up my drawers and opened the window wide so it would look like an outside job."

Jerry said he was now earning big bucks, as much as fifty dollars a night, plus expenses, appearing in four-round preliminaries on club fight cards in Chicoutimi, Three Rivers, and Shawinigan Falls. But I shouldn't bother looking for his moniker in the sports pages, he added, because he fought under assumed names, a different one each time. There were two reasons for that, he explained. One, it wasn't legit: he was still too young to appear on pro cards; and two, he didn't want to lose his amateur status, what with the Olympics coming up in England the next year. However, he had already won a bout on a card featuring Gus "Pell" Mell in the main event, and he now worked out in the same gym as Maxie Berger and Lou Alter. Peachy guys, he said.

◇ *Four* ◇

ONE SUMMER AFTERNOON MANY YEARS AFTER I HAD moved to England, a married man now, already the father of three children, I was informed that our eleven-year-old boy had been caught pinching a Billy Bunter comic book from our local newsagent on Kingston Hill, Surrey. I was obliged to admonish him, warning that such shocking behavior could lead to an arrest if there was a next time. He fled in tears. Feeling absolutely rotten, I poured myself a large scotch and retreated to our garden. I easily conjured up a picture of Jerry, Hershey, Myer, and me stopping at Wilensky's for hot dogs after a shoplifting expedition to Woolworth's, surreptitiously loosening the caps on the salt and pepper shakers before quitting the counter, and then loping through the lane, horsing around, quietening down only as we approached the corner of Jeanne Mance, where my grandfather might be seated on his balcony, savoring the evening breeze.

Brooding over the troubling image of my grandfather, *Der Kanader Adler* on his lap, I tried to reconstruct his Friday. He would have risen at 5:30 AM, put on his phylacteries and prayer shawl, and said his morning prayers, swaying to and fro before the wall facing Jerusalem, and, following a quick breakfast, he would have been driven to the junkyard near the waterfront by either my father or my uncle Joe. His Friday at the yard would have ended at 4:00 P.M., enabling him to return home and bathe and dress for the Sabbath, which began at sunset. Then he would have joined the unmarried children who still lived at home, five boys and three girls, to attend to his wife's blessing of the Sabbath candles in the dining room. They would all have sat down to a heavy meal and only afterward would my grandfather have gone to sit on the balcony with his newspaper. I now wondered whether most of the time he had not been angrily ignoring me in the lane, as I fancied, but had simply been dozing.

The truth is, I hadn't joined Habonim in the first place because of an overwhelming commitment to Zion. I had done it to spite my grandfather. I was also flattered by Jerry Greenfeld's attention. There was another consideration: I longed to meet girls who could stay out after ten o'clock at night. And according to the disapproving gossip I had overheard in the Young Israel Synagogue, the girls in the movement, especially those who were allowed to sleep over at our Camp Kvutza, where there was no adult supervision, practiced "free love." Mind you, in those days this promise of sexual whoopee translated into no more than some necking, within vigorously defended territorial limits, usually on a front porch at night, after the overhead light bulb had been loosened, but with couples still leaping apart abruptly when footsteps were heard or a car turned the corner — and even this much certainly never on a first date. A date often meant taking in a double feature at the Rialto, and a good indicator that your girl might be in the mood for a bit of monkey business was that she agreed to seats in the last row of the balcony. Unfortunately the *chaverta* who came to tolerate my kisses wore braces on her teeth, which pinched my lips.

Another rumor about the girls in the movement (this one, given my upbringing, suggesting behavior even more wanton) turned out to be absolutely true. Treat one to a nosh at The Hut and, without any qualms whatsoever, she would order forbidden foods: a toasted bacon-and-tomato sandwich or possibly even a shrimp cocktail, the very height of sophistication.

Habonim converted me into a zealot for Zion. I demonstrated. I badgered my aunts and uncles to join a boycott against British goods. I put in hours on our Gestetner, churning out propaganda that could be handed out on *goyish* street corners. Friday nights, impatient for informed analysis of the latest crisis, we waited outside the house on Jeanne Mance Street for the older *chaverim* to appear. Isaac Reisler. Gdalyah Wiseman. Bill Kofsky, Ezra Lifshitz. Sol Cohen, the most thoughtful, and his fiancée, Fayge Kravitz. Fayge was intelligent, awfully pretty, and encouraging even when we were confronted by the most depressing news from the Yishuv. We adored her. And that summer in 1947 a flood-tide of rumors and reports began to wash over us. Harry Truman, according to Isaac Reisler, *had* to support the partition of Palestine into Jewish and Arab states, because he couldn't win the 1948 election without the Jewish vote in New York, Pennsylvania, and Illinois. But Gdalyah Wiseman feared that the anti-Semites in the United Nations would see to it that Palestine became a federated binational state, with the Jews condemned to minority status even in Zion.

One night we learned that the United Nations Special Committee on Palestine (UNSCOP) had appointed two sub-committees. The first was to draw up a partition plan and the second a draft for the recognition of Palestine as a single unitary state. The chairman of the first committee was Lester "Mike" Pearson, then Canada's Under Secretary of State for External Affairs. In his memoirs, he later wrote: "I must admit that I became emotionally involved in a very special way because we were dealing with the Holy Land — the land of my Sunday School lessons. At one stage in my life I knew far more about the geography of Palestine than I did about the geography of Canada. I could tell you all the towns from Dan to Beer-Sheba but certainly not all from Victoria to Halifax. I think that in the back of my mind I felt I was concerning myself with something close to my early life and religious background. Although this was only an ancillary factor, it made the dispute much more real in my mind than, for instance, Korea. I do not recall ever getting very worked up about Korea when I went to Sunday School."[1]

The plan submitted by Pearson's subcommittee was approved by UNSCOP on November 25, 1947. It called for an end to the British Mandate no later than August 1, 1948, and the partition of Palestine into Jewish and Arab states, with Jerusalem remaining under U.N. control. Four days later the U.N. General Assembly voted, and the result was thirty-three in favor, thirteen against, and ten abstentions.

In our neighborhood, people charged out into the streets to embrace. Sticky bottles of apricot brandy, left over from a bar mitzvah here, a wedding there, were dug out of pantries, dusted off, and uncorked. Men and women who hadn't been to a synagogue since last Yom Kippur surprised themselves, turning up to offer prayers of gratitude and then toss back glasses of schnapps with slices of schmaltz herring. Horns were honked. Photographs of Chaim Weizmann or Ben-Gurion, torn from back issues of *Life* or *Look*, were pasted up in bay windows. Blue-and-white Star of David flags flapped in the wind on some balconies. Many wept as they sang "Hatikvah," the Zionist anthem. In New York, members of Habonim and Hashomer Hatza'ir joined hands to dance a hora in front of the New York Times building. In Montreal, we gathered at the house on Jeanne Mance Street, linked arms, and trooped downtown singing *"Am Yisrael Hai"* ("The People of Israel Lives"), and then danced the hora in the middle of St. Catherine Street, just outside the Forum, bringing traffic to a halt.

On May 14, 1948, in Tel Aviv, David Ben-Gurion proclaimed the State of Israel, promising that it would be "a beacon to the nations." But no sooner did the British Mandate lapse the following day than Israel — that rib torn or redeemed, depending on where you paid your dues, from the body of Arabia — was attacked by five Arab states. Egyptian planes bombed Tel Aviv. Ben-Gurion's first radio broadcast as prime minister of Israel was delivered from an air-raid shelter.

We seldom missed the radio news now, and were overjoyed to hear one day that former Flight Lieutenant George "Buzz" Beurling, born and bred in Montreal's working-class suburb of Verdun, was going to fight for underdog Israel. Beurling, who had been rejected as unqualified by the RCAF in 1939, had gone on to fly a Spitfire for the RAF, becoming "the Knight of Malta," officially credited with thirty-one and a third kills, all but two of them in dogfights over that island.[2] He was awarded the DSO, DFC, DFM, and bar. Canada's most celebrated war hero would be our very own knight-errant — a considerable morale booster. Yet what we heard from older *chaverim* was somewhat less inspiring. The Israelis, we were told, fearful of an Arab propaganda coup, had outbid them for Beurling's services.

After all these years, the truth remains murky. The Montrealer who recruited Beurling for the Haganah, Sydney Shulemson, himself a World War Two hero and winner of the DSO and DFC, insisted as late as 1980 that no promise of money was involved in the enlistment. This claim was supported by Ben Dunkelman, a major with the Queen's Own Rifles during the war, who went on to fight in Israel's War of Independence. He told Beurling's biographer, Brian Nolan, that before accepting the pilot's offer to serve, he asked him, "Why are you so interested in helping us?"

Beurling purportedly replied, "You people have been without a state for thousands of years, wandering homeless and persecuted. I would be helping to fulfill the prophecies and teachings of the Bible."[3]

However, before coming to an arrangement with Shulemson, Beurling had bragged at the Montreal Press Club that the Arabs had offered him $5,000 a month to fly for them. He told a journalist who was preparing an article on him for *Maclean's*, "I know it may sound hard, but I will drop bombs or fire guns from a plane for anyone who will pay me," and that he would fly "for the one who will pay the most."[4] And after the Haganah ordered him to Rome from New York, where he had been awaiting their summons, his girlfriend saw him retrieve an airmail envelope bulging with money from a safe at the Henry Hudson Hotel.

In any event, Beurling, who was twenty-six years old in 1948, never got to fly for Israel. On May 20, he and Leonard Cohen, another RAF veteran of Malta, took off from Urbe airfield, just north of Rome, in a Norseman that had recently been acquired from the Haganah. The plane burst into flames at three hundred feet and exploded on landing. Both pilots died in the inferno. Two and a half years later, their remains were flown to Israel and were buried, with honors, in Haifa's military cemetery at the foot of Mount Carmel, near the cave of the prophet Elijah.

ON FEBRUARY 2, 1949, Israel officially incorporated the sectors of Jerusalem it held into its territory, and by July it had concluded armistice agreements with Egypt, Lebanon, Jordan, and Syria, although this did not commit any of these states to the recognition of Israel's right to exist.

In those hallelujah days of Habonim, in that time of moral certitude, a two-thousand-year-old dream fulfilled, I was, like the other *chaverim*, insufferably condescending to our peers in the neighborhood. They seemed so out of touch with Zion and the lessons of history, so blind. The majority were spending long nights studying for their university entrance exams, plotting future careers as doctors, dentists, lawyers, and notaries in what we scorned as the wasteland of the Diaspora. We needled all of them for being assimilationists, reminding them that no Jews had been more integrated into their society, or felt safer, than the Jews in Germany. Our heated ideological quarrels could flare up anywhere: between the stacks of the YMHA library, leading to our eviction; late on a Saturday night at a table in Ben Ash's Delicatessen on Park Avenue, ruining a double date, the girls tearful; at a Passover Seder, our elders shocked by the inevitable decline into coarse language from whoever got shoved into a dialectical corner.

The brightest and the best of our older *chaverim*, now in their early twenties, departed for the *hakhsharah* in Smithville to prepare themselves for *aliyah*: among them, Isaac Reisler, Bill Kofsky, Gdalyah Wiseman, Ezra Lifshitz, and Sol Cohen and Fayge Kravitz. None of them believed they would be sailing into a tranquil Zion, but I doubt whether any of them expected that, as Paul Johnson wrote in his *History of the Jews*, "to use Palestine to settle 'the Jewish problem' might, in turn, create 'the Arab problem.'" However, a prescient essayist, Asher Ginsberg, who was born in the Ukraine in 1856 and did not settle in Tel Aviv until 1922, had anticipated the tribal turmoil to come. Ginsberg, who wrote under the pseudonym Ahad Ha'am (One of the People), favored "cultural" rather than "political" Zionism. After an early visit to Eretz Yisrael, he published an article in 1891 in which he wrote that it would be an error to dismiss the Arabs as stupid: "... the Arabs, like all semites, possess a sharp intelligence and great cunning.... [They] see through our activity in the country and its purpose but they keep silent, since for the time being they do not fear any danger for their future. When, however, the life of our people in Palestine develops to the point when the indigenous people feel threatened, they will not easily give way any longer. How careful we must be in dealing with an alien people in whose midst we want to settle! How essential it is to practise kindness and esteem towards them!... If ever the Arab judges the action of his rivals to be oppression or the robbing of his rights, then even if he is silent and waits for his time, the rage will stay alive in his heart."[5]

There was another dissenter. In a 1938 interview, Albert Einstein said, "I would much rather see reasonable agreement with the Arabs on the basis of living together in peace than the creation of a Jewish state ... my awareness of the essential nature of Judaism resists the idea of a Jewish state with borders, an army and a measure of temporal power, no matter how modest. I am afraid of the inner damage Judaism will suffer — especially from the development of a narrow nationalism within our own ranks."[6]

◇ *Five* ◇

J ERRY, HERSHEY, MYER, AND I ONCE ASSUMED THAT
we would ramble through the rest of our lives as pals. When
we were still in ninth grade, a year or so before our carefully
collected two hundred dollars vanished, Jerry and I used to spot
pins two nights a week in Joslin's bowling alley on Park Avenue,
where we also charted possible futures together in Eretz Yisrael.
We each handled two alleys and often bet a dime on whether
the next ball bowled toward us would scatter an odd or even
number of pins. Gambling, said Jerry, was in his blood. Most
evenings his father, who worked as a cutter at Grover's Knit-to-
Fit, took a streetcar directly from the factory to the Blue
Bonnets racetrack. When the trotters were not in season, he
could be counted on to find a crap game somewhere or other.
He was a solitary drinker, his preferred tipple a glass of Labatt's
beer fortified by two inches of *alcool*. One evening, calling for
Jerry at his home, I was startled to come upon Mr. Greenfeld
brooding in the dark in the living room. "Hey, you boys gonna
get laid tonight?"

"No."

"Probably wouldn't know how yet. Hey, don't run away. I don't bite. Come here, kid. You understand Yiddish?"

"Some."

"Before you even know it you're an *alter kocker* like me and you can't even piss right any more. Are you scared of me?"

"No."

"Oh, I've got it. Friday night." He rose uncertainly out of his easy chair and began to whoop and kick his heels, dancing his version of a hora. "You're one of those Jewish red Indian kids who's gonna make a safe home for us in Palestine."

"Maybe."

"*Shmocks* is what you are."

Suddenly Jerry was standing there, bristling. "I want some money for supper," he said.

Mr. Greenfeld pulled out his trouser pockets to show that they were empty.

"Go to hell," said Jerry.

"See how he talks to his father."

"Come on," said Jerry. "Let's get out of here. I'll be lucky if I don't have to mop up the toilet when I get home."

"Tich tich tich."

Before the rest of us had even graduated from Baron Byng High School, Jerry scampered out west to seek his fortune. After graduation, Myer elected not to continue with his studies. Instead, he took a job as an usher at the Rialto, and I hardly ever saw him any more. Hershey went on to McGill, where he hoped to major in English literature. McGill's Jewish quota was still intact in those days and my matriculation results weren't nearly good enough for me to seek admission; I had to settle for the less desirable Sir George Williams College. Hershey and I, no longer Friday night regulars at Habonim or students at the same school, made an effort to remain friends all the same. One evening I went to his place for a beer. "Obviously," I allowed,

"McGill has more prestige, but Sir George is truer to our working-class origins and socialist beliefs."

Hershey said that his most stimulating course, conducted by a professor with a degree from Oxford, dealt with nineteenth-century English poetry. "But the other day I had to admit to him that I was unable to respond to the poetry of William Wordsworth. However, I suspect it may not be that his poetry is *passé*. I fear it could be some inadequacy in me."

Months passed before I ran into Hershey again, this time at the Café André on Victoria Street, then a favored student haunt. He wore a white sweater with a big red felt M sewn onto it and sat drinking beer with a bunch of fraternity boys. Thumping the table, they sang:

> If all the young ladies were little white rabbits,
> and I was a hare,
> I'd teach them bad habits. . . .

I was wearing a navy blue beret (the real McCoy, made in France) and had already written my first poem in lower-case letters. Hershey and I waved at each other, but he didn't come to my table, and I didn't go to his.

LEAVING HABONIM, wrote Marion Magid, "I learned that Yeats was not pronounced 'Yeets.'"[1] I myself found more recognitions in the poetry of W. H. Auden, one of a slew of names new to me, than I ever had in that of Chaim Nachman Bialik. I discovered that John Dos Passos of the *U.S.A.* trilogy spoke my language, but that Isaac Leib Peretz didn't, and I was too young to grasp that I could accommodate both streams.

Montreal, then as now, was not so much an integrated city as a sequence of alienated, self-contained tribal bastions — French, WASP, Jewish — enriched in recent years by settlements of Italians, Greeks, Portuguese, and Haitians. Growing up, I was nourished and to some extent misled in a warm world that was just about entirely Jewish, and enjoined to be suspicious of those who weren't. At Sir George, moving timorously to begin with, I made my first gentile friends. Terry, Florrie, Kay, Phil, and Stu became my guides to *goyish* culture. Through them I was introduced to *Penguin New Writing*, Bloomsbury, the films of Roberto Rossellini, Tennessee Williams, the Saturday afternoon Metropolitan Opera broadcasts, *The New Yorker*, e.e. cummings, and the Sadler's Wells Ballet on its visit to Montreal. Stu and I couldn't afford tickets to the ballet, so we mingled with the crowd outside during a first-act intermission, and then strolled back with them into the theater and found a place to stand.

My ride into *goyish* culture was exhilarating, but there were disconcerting bumps on the road, some encountered then, others later. I had to pardon Evelyn Waugh, whom I cherished above all other modern British novelists, his scorn for "jew-boys." Then there was the case of George Orwell, whom I took to be the writer a latter-day Diogenes might have sought as he set out in daylight with his lighted lantern. On October 25, 1941, Orwell wrote in his *Wartime Diary*: "The other night examined the crowds sheltering in Chancery Lane, Oxford Circus and Baker Street Stations. *Not* all Jews, but, I think, a higher proportion of Jews than one would normally see in a crowd this size. What is bad about Jews is that they are not only conspicuous, but go out of their way to make themselves so. . . ."[2]

Dostoievsky was convinced that the Jews reigned over the stock exchanges, controlled capital, and were the masters of international politics. In his *Diary of a Writer*, he wrote that the reign of the Jews, their complete reign, was approaching: "Even in my childhood I have read and heard a legend about Jews to the effect that they are supposed to be undeviatingly awaiting the Messiah, all of them, both the lowest Yiddisher and the highest and most learned one — the philosopher and the cabalist — rabbi; that they all believe that the Messiah will again unite them in Jerusalem and will bring by his sword all nations to their feet. . . ."[3]

Welcomed into neighborhoods hitherto unknown to me by my new friends, I found that "among them" living rooms were not out of bounds, kept clean for special occasions, and that it was not the rule to maintain cellophane wrappings around lampshades. But my emancipation, as it were, came with culinary penalties. Invited to dinners here and there in Montreal's Presbyterian redoubt of Notre Dame de Grâce, I learned to tolerate tinned soup into which, in lieu of kasha or *kreplach*, you were expected to break Ritz crackers that quickly turned to slush. This was invariably followed by a leathery roast, untainted by garlic, served with potatoes boiled beyond the crumbling point. To my astonishment, anecdotes about my Hasidic childhood were considered entertaining. I had been raised on the dictum that it was hard to be a Jew (*siz shver tzu zein a Yid*) but, at least in some quarters, it was also considered a novelty. A story I burnished into a real knee-slapper was the one about how I used to be sent, as a child, to the home of a *shammes* (sexton) on City Hall Street, to pick up our Passover wine. The old man would bundle the bottles into newspapers before slipping them into a heavy-duty brown bag — not to ensure them against breakage, but to make them proof against the evil eye. If a *goy* so much as glanced at an uncovered bottle in passing, it was instantly rendered *trayf*, unclean, and had to be poured down the sink. Another tale that went over big was the one about how, late one afternoon during the Ten Days of Awe which culminate in Yom Kippur, I had to rotate a squawking chicken over my head while pronouncing a blessing that enabled me to shift all of my previous year's sins onto the bird. This led to a discussion of *The Golden Bough*, Aztec rituals, and voodoo rites. Walking home alone, I felt that I was the one who was now *trayf*.

In 1950, I dropped out of Sir George Williams, sailing for Paris rather than Tel Aviv. Staring into the molten, heaving seas late at night on the deck of the *Franconia*, I feared that any minute I might be confronted by Ezra Lifshitz or Fayge Kravitz. "You're heading for the wrong port, *chaver*. Shame on you."

After a couple of years on the Continent, I moved on to London, where I was rooted for twenty years. In 1956, shocked by the revelation that the British had invaded Suez in collusion with the French and the Israelis, I joined thousands of others in Trafalgar Square to listen to Nye Bevan's speech. Marching on Downing Street, we chanted, "Eden must go! Eden must go!" But secretly I was thrilled by the Israelis' brilliant campaign in Sinai, and by Moshe Dayan, the one-eyed general, our protector, who had just possibly been raised to life by a rabbi, a Ba'al Shem, schooled in kabbalistic lore, inserting the secret name of the Holy One into his mouth, the letters in the correct order.

ON MAY 16, 1967, President Gamal Abdal Nasser declared a state of emergency in Egypt. Syria, Jordan, Iraq, Saudi Arabia, and Kuwait also mobilized. The peace-keeping United Nations Emergency Force (UNEF) withdrew from Gaza. The number of Egyptian troops deployed in Sinai swelled from thirty-five thousand to eighty thousand. On May 26, Nasser declared that if war came, Israel would be totally destroyed.

In London, contemplating the battle odds, we anticipated an apocalypse, and another Babylonian exile for those who survived the inevitable massacre. An official of the Israeli embassy phoned me to ask if, in common with other Jewish writers, I would sign a letter to the *Times* stating that Israel, a country smaller than Wales, was in immediate danger of being overrun by the massed Arab legions of five nations and was in urgent need of support from other democracies.

"Of course I'd be glad to sign such a letter," I said, "but given my Jewish name, and those of the others you've mentioned, our protest would seem no more than a reflex action. I happen to know Sean Connery" — then at the height of his James Bond fame — "and it's possible that he would also be willing to sign the letter."

"Sean Connery," he said, "is not an intellectual."

The first flutter of reports to emerge out of the Middle East, after fighting broke out early on the morning of June 5, were contradictory. Robin Day — host of *Panorama*, BBC TV's flagship news commentary program — relayed without comment the Arab boast that they had already destroyed at least 160 Israeli planes. *Panorama*'s Beirut correspondent, Ivor Jones, suggested there was substance to stories that most of Israeli Jerusalem had been taken by the Jordanian army. The optimistic pitch of the first fragmentary reports out of Israel to elude the censors was too much for Neville Brown, defense correspondent for the *New Statesman*, who dismissed Israeli claims of successful airstrikes as wildly exaggerated. "If they have destroyed fifty or sixty planes," he said on BBC TV, "they have done rather well."[4] The one report that hardly anybody credited — certainly not those of us who were constantly on the phone to each other, one eye on the television set — came from Michael Elkins, a BBC correspondent in Jerusalem. Elkins's bulletin was rendered immediately suspect by his American accent, a sure symptom of hyperbole, and was broadcast only after the BBC newsreader warned that it was unconfirmed.

"Less than fifteen hours after the fighting began, Israel has already won the war," said Elkins. "Egypt is no more a fighting factor.... It's the most instant victory the modern world has seen."[5]

By the end of the second day of the war, there was no longer any doubt: Israel, its planes sweeping in low from the sea, had destroyed 309 Egyptian aircraft. In other sorties, 29 Jordanian, 17 Iraqi, and one Lebanese airplane had also been knocked out. The next day I flew to Montreal to attend my father's funeral. I was sitting *shivah* (the seven days of mourning immediately following the funeral) in an apartment with my brother, my father's eighty-five-year-old mother, his seven surviving brothers and six surviving sisters, when Colonel Mordechai Gur's paratroopers stormed the Old City of Jerusalem. We gathered round the radio to listen as General Schlomo Goren, the Chief Army Rabbi, stood by the Wailing Wall and blew the shofar, the ram's horn trumpet. My grandmother lamented between sobs that Moishe, her firstborn child, had not lived to hear it.

One afternoon I slipped out of the apartment to meet Hershey Bloom in a downtown bar, to raise a glass to Israel's incredible triumph and to the hope that all of our *chaverim* who had made *aliyah* had survived the conflict. Hershey had married Hanna Takifman and they had two children, Craig and Lucinda. He had become a dentist and had bet most of his inheritance, he said, on farmland on the outskirts of the burgeoning city, confident that it would quadruple in value as the city's growth continued.

"Remember Jerry Greenfeld?" he asked.

"Sure I do."

"And how you thought maybe he hadn't stolen the money that time, you *putz*, but there had actually been a robbery?"

"His father maybe."

"Or the tooth fairy. Well, our old *chaver* literally came in out of the rain one night a few years back, rang our doorbell and asked if I could put him up for the night. He told me some *bobbe-myseh* about how well he was doing in Calgary, where he was deeply involved in the oil patch. Translated, that means he had been pumping gas at an Esso station until they found out he was diddling the cash register. Anyway, he said he had flown into Montreal on a moment's notice, ho-ho-ho, for an urgent meeting with the Royal Trust people, but he had been mugged on Sherbrooke Street — cash, credit cards, everything gone — just as he was going to take a room at the Ritz, and he couldn't possibly straighten out the mess until tomorrow morning. But the next morning, before the rest of us had even wakened, he was gone, and so were my typewriter, my golf clubs, a pearl necklace of Hanna's, a sterling-silver tray, and a few other things. And now I hear that he's gone and joined the army and he's stationed in Germany."

◦ *Six* ◦

ONE EVENING A COUPLE OF YEARS LATER I AN-
swered the phone in our home on Kingston Hill,
Surrey, and suppressed a groan when the voice on the other end
said, between giggles, "Hello there, Mr. Big-Time Operator,
some guys remember you when."

"Who is this?"

"A voice out of the past, but you'll never guess who in a
thousand years."

"I'm not a fan of these kinds of games."

Helping me out, he began to sing "*Am Yisrael Hai.*"

"Oh my God, it's Myer," I said, pleased.

"Kee-rect! Only I haven't been called that in years. I'm
known as Woodrow now. Or Woody, which I prefer."

I invited him to meet me for drinks at the White Elephant
Club, on Curzon Street, late the following afternoon. The first
thing Myer, rosy-cheeked, still charged with good nature, and
ever the barber's son, said to me after we had embraced was
"I'm glad to see somebody has managed to keep his hair. There
are experts who swear by chicken shit. You rub it into your

scalp. Imagine that. What do you use?"

"I don't. How's your father?"

"In the pink. My mother passed away years ago. A massive heart attack. Otherwise there was nothing wrong with her. I keep him in a condo in Miami, where he cuts whatever hair the other old farts still have, and he even has a girlfriend who cooks him kishka, flanken, *lokshen kugel*, chicken in the pot with matzoh balls, it's a pleasure to visit. I wish my wife could do the same instead of *médaillons de veau* — you've got to turn over spinach leaves before you can even find it on the plate. She's a *shiksa*. We have one kid. Patsy. After Patsy Cline. You a member here?"

"Yeah."

"Then good for you, you must be earning a nice living, even writing such crap, as if the Jews didn't have enough trouble without you. What do you make on a book?"

"It varies a good deal."

"So give me a for instance. Say the last one. A ballpark figure."

"I don't remember."

"He doesn't remember. I've caught you on TV a couple of times. Every time you appear your sales must take a dive. If I were your publisher I'd hide you in a cupboard. I've read all of them. Your books. Most. Some I enjoyed more than others. Hey, I went into a bookshop in your behalf yesterday, Hachit's or whatever, and I asked for your latest. Not in stock. But they could order it for me. Oh yeah, how long would it take? Three weeks. Too bad, I said, I'm staying at the Savoy, you see, and I wanted a hundred copies, but I'm leaving at the end of the week. In that case, sir, let me make a phone call and see what I can do. Go ahead. But he hesitated. Do you mind my asking, sir, what you'd want with a hundred copies? Sure. I'm going to read one and shove ninety-nine others up your arse-hole. Boy, are they ever cold fish here. The British, I mean. How can you stand it? They look at you, it's like they smelled something bad."

Myer was wearing a suede jacket with fringes running across the chest and back, a string tie, initialed cufflinks, a pinkie ring, and tooled western boots. "I thought I'd open a bank account while I was here," he said, "you know, in case I wanted stuff shipped home, so I popped into Barclays, pulled out a wad of traveler's checks, and said I wanted to open an account. This little guy, he could have stepped right out of an Ealing comedy with that accent, he says, jolly good, or some shit like that, but we shall require three references, sir. What are you talking *references?* I'm not hitting you for a loan. I'm offering to keep *my* money in *your* bank. How's about you supplying me with references? He didn't even crack a smile."

"Why did you change your name to Woodrow?"

"Myer's so Jewy. 'Myer, finish what's on your plate.' 'Myer, play with a cat, you'll forget everything you learned.' Myer this, Myer that. I always hated it. Names. *Oy oy.* Have I got a story for you. But I don't want to read it in one of your books one day, you *mamzer.* Here goes. The story. My father, you know, he's reached an age when you ask him who he had lunch with yesterday you draw a blank, but he can tell you exactly where he was on October 8, 1908. Anyway, one day he told me that when he was seven years old and his father registered him for school, the teacher asked, First name, please? My grandfather said, Yehoshua. And how do you spell that? My grandfather looked her in the eye and said, You're the teacher. You spell it."

"Are you still a Plotnik?"

"That's the family name," he said, affronted. "Tell me, you play around?"

"Myer, it's good to see you."

"Come on. I won't tell."

"No."

"If you're telling the truth, I've got to hand it to you for self-control. The broads in here. Yum yum. Me, I'm weak. Last time Melanie caught me cheating she made me go to a marriage counselor. That little *shmock* for a hundred bucks he tells me I screw around because I'm sexually insecure and have to prove my manhood to myself. Hey, I said, what do you do for laughs? Jog? Eat a yogurt?"

"Do you realize the last time we saw each other you were still an usher at the Rialto?"

"And you were at that loser's college, but still too snobbish to hang out with me any more."

"That's not true," I lied.

"Never mind. Forget it. Hey, you are looking at a guy who has seen *Red River* maybe a hundred times. You want to test me on some of the dialogue?"

"No thanks."

"Or *The Snake Pit*. Remember that one? *Oy.*"

Then, without prompting, he told me his story.

"There I was, an usher dressed like a guardsman in an operetta, earning *bupkes*, when one day Irv Bishinsky came to town to check out the theaters in the chain. I was summoned to the office and he sent me out for a coffee without even looking at me, his shnoz already buried in the books. I got him a coffee and brought him a hot bagel with it, and a small package of cream cheese. He snorted, still not looking me in the face, but before he left the Rialto I was sent for.

"'You're Plotnik,' he said.

"'Yeah.'

"'And obviously you read the trades or you wouldn't know what I liked.'

"'Yeah.'

"'So why is such a bright Jewish boy working as an usher?'

"'I needed a job.'

"'Ride downtown with me.'

"'My shift doesn't end until seven o'clock.'

"'*Hok nit kain tchynik.*'

"So we drove downtown together and he asked me what my father did for a living, if I loved my mother, did I drink or *shtup* any of the usherettes. Then he invites me to dinner at his hotel. The Laurentian, class in those days, but it's gone now, eh? And he tells me how he struggled to get where he is, overcoming many obstacles. Anti-Semitism. An allergy to cat fur. A wife with a fear of elevators — she has to see a doctor, first question is, what floor is he on? And suddenly he makes me lean close to him and asks me to exhale. So I did. *Feh!* he says, making a face. In the future, he says, I should remember to take something for my breath every morning, because we're both in show business, meeting the public at all hours of the day. Personal hygiene. Never underestimate it. Then it's good night, kid, and I figure that's it. But a month later I was made manager of the York on St. Catherine Street, and I had to fire the girl in the ticket booth, sticky fingers, and make a few other changes, and the receipts reflected it. Within six months Irv brought me to the head office in Toronto. Thank God I must have chewed through three packs of Dentyne on the train. Lean close and breathe out, he says. I did. That's the ticket, kid. And I was put in charge of checking out our theaters in Ontario. I was now earning good money. I had the use of a company car, a Buick. But overnight in Hamilton or Kingston, or in Toronto even, I didn't know anybody, so I started to hang out in bars and coffeehouses at a time when folk singers were becoming the rage. As a hobby, just for the hell of it, I began to manage a singer here, a singer there, and then a couple of groups. One night in a club in London — the Ontario one, not this — I lucked out. I caught The Highlanders. For their first set they're doing Scottish folk songs and sea-shanties and most of the college kids in the audience don't stop yakking away at their tables. But for their second set they're into their Woody Guthrie shtick, and miners' protest songs, and let's hear it for the *shvartzers* or the Mohawks, and those middle-class white-bread kids in the audience who are afraid to even jaywalk are coming in their pants. I signed up The Highlanders and booked them into college towns only, building from there. They caught fire. Soon I was so busy I had to quit my job and handle The Highlanders full-time. Irv was not only understanding, but went out of his way to set us up with guys in the record biz. In 1967 we played Expo in Montreal, SRO every night. Rave reviews. That got us our weekly TV show on CBC, the ratings are better than ever, and we're touring eight cities in England and Scotland, every concert being taped. And that's why I'm here."

We began to reminisce about Habonim, the four of us strolling toward the house on Jeanne Mance Street, puffing on Sweet Caps and shooting the breeze.

"Have you ever heard from Jerry?" I asked.

"He joined the army, you know."

"I heard."

"At least they taught him a trade. He's a mechanic. Last I heard he was shacked up with somebody in Regina, but he moves around a lot, so who knows where he is now? But listen to this. I phoned Hershey on his thirty-seventh birthday. Hey, how come *you're* answering the phone? Don't you remember you were supposed to die of a heart attack today? Welsher! He didn't even laugh. No sense of humor. As for you, I'm really glad to know you're married with children."

"Oh. Why?"

"When you were at Sir George Williams and began to hang out with all those la-di-da *goyisher*, quote, poets, unquote, a lot of us thought you'd become a *faygeleh*. Hey, don't be offended. I understand she's some looker. The missus."

"Yes. Certainly."

"Then what's she doing with you?" he asked, bouncing a mock punch off my shoulder, Jerry's gesture. "In the old days you could never even get a decent date. Remember Charna Farber?"

"Damn right I do."

"You have no idea what we had to go through with that one before she'd go to Commencement with you. 'I won't be able to wear my high heels, we'd look ridiculous together on the dance floor.' And then Stan Malkovitch marries her and croaks, leaving her zillions, and now she lives in New York, on Park Avenue yet, and you want to run for Congress you'd better make nice to her, she's a big contributor to the Democrats. Hey, there's nothing to compare to a Jewish childhood. Right?"

"Right."

"But only you understood you write it up, changing the names, telling a few lies, adding some *shmutz*, and there's big bucks in it. Don't look at me like that, I give you credit. I should have thought of it myself."

"Myer, in the late watches of the night, do you ever regret that the four of us never made *aliyah* together?"

"And live on a kibbutz? Jerry would've been stealing eggs from under the chickens and selling them on the roadside."

"It didn't necessarily have to be a kibbutz. We might have gone into business together in Tel Aviv."

"I've been there, thank you very much. If you're going, don't forget to pack a lunch. Or don't eat anywhere but in Arab restaurants."

IN 1972, my wife and I quit London and settled into a house in Montreal with our five children. Late one night, twelve years later, Florence and I were reading in bed when the phone rang. It was 12:45 AM. A voice unfamiliar to me said, "I'm afraid I've got bad news."

Our youngest child was asleep in another room, but the others no longer lived at home. I hastily tried to work out what they could possibly be up to at this hour in Toronto, Boston, New York, or London.

"Jerry Greenfeld died this morning."

"Oh," I said, enormously relieved, "I'm sorry to hear that."

"He never stopped talking about you. I hope you can come to the funeral. Say a few words."

"Where are you calling from?"

"Whitehorse."

"No," I said sharply, ashamed to have caught myself out relieved by Jerry's death, "I can't possibly come to the funeral."

"I beg your pardon, sir. I know how important you are, sir. And how nobody ever heard of Jerry."

"You don't understand. I have no idea what he told you, but I haven't seen or heard from Jerry in almost forty years."

"Jeez, I'm sure a lot of your readers would like to know what a horseshit liar you are. You know what you can do? You can go fuck yourself," he hollered, and then slammed down the receiver.

I explained to Florence what had happened, and went into the living room to pour myself a large scotch and water.

All I had owned in the old days was a cheap first-baseman's mitt that I had acquired in a trade for eight different sets of British colonial stamps commemorating the coronation of King George VI. After catching for Jerry in the lane, helping him with his fastball, I had had to soak my red throbbing hand in ice water. He threw that hard.

Jerry was only fifty-three years old in 1984. My age. I put out my cigarillo, stood up, and attempted to touch my toes, unaware that Florence was standing there until I heard a small cough that just could have been a suppressed giggle. "What's so goddamn funny?" I asked.

"Come to bed."

"Soon."

I sat in the living room for hours, recalling Habonim days, pondering what might have been had Jerry, Hershey, Myer, and I actually made *aliyah*.

I had been to Israel once, in 1962, but at the time I hadn't sought out Ezra, Gdalyah, or Sol and Fayge, feeling that I had failed them somehow, disembarking at the wrong port years ago. Pouring myself another scotch, I resolved to make a second trip to Israel, if only to find out what had happened to my old *chaverim*, whom I had known when they were young, when everything was possible. Were they at ease in Zion? Or did they regret having made *aliyah*?

Eight years would pass before I was able to make that second trip to Eretz Yisrael.

◊ *Seven* ◊

O N MY FIRST TRIP TO ISRAEL, IN THE SPRING OF
1962, I flew out from London for a month's stay, on
assignment for *Maclean's* magazine. The shuttlebus from Lod
Airport to Tel Aviv, a Volkswagen, was driven by an Ethiopian
Jew. "How do you like it in Israel?" he asked immediately.

"I only just got here," I said.

The bubbly American boy who plunked himself down be-
side me said, "I've been here for three days. Leaving tomorrow.
I'm on a world tour. Tonight I'm going to see *Breakfast at
Tiffany's.*"

On the Allenby Road, kids with transistor radios clapped to
their ears, lottery-ticket sellers, youngsters with tiny knitted
kipas fastened to their heads with bobby pins, and shoals of boys
and girls in uniform passed to and fro. The Yiddish restaurant I
stopped at was typical of its kind anywhere. Wine-stained linen
tablecloths, toothpicks in shot glasses, the familiar sour shuffling
old waiter with his shirttail hanging out. "Sit down," somebody
said. It was Mr. Berman, who had sat immediately in front of me
on the flight from London. "This is your first time in Israel?"

"Yes it is."

"All cities are the same, you know. A main street. Hotels. Restaurants. And everybody out to clip you. Here they're champion clippers. Me, I'm in sporting goods. I sell guns, tents, sleeping bags." He laughed, inspected his spoon, wiped it on the edge of the tablecloth, and began to chop his strawberries in sour cream. "You'd never catch me spending a night in a sleeping bag. People are crazy. I should complain." He was leaving for Tokyo in the morning. "The girls in Tokyo are the best. They're ugly, but you can get used to them. Used to them? It's easy. They wait on you hand and foot."

Sonny Idelson, an Israeli living in Montreal, had written to his friend Bill Arad to say that I would be in Tel Aviv. Arad took me to the California, a café favored by young journalists and artists. I told him that I intended to look up Uri Avnery, the editor of *Ha'olam Hazeh* (*This World*), a weekly magazine.

"He's a pornographer," said Arad. "Clever, but irresponsible. Don't believe anything he tells you about Israel."

Arad introduced me to a young journalist. Shlomo. "Do you really call yourself 'Mordecai' in Canada?" he asked, making it sound like an act of defiance.

"But it's my name," I said, feeling stupid.

"Really? In Canada? Isn't that nice!"

The bubbly American boy was waiting at the bus stop.

"How was the movie?" I asked.

"It was really something. I'm on a world tour, you know."

"You told me."

"I leave for Bombay at three o'clock tomorrow afternoon."

What's playing in Bombay, I wondered, but I didn't say it. Instead I said, "Enjoy yourself."

"I'll only be there overnight."

It was not yet midnight; I decided to give the Hotel Avia's Jet Club, Open Nightly, a whirl. The bartender turned out to be an admirer of Uri Avnery. "The government," he said, "would rather hang him than Eichmann. Shimon Peres hates him."

Peres, then Assistant Minister of Defense, was one of Avnery's targets. It was *Ha'olam Hazeh* that had first revealed that Israeli-made arms were being used by the Portuguese in Angola. The bartender was distressed, because he felt Israel had become identified in the Middle East with repressive colonial powers. "Uri," he said, "was the only journalist here with guts enough to come out for an independent Algeria. The other papers stuck by France."

The bartender assured me that Israel kept a cultural attaché in Stockholm whose sole purpose was to lobby for a Nobel Prize for S.Y. Agnon. "Buber would have got one last year," he said, "but Hammarskjöld died as he was translating him."

Bill Arad and I met again late the next afternoon. Out for a stroll, we came upon the new Haganah House. "I'm paying for it," he said. "We might as well look inside."

Like most Israeli men of his generation, Arad had first fought alongside the British, in World War Two, and then against them during the last years of the Mandate. Many of the devices that had been used to conceal arms in the run to Jerusalem in the dying days of British rule were on display in the museum: an oxygen tank with three rifles inside, a boiler stuffed with a machine gun. I also saw a Davidka.

When morale in Jerusalem was probably at its lowest, in 1948, as the shelling of the Holy City reached such a pitch that the projectiles were falling at a rate of one every two minutes and the Jews inside had nothing to reply with, a young engineer, David Leibovitch, invented a homemade weapon that came to be known as the Davidka. Dov Joseph, who was military governor of Jerusalem during the siege, wrote in *The Faithful City*: "It was basically a kind of mortar which used a six-inch drainpipe.

It fired a bomb of nails and metal scrap which exploded with some force and — what was more important — with tremendous noise and fury. Its effect on the Arabs was sometimes considerable...its noise frightened them almost as much as its projectiles hurt them, and it gave great heart to the people of Jerusalem when real artillery shells were falling on them."[1]

Back at the California, Arad and I fell in with two young architects. One of them was convinced that the Eichmann trial, which had just finished, was a mistake. "It dragged on and on, cheapening things."

"But we had to have a trial to educate the young," said Arad. "They have no respect. They don't understand why the Jews in Europe didn't rebel."

"We're a new kind of Jew here," said the other architect, "don't you think?"

On Sunday I moved to the Garden Hotel in Ramat Aviv, where many foot-weary, middle-aged tourists were sunning themselves by the pool.

"The ones I saw in Jerusalem, they're poor kids," said a lady. "They don't even know what a handkerchief is, should I chase them away? They're sneezing and blowing and coughing all the time."

A card player looked up from under his baseball cap long enough to say he was taking the tour to Eilat the next day.

"If you're constipated," Mr. Ginsburg told him, "the water is good for you, if not — pardon me the expression — you'll get the diarrhea."

Mr. Ginsburg, chewing on an unlit corona, fond of massaging his big bronzed belly, questioned each new arrival at the pool. Shooing flies away with his rolled newspaper, pondering his toes as he curled and uncurled them, he'd ask, "And where are you from? Ah-ha. And how long are you here for? I see.

Longer you couldn't stay? And tell me, you came over here on one of our planes, you liked it? You were impressed? This country, it's a miracle. So? The only thing I got a complaint is the hotelkeepers they make the monkey business. I been here seven years ago and what they done since it's remarkable. I'm not a millionaire, and I'm not poor. I spend? It's the children's money. Do I want to be the richest man in the cemetery? The less I leave, the less the children have to fight over, God bless them. So, Mr. Richler, you're enjoying here?"

In Jerusalem, bouncing in a taxi badly in need of new shock absorbers (never mind a muffler job), bound for the Hebrew University, we passed a prison block. "Today he's in there," said the driver.

"Who?"

"The Eichmann."

With Yitzhak, a law clerk who had just completed a month's military duty on the Jerusalem frontier, I climbed a rock-strewn hill to an abandoned courtyard where the Israelis and Jordanians occupied sandbagged positions about a hundred yards apart in the then-divided city. "When I served here," said Yitzhak, "we used to gossip every morning and throw fruit back and forth."

From the lookout at Ramat Rachel, he pointed out the inaccessible Mount Zion, the hill where Solomon's tomb is supposed to be, and the road to Bethlehem.

Another day I went to meet Tovia Shlonsky, then a young lecturer at the Hebrew University. He told me how much he admired Bellow, Malamud, Roth. "Unfortunately, they are not much read here." He laughed, embarrassed. "The young think of them as ghetto writers."

One Saturday Tovia picked me up at noon and we went to visit a young couple he knew who had just built a house in Abu Tor, on the frontier with Jordan, overlooking an Arab village on the mountainside and the Old City. As we sat on the terrace, sipping Turkish coffee, we could hear the Arabs on the other side of the frontier being summoned to prayer. "At night we can listen to their drummers," said Miriam. "Children often stray across the frontier. The Arabs are very good about it. They always give the kids candy, treat them well, and return them. But if an adult wanders across he's beaten up. Not gratuitously. For information."

Miriam missed her old Muslim neighbors and regretted that Jerusalem had not been made an international city. A youth group wearing soft blue sun hats, neckerchiefs, shorts, and back-packs marched past below, singing vigorously. "Just consider our splendid view. We can see the Old City, the Arabs...but the poor Arabs," she said, indicating the martial group below, "this is all they can see."

Hadera, a sun-baked industrial town only an hour's run from Tel Aviv on the coastal plain, enjoyed the rare distinction, for Israel, of not being listed as "a place of interest" in any official guidebook I had seen. My cousin Shmul lived there. When I arrived, Shmul's shop, the Hadera Locksmithy, was closed. He wasn't at home either. But his wife, Sarah, let me into their apartment. Sarah was a New Yorker. She and Shmul were Orthodox. They had met on a kibbutz, on their first trips to Israel some years before, and then again in New York, where they were married and had a child. Shmul had learned his lock-smith's trade in New York, bought equipment on credit, and returned to settle in Hadera with his wife and child. Sarah was troubled by her Moroccan Jewish neighbors. "A problem? Wherever you have black and white there's a problem. With the least excuse," she said, "they take out a knife. The worst are the ones from the Atlas Mountains. They've just come out of the caves."

My cousin Shmul, the son of my father's eldest sister, no longer called himself Herscovitch. Following a popular immigrant custom, he had given his name a clearer Israeli ring: he was now known as Shmul Shimshoni.

"When I first came to Hadera," said Shmul, after he finally turned up, "the locals thought I was crazy. For forty years, they said, there has never been a locksmith in town, what do we need one now for? Then, out of sympathy for a new man, one by one they looked for something in their attics to bring into my shop. My first customer brought me an old suitcase, the case was locked and the key was lost, he asked if I could open it and make a new key. When I did it for him, he was amazed. He had to go home to get money to pay me. Over here, we believe in letting the other man live. As long as you're not a pig, everybody helps out."

Sarah added, "Don't forget, we didn't have to come here. Not like the European Jews."

Mr. Ginsburg was lying in wait for me in the lobby of the Garden Hotel. "So, Mr. Richler, walk, walk, see, see. Quite a country, eh? But you know how long this hotel would last in Miami? Six days — and boom, bankrupt. Or maybe you think it's right, I have donated so much to build this country, it costs a man thousands to come here, maybe you think it's right they should charge me extra if I want a cup of tea after my dinner?"

I assured him that hotelkeepers were the same everywhere; they would charge him for his tea in Italy too.

"Who cares Italy?" he said, disgusted.

When I finally caught up with Uri Avnery, I told him that Mr. Ginsburg felt unwanted in Israel.

"For the middle-aged tourists from America," said Avnery, "the old-time Zionists, this has to be a paradise, and no criticism is possible. They come here as to heaven on earth and they want it pure, not filled with quarreling human beings. Those old men would cut off their fingers for Israel. It's true they wouldn't settle here, but they will pay for it. They are, in a sense, the backbone of the Israeli economy. But as far as most Israelis are concerned, your middle-aged tourists are shirkers for living abroad. They come here to be delighted by Jewish cops, a Jewish army — well, they have to pay for it."

Avnery's office had been bombed twice. He had been beaten up. He described *Ha'olam Hazeh* as one third sex and sensation, one third *Time*-style, and another third modeled on *L'Express*. "Ours is the only true opposition paper," he said.

When *Ha'olam Hazeh* charged that Israeli-manufactured arms were being used by the Portuguese in Angola, the report was denied by the government. But Avnery insisted and other, more reputable journals were obliged to investigate the claim. They came back with concrete proof that the story was true. "The government," said Avnery, "then explained they had sold the arms to Germany and had no idea where or how they would be used. That much is true. But what is also true is, they must have known Germany had no need whatsoever for Israeli arms. They buy them for show, out of guilt. Also, they are too clever to send their own arms for use in a dirty colonial war. So once more we get the worst of both worlds."

We drove past Ben-Gurion's house. Ben-Gurion, who was then still prime minister, had three homes: an official residence in Jerusalem, his own house in Tel Aviv, and his desert retreat in Kibbutz Sde Boker. "He really hates the desert," said Avnery, "but he is a man with a rare sense of style. If he is going to be interviewed on American TV, he flies out to the desert by helicopter a half-hour before the camera crew. A half-hour after they've left, he's back in Tel Aviv. Nobody here can touch him politically."

The Israeli economy, Avnery argued, was totally unrealistic, dependent on international loans, German reparations money, and continued help from Zionists abroad. "Israel insists on be-having as if it was not a Middle Eastern country," he said. "The Jews will continue to pretend they are a Western power. Nobody is really interested in what goes on in Alexandria and Beirut, so close by, but they will go rushing off to New York and London, where they can parade as heroes in the Jewish communities. From the beginning, going back to the earliest settlements, there has never been an attempt to assimilate with the Arabs." Finally, Avnery had to laugh at himself. "You know, I love it here. In London, where you live, everything's been done. Here we'll see."

⬦ *Eight* ⬦

A GALLUP POLL PUBLISHED BY THE ISRAELI DAILY *Ha'aretz* in 1990 claimed that the longing of Israelis to escape their country exceeded even that of East Europeans. According to Matti Golan, a former editor of *Ha'aretz*, some 500,000 *yordim* ("those who go down") have emigrated from Israel since the state was established, and the Council to Combat Yerida has estimated that by the year 2000 more than 800,000 Israelis will have abandoned the country. Even now, approximately 20,000 depart every year, wrote Golan in *With Friends Like You: What Israelis Really Think About American Jews*, "ten percent of whom are scientists, doctors, engineers, computer experts, and other technological professionals...the cream of our young people have had enough and don't know why they should bear the burden any longer. A U.S. green card has become the new Zionist dream of the average Israeli."[1]

On a visit to the United States during his first term as prime minister, Yitzhak Rabin denounced the *yordim* as "the dregs of Israeli society." But he apologized in a 1991 interview he gave the *Los Angeles News*, a Jewish community newspaper. "What I said then doesn't apply today," said Rabin. "The Israelis living abroad are an integral part of the Jewish community and there is no point in talking about ostracism."[2]

Among the *yordim* I count two of my oldest and most cultured friends in Montreal, Sonny Idelson and his wife, Bella, who immigrated to Canada in the fifties. Sonny, who was a building developer until he retired, is a voracious reader, fluent not only in Hebrew and English but also in Latin, French, Spanish, Italian, and Russian. His father was Israel's first official government printer. He and Bella usually spend a month in Israel every winter. Sonny feels most at home in the seedier old neighborhoods of Tel Aviv, on Ben Yehudah and Dizengoff streets, where, he once told me, "The paint is peeling, the bricks are crumbly, everything is in need of repair, and the old men used to settle into a sidewalk café at ten o'clock in the morning, order a cup of lemon tea, and sit there all day, arguing politics and making snide remarks about the tourists who passed. The *Americanishe gonovim.*"

Before leaving for Israel in 1992 I arranged to meet Sonny for lunch, just as I had done before my first trip. We were going to eat at Moishe's on the Main. Garish it may be, but it's a Montreal institution, the best steakhouse in town. It was called the Bucharest when I was a boy, but after Romania came into World War Two on the wrong side, its rambunctious proprietor, the late Moishe Lighter, renamed the restaurant after himself. Later he introduced a claret on his *carte de vin* called Cuvée Moishe, the label adorned with his smiling face. While I waited for Sonny, a waiter came over to chat about the old days when we all lived in the neighborhood.

"Remember Sid Horowitz?"

"I don't think so."

"Sure you do," said the man at the next table. It was Marty Hoffman, Baron Byng, class of '48. Now sole proprietor of

Pantalon Picasso — Picasso Jeans. Made by prisoners in China, shipped through Hong Kong. No strikes, no late deliveries. "*Langer loksh* Horowitz. He was with the Y basketball team the year they won everything."

"He came in here yesterday with his new wife," said the waiter, "a *shiksa*, Yolande — maybe twenty-five years old, she's already got a bun in the oven — *and he's wearing a rug*. Hey, I had to be careful not to seat him next to an air-conditioning vent. Excuse me."

Marty asked, "Weren't you in Hashomer Hatza'ir with Shloime Scheiderman?"

"No, I was in Habonim."

"*Pam achas bochur yatza*," he sang, "*bochur v'bachura....* He was in from Toronto last week. He calls himself Cy Taylor now. He's with Stikeman Elliott, one of their tax mavens. A partner. These days I go to Toronto and I can see more kids we grew up with than I do here. Fucking Parti Québécois, they're ruining the city. Boogie Friedman. Remember him?"

"Boogie Friedman?"

"Cancer of the pancreas. I ran into him at the Friends of the University of the Negev dinner. Hershey Bloom was getting an honorary degree, he can afford it, and he looked awful, Boogie, he was wearing a yarmulke and he said the *hamotzi* before eating. You think that'll help? Let me try another one on you. Fishel Shechter?"

"Sorry."

"Yeah, yeah. Come on. His father used to go from pool-room to poolroom here with his little suitcase of socks and ties. Factory seconds. Fishel's waiting for a heart transplant. Every night before he goes to sleep he prays some healthy young biker will hit a tree and they'll call him in for a refit. Me, I'd be scared of AIDS. You?"

"Me what?"

"Your health."

"I'm in the pink. Honestly."

"The way you smoke those little cigars? Sure sure. *Fuck 'em!*"

"Who?" I asked, startled by his vehemence.

"Jacques Parizeau. Camille Laurin. The PQ. *Oysvorfs. Mamzerim.* A *choleria* on them!"

Then the waiter was back with more names recalled from the good old days. Charna Rosen, Grepsy Sussman. Moish Bercovitch, who was doing time. Dr. Phil Gold, a credit to us. And Baron Byng's most famous graduate, William Shatner, Captain Kirk of *Star Trek*.

Foolishly, I tried to trump that one. "Do you know who used to live right around the corner from here on Napoleon Street?"

"Sure. The Kushners. They were in footwear. Retail."

"Saul Bellow," I said, "right around the corner. When he was a boy."

"Bellow?" the waiter asked, puzzled. "Now you've got me. What was his father in?"

"*Oy vay,*" said Marty.

"Listen here," said the waiter, "who can remember everybody?" And then he was off again.

"I phoned you on Super Sunday," said Marty. "I had your UJA card. You said, 'Sorry, I can't talk now, I'm just rushing off to the airport.' You're supposed to be a writer. Couldn't you come up with a better line than that?"

"Next time," I said.

"So let me tell you a story. A middle-aged Jewish couple is on a jumbo jet flying to Japan. Somewhere over the Pacific they run into engine trouble. The pilot, a real genius, manages to bring the plane down on a remote spit of sand, a little pimple of an island in the middle of nowhere. They'll never find us here, the husband says. Wait, says the wife, have you honored your United Jewish Appeal pledge card? Not yet, says the husband. Then there's nothing to worry about, she says, they'll find us."

"But I never made a pledge. In fact, I contribute to the Peace Now people instead."

"In that case, my friend, why don't you go right to their head office?"

"I don't understand."

"Arafat."

SONNY, WHO HAD BEEN caught in a traffic jam, finally arrived, offering apologies. Following his ritual denunciad of Shamir, Rabin, and Israeli policy toward the Palestinians, he warmed to his pet peeve, the *haredim*, the ultra-Orthodox. *Haredi* is Hebrew for "trembling" or "fearing," and the *haredim* are the God-fearing. "Our ayatollahs," said Sonny. Then he rounded off his show of distaste for the *haredim* with an anecdote that betrayed an affection for their savvy. "A few years ago," he said, "some of the boys I went to school with were putting up a hotel in Jerusalem. The *haredim* turned up every day and watched and waited but didn't make a move until the sixth floor had gone up. Then they paid the boys a visit. This hotel will have to come down, they said, because it is being built over a graveyard. Now tell me where you can build in Israel without bones underneath. The whole country's a graveyard. So what could be done? The boys were presented with a list of yeshivas and their financial needs. After some hard bargaining, the extent of the required donations was agreed to by both parties. But that wasn't all. To be permitted to build over a graveyard, the *haredim* said, they must drill holes in the foundation so that the souls of the departed could escape for fresh air. Of course, the boys said.

Naturally. We should have thought of that in the first place. So the architects were called in. Building plans were unrolled. How big is a soul, the boys asked. Sometimes as small as a fingernail, they were told, but other times as large as a fist. The haggling went on for weeks and finally the number and size of the holes were agreed upon and construction was resumed."

If the *haredim* were sneaky smart, I pointed out, sometimes it was in a worthy cause. Take, for example, a story that Rabbi Ovadia Yosef, the former Chief Sephardic Rabbi of Israel, likes to tell about the third Lubavitcher rebbe, Rabbi Menachem Mendel, the Tsemach Tsedek — a story I cribbed from David Landau's admirable *Piety and Power: The World of Jewish Fundamentalism*:

One day he [Rabbi Menachem Mendel] said to his servant: "Let's go." He didn't say where, and the servant, of course, didn't ask.

They reached the home of a certain bank manager, a non-Orthodox man. But he was respectful. He welcomed the Rabbi, offered him refreshments. The Rabbi just sat, and said nothing. The host felt it impolite to ask the Rabbi what had brought him, so he asked the servant. "I don't know either," he said. So they all sat in silence.

After some time, the Rabbi rose, said to the servant: "Let's go," and headed for the door. The bank manager could no longer restrain himself and asked, very politely, to what had he owed the honour. So the *Tsemach Tsedek* said, "Our Talmud tells us, Just as it is a *mitzva* [a good deed] to say something that will be listened to, so too is it a *mitzva* not to say something that will not be listened to. If I stay at home, I can't fulfil that *mitzva*. So I come here, I sit with you, and I don't say something that will not be listened to. Having done that, I'm now leaving."

The manager, of course, demanded to know what it was he wouldn't listen to. After much pressure, the Rabbi told him: a poor widow could not afford the repayments on her mortgage. "And your bank has sent her an eviction notice. Where is your mercy? The Torah commands us to protect the widow...."

The manager remonstrated that it was not his bank, and he had to follow procedures.

"There you are! I knew you wouldn't listen. But now you've foiled my intention of fulfilling the *mitzva*!"

In the end, Yosef concluded the story, the manager paid the debt from his own pocket, and the Rabbi blessed him with lifelong prosperity.[3]

Sonny inveighed against the two main political parties representing the *haredim*: Agudat Yisrael, the voice of the ultra-Orthodox Ashkenazim, Jews of Northern European descent; and Shas, the self-styled "Torah Guardians" of the Sephardim, some of them Spanish, but most of North African or Middle Eastern origin. Agudat Yisrael was founded at the turn of the century to combat the "Zionist heresy," a secular impediment to the coming of the Messiah. And Shas, so far as Sonny was concerned, had been formed in 1984 only to lobby for a shift of religious slush funds from the Ashkenazim, the traditional insiders, to the much less favored Sephardim.

Given that, for the last twenty years, Israelis have split their vote just about evenly between Likud and Labor, denying either party a clear mandate, the country has had to muddle through by tolerating one or another form of disabling compromise. Either the two major parties have been joined together in a national government, their leaders alternating as a prime minister held on a short string, or both Likud and Labor — donning yarmulkes and proffering loot bags — have pursued the religious parties with an eye to forming a coalition government. In turn, the religious parties flirt with both Likud and Labor, eventually blessing whichever delivers the best ministries and the most largesse, and snuggling into its lap.

Shas, a member of the last Likud coalition, had now switched to Labor, which had won the most seats — 44 out of the Knesset's 120 — in the election held on July 2, 1992. Three of Shas's six members now seated in the Knesset were under investigation for corruption that allegedly took place while they were serving in the previous government, and the party itself had been fined three million shekels for improprieties. But Sonny's greatest anger was reserved for the pronouncements of Rabbi Eliezer Schach, founder of Shas, and religious mentor to that party as well as the smaller Degel Hatorah Party. In December 1990, the Lithuanian-born, ninety-seven-year-old rabbi addressed a gathering of students in the yeshiva over which he presided, the Ponivezh in Bnei Brak. "The nation's chosen," he said, "are not those elected to the Knesset, but those studying in yeshivot," and he denounced the Knesset "for not dealing with the true emergencies of this nation, but with how to protect pig growers."[4]

However, it was another statement, reprinted in the *haredi* daily *Yated Ne'eman*, that created a scandal in Israel and the Diaspora. The rabbi asked his students, "Does anyone here think that before the Holocaust, which exacted so terrible a price and left no family untouched, all the Jews of Europe were righteous, God-fearing folk? There was a drift away from our faith and way of life. What happened was divine retribution for the accumulated weight of years of drawing away from Judaism."[5]

Shas activists had provoked secular Israelis at least twice before.

In an interview with the Jerusalem newspaper *Kol Ha'ir* in December 1984, Shas Member of the Knesset (MK) Shimon Ben-Shlomo had ventured that the main cause of the death of 603 Israeli soldiers in Lebanon had been the sexual licentiousness of women in the army, an institution that many *haredim* regarded as a state-sponsored quagmire of promiscuity. Rabbi Yitzhak Peretz, then a Shas Minister without Portfolio, dissociated himself from Ben-Shlomo's charge. But a year later, filling the office of Minister of the Interior, he told a television interviewer that the investigation into the cause of a school bus collision with a train on the railway crossing at Petah Tikva was irrelevant. The accident, in which children and adults had been killed, was, he said, "divine retribution for the breach of the Sabbath in Petah Tikva."[6]

Following Labor's electoral triumph, on July 2, 1992, ending fifteen years of Likud rule, Yitzhak Rabin forged a querulous coalition that included Shas on the right and the Meretz Party, which had won twelve seats, on the left. The price paid to Shas, the appointment of Arye Deri as Minister of the Interior, did not delight secular Israelis, and the announcement that Shulamit Aloni, a Meretz MK, would be the new Minister of Education made for frenzy among the *haredim*. Ms. Aloni's assumption of that portfolio, said Rabbi Schach, would result in over a million Israeli children being forced into apostasy, and that was worse than what had happened to Jewish children during the Holocaust.

The continuing quarrel between ultra-Orthodox and secular Israelis took another turn on October 5, 1992: MK Yael Dayan was photographed sunbathing in a bikini on a beach in Tel Aviv on Yom Kippur, which many *haredim* took as a deliberate provocation. Later in the month, Shulamit Aloni was accused of dining in non-kosher restaurants and of having held meetings on the Sabbath during an official visit to Germany.[7]

Reading about the defiant behavior of Yael Dayan and Shulamit Aloni in the fortnightly *Jerusalem Report*, I was spun backward in time, a thirteen-year-old again, eating my first toasted bacon-and-tomato sandwich, not altogether sure that I wouldn't be struck by lightning when I emerged from Horn's Cafeteria on Pine Avenue. My initial experience with hashish, on the terrace of the Café de Flore on Boulevard St. Germain, did not leave me nearly so guilt-ridden. But it was one evening in Paris, in 1951, when I grasped how far I had strayed from childhood religious observances. I had offered to take a Texan friend, who had never eaten a Jewish meal, to dinner in a kosher restaurant. As we strolled along the Seine on the *rive gauche*, crossing the bridge to Ile St. Louis, coming out in the Jewish quarter on the other side, I extolled the merits of gefilte fish, horseradish that made your nose tingle, stuffed derma, and boiled flanken. But the restaurant I favored was closed. It was Yom Kippur. A sign in the window, which I took to be a personal rebuke — surely set in place by my paternal grandfather's ghost, a *dybbuk* in quest of winter quarters — expressed the wish that all of the restaurant's clientele would be written down for a good year in the Book of Life: *L'shana tova tikatevu.*

RABBI ELIEZER SCHACH'S 1990 vision of Hitler as the unwitting instrument of a vengeful Jehovah not only infuriated secular Jews but also distressed the Lubavitcher rebbe in Crown Heights, Brooklyn. Addressing a group of his followers, Rabbi Menachem Mendel Schneerson said, "All those who suffered during the years of the Holocaust were holy and pure, and they didn't die because of any 'settling of accounts.' What person can make accounts for God?" The rabbi went on to say, "We don't have the power to understand why God allowed these sufferings to occur. But just because we don't understand, does this mean we may say that these events were, God forbid, a punishment? No."[8]

In an acrimonious eight-hour debate in the Knesset, Deputy Housing Minister Avraham Ravitz, of the Degel Hatorah Party, sprang to Rabbi Schach's defense. The rabbi's warnings of divine retribution for backsliding, he said, were no different from those of biblical prophets. He was right. Reminding the people of God's terrible vengeance for transgressions has many biblical and rabbinical precedents, including the warning against dishonoring the Sabbath issued by my grandfather, the Skaryszewer Illuy.

An earlier case was the Damascus affair. On February 5, 1840, Friar Thomas, an Italian monk, and Ibrahim Amara, his Muslim servant, disappeared in Damascus. Seven Jews were accused of murdering the pair in order to drain their blood to make matzohs for Passover. The seven Jews were imprisoned and tortured, and sixty-three children were seized in the hope that this might force their mothers to reveal the hiding-place where the blood of the two victims was stored. There were protests from prominent Jews in England and France, and eventually those prisoners who had survived were released. But then Rabbi Judah ben Solomon Hai Alkalai, the Sephardic rabbi of Semlin, on the Danube, peered into the entrails of the affair and concluded that it had been God's way of chastising the Jews, "complacent dwellers in foreign lands," and goading them into a greater awareness of "the remoteness of Jerusalem."[9]

And of course there was also the prophet Jeremiah, who proclaimed Nebuchadnezzar God's chosen scourge for punishing Judah, and welcomed the coming destruction of Jerusalem by Babylon: "And afterward, saith the Lord, I will deliver Zedekiah king of Judah, and his servants, and the people, and such as are left in this city from the pestilence, from the sword, and from the famine, into the hand of Nebuchadnezzar king of

Babylon, and into the hand of their enemies, and into the hand of those that seek their life; and he shall smite them with the edge of the sword; he shall not spare them, neither have pity, nor have compassion."

Jehovah was enraged and punished Judah for worshipping Ba'al in the high places of Tophet, where sons and daughters were burned in the fire, "which I commanded them not, neither came it into my heart."

⋄ *Nine* ⋄

FLORENCE AND I ARRIVED IN ISRAEL ON OCTOBER 11, 1992, flying in from Frankfurt. We were met at Ben-Gurion Airport late in the afternoon by a driver who was to take us to Mishkenot Sha'ananim, the municipal guest house for visiting artists and intellectuals in the charming Yemin Moshe neighborhood of West Jerusalem, a distance of 30 miles. Once we had put the Philistine coastal plain behind us, we emerged into winding hills. Close by Bab el Wad, the six rusting, burned-out chassis of trucks that I had first seen in 1962 still lay by the roadside. They were a memorial to the Passover convoy of three hundred trucks that had left Tel Aviv on April 20, 1948, laden with chickens, eggs, sugar, and matzohs, bound for the besieged Jews in the Old City. Unfortunately, Operation Nachshon, which had preceded the convoy and was supposed to have wrested control of the road from the Arabs, had failed. In a battle that lasted all through the day, three Jews in the convoy were killed, thirty were wounded, and six trucks had to be abandoned. The rest of the trucks got through, but afterward control of the road reverted to the Arabs, and 280 of the Passover convoy's drivers were stuck in the Jewish quarter for months.

On the approaches to Jerusalem, the summits of bony hills that had been all but bare in 1962 now bristled or were adorned — depending on whether you were a grieving Palestinian or an unashamed advocate of a Greater Israel — with new suburban settlements: Ramot, Har Nof, Mevaseret Zion. Entering the city, we encountered a forest of industrial cranes stooping over building sites here, there, and everywhere. All the new completed high-rise apartment towers and hotels had been constructed, or at least faced, with the local limestone, which seems to sparkle as the sun sets.

In 1860, Yemin Moshe, with its landmark windmill, its arms now stationary, became the first quarter outside the swarming confines of the Old City to be settled by Jews. It was inaugurated by the construction of Mishkenot, which was commissioned by the British philanthropist Sir Moses Montefiore but never became the hospital he had intended. Instead, its row of twenty-four terraced apartments — each one opening onto a communal stone terrace overlooking Mount Zion, the Jaffa Gate, and the walls of the Old City — was divided equally between Ashkenazi and Sephardic Jews. In later years it fell into a state of disrepair until, in 1973, it was restored and opened as an official guest house.

Our driver deposited our luggage in Mishkenot's lobby and was gone. Only after we had moved into our apartment did I grasp that he had forgotten my new gunmetal-gray Smith Corona XD 5500 electric typewriter; it had been left on the airport cart in the parking lot. In Frankfurt, my typewriter in hand, I had been yanked out of the queue for the flight to Israel and escorted to a small room where my machine was vacuumed and X-rayed before a security seal was fixed to it and I was allowed to proceed. I called the front desk at Mishkenot and they got in touch with the airport police. A half-hour later Estée Du-Nour, director of the guest house, reported back. "I've got good news and bad news for you," she said. "The good news is that they found your typewriter. The bad news is that they blew it up."

At a dinner party that night I learned that schoolchildren in Jerusalem are trained to summon the police immediately on discovering an unattended parcel or carton anywhere on the street. Within minutes a police van will heave to, police with loudhailers will clear the area, a ramp will be lowered from the rear of the van, and a robot will be sent out to deal with what could be a bag of groceries or dirty laundry or, just possibly, a bomb. Another guest at the dinner party, an archeologist, told us about an associate who had forgotten his briefcase on a bus. It was reported to the driver, everybody disembarked, and the bus was driven to a secluded area. And then the man's Ph.D. thesis, the work of several years, was blown to bits.

Our hostess lived in a nondescript concrete apartment block in Jerusalem's Ramat Eshkol district. "People are beginning to look for apartments elsewhere," she said, "because the *shvartzers* have begun to move in." In Israel, *haredim* are variously known as *shvartzers*, blacks, or black-coats. "You're going to think this is terrible of me, but the truth is, they smell so bad. They can't help it. Those clothes. This heat. What can I say? Then I take out the car on a Saturday morning and there they are with their ten children, shaking their fists at me and shouting, *Shabbes! Shabbes!* You know, one day, at the rate they're going, they will outnumber all of us, and what then?"

I asked our hostess's daughter, a bright teenager fluent in English, if she knew any Arabic. "No," she said, and neither did she have any Arab friends.

"We will have to give up the Golan," our hostess said, "but don't think I'm not afraid. It will put the Syrians only sixty-five kilometers from Haifa, and there's a big difference between sixty-five kilometers and seventy-four."

The archeologist pointed out that there was an ongoing dispute in Israel between building developers and those determined to preserve the country's cultural heritage, who had declared more and more sites inviolate. "And now," he said, amused, "we have Christians here searching caves for the ashes of the red heifer."

For the building of a Third Temple, in anticipation of the coming of the Messiah, tradition demands the recovery of crucial elements supposedly preserved from the Second Temple in 70 A.D., among them the Ark of the Covenant and the ashes of the red heifer. The ashes, mixed with water, would be required for purifying the defiled site prior to construction. In ancient Jewish ordinance, only male animals were usually acceptable for sacrifice in regular sin-offerings for the congregation, but an immaculate red heifer was typically required for ritual purification of objects and sites — a heifer "upon which a yoke had never been set." Hence Orthodox fascination with the Qumran scroll that says where the ashes of such a beast were hidden, and archeological interest in ossuaries and the tombs of priests, as well as Israeli agronomists' current attempts to breed a perfect red heifer. (Perfect, for the Talmud warns that even one white hair would disqualify the animal.) In 1989, Orthodox rabbis were dispatched to Europe to obtain frozen embryos to begin a breeding program.

BACK IN OUR apartment, unable to sleep, I read *The Jerusalem Post* in bed. Rioting had broken out in Gaza in support of a fourteen-day hunger strike by more than 3,000 security prisoners. Police Minister Moshe Shahal had met with five Gaza lawyers and told them, "We will try to answer any humane and legal needs of security prisoners, but we refuse to pander to the unreasonable and political needs of an extreme few, especially concerning convicted murderers and terrorists."

There were an estimated 13,000 security prisoners in Israel. Freih Abu Meidan, chairman of the Gaza Bar Association, said he did not question the authorities' right to imprison people. The problem, he said, was the plight of 105 prisoners in Ramallah and Beer-Sheba who were being confined in underground isolation cells, some in chains.

More than forty people had been injured in the rioting in Gaza City, whose downtown area, according to *The Jerusalem Post*, "was strewn with more rocks than at any time since the early days of the *intifada*." A border policeman had been wounded by a flying rock and a thirteen-year-old Palestinian boy had been shot in the abdomen. In Beita, south of Nablus, border policemen and soldiers fired on rock-throwers who had refused to disperse. Two sixteen-year-old boys were wounded in the legs and Amer Abdullah Hamayel, who was twenty-three, was killed.

The *Post* also paid tribute to cartoonist Noah Mordechai Birzowski, who had just turned seventy-five. A contributor since 1940 to the *Palestine Post*, as it then was, and other Israeli newspapers, Birzowski signed his name Noah Bee. One of the cartoons reproduced for the tribute was in two frames with the headnote "FINAL SOLUTIONS." The first frame showed Jews in striped concentration-camp uniforms, lining up to be consumed in a crematorium, smoke billowing out of its tall chimney. The second frame was a drawing of a couple being married in church, standing before a crucifix, with the footnote "INTER-MARRIAGE." I did not wake up Florence, my Protestant bride of thirty-three years, mother of our five children, to show it to her. However, it did occur to me that had Bee been a cartoonist for the *Catholic Herald*, and had he drawn a mixed-marriage couple clasping hands before a Star of David and equated it with genocide, the B'nai Brith Anti-Defamation League would have been on his case in a jiffy, accusing him of racism. Actually, our half-breed children — three boys and two girls — solved the problem of their dual religious provenance years ago. When our elder daughter, Emma, was a mere ten-year-old, she informed her brothers, "You guys are Jewish, but the girls aren't."

Finally I drifted off to sleep, conjuring up an image of Major General Orde Wingate in Palestine in the thirties, lying naked in his tent, combing out his pubic hairs with a tooth-brush, as was his habit, and instructing eager Jewish youngsters, Moshe Dayan among them, in guerrilla night tactics. Wingate, who went on to become a World War Two hero in Burma, leader of the irregular Chindits, a mixed force of British and Gurkha troops, had a Hebrew code name in Palestine in the thirties: *HaYadid*, the friend. On December 1, 1937, he wrote to his cousin Sir Reginald Wingate: "The administration of Palestine and Transjordan is, to a man, anti-Jew and pro-Arab. This is largely due to the fact that we seem to send only the worst type of British official to Palestine. They hate the Jew and like the Arab who, although he shoots at them, toadies to them and takes care to flatter their sense of importance."[1]

Wingate was a first cousin of T.E. Lawrence, and was given to messianic fantasies; he dreamed of being a latter-day Moses, leading the Jews in a military campaign to re-establish them in their historic homeland. Instead, he died in an airplane crash in Burma in 1944. During the War of Independence, his widow flew over the battle in progress at Degania and dropped her hus-band's Bible on the field.

LATE ONE AFTERNOON, a week after our arrival in Israel, I sat on a terrace set on a height overlooking Hinnom, or Wadi al-

Rababi, Jeremiah's "valley of slaughter." The valley, the very mouth of Hades in Jewish tradition, is known as Gehenna (hell) to both Jews and Arabs. Children were once sacrificed here in an open fire-pit, a tribute to Moloch. According to Plutarch, Moloch's priests used to beat drums to drown out the wailing of the children in the flames. As late as the eleventh century, there were people who maintained that, standing on the height, they could still hear the cries of those in Gehenna ascending from below.

Since 1981, the height has been the site of the Jerusalem Cinémathèque, and I was seated on its Liv Ullmann Terrace and Café-Restaurant with the center's soft-spoken, silvery-haired director, Lia van Leer. Our view was remarkable. We looked out on the western wall of the Old City, Mount Zion, and the seemingly endless scorched hills of the Judean Desert, pink under the lowering sun. A three-hundred-yard cable still ran from the Ophthalmic Hospital, on our side of the valley, across to Mount Zion. During the siege of the Jewish quarter by the Arab Legion in 1948, the cable was lowered during the day, when it might be seen, but raised at night, to carry a trolleycar of food and ammunition to Mount Zion and bring back wounded soldiers.

The Jerusalem film center's archives are the repository of over 10,500 prints, the largest collection extant of Israeli films and other films of Jewish interest. It includes the first Hebrew fiction feature produced in Palestine, *Oded the Wanderer*, as well as the first Yiddish silent dramas shot in either Poland or America. The center's documentary riches reach back as far as turn-of-the-century Palestine, through the years of illegal immigration during the British Mandate, to battle footage of the War of Independence and after. Mrs. van Leer told me that in 1981, when the center was still being constructed in a restored nineteenth-century building, she was visited by a rabbi. "He wanted me to put in a revolving door, just like at the Hadassah hospital, so that wandering souls rising from the valley below could not be trapped inside the cinémathèque." But her real troubles began when it was announced that the center would be open on the Sabbath. This at a time when, in deference to the *haredim*, every Jewish-owned store, cinema, café, or restaurant in Jerusalem shut down at sundown on Friday.

"Tel Aviv was one thing," said Mrs. van Leer, "but when word got out that I was going to offer screenings *here* on Friday nights, a rabbi phoned and said the *haredim* could afford to pay me to keep closed on *Shabbat*. I said this was a cultural institution and I refused. In that case, I was told, I mustn't charge for tickets and I had to hire a non-Jewish projectionist. When I didn't comply, yeshiva *buchers*, the male students of the talmudic academy, used to gather outside here on Friday nights shouting, *Shabbes! Shabbes!* at cinema-goers, and sometimes even throwing stones. Then, after the *intifada* started, the *haredim* put up posters in the city saying it was my fault, the *intifada* was God's punishment for my opening the cinémathèque on the Sabbath. It's terrible, but I really can't stand the black-coats. Once I was getting into my car when I saw one of them rushing toward me. I immediately began to raise my window. But it turned out that all he wanted to do was return my eyeglasses case. He was a nice man."

◇ *Ten* ◇

D URING THE WAR OF INDEPENDENCE, HAGANAH DE-
fenders, stubbornly entrenched in the Yemin Moshe
quarter throughout the conflict, were in a position to block any
attempt by the Arab legion to break out of the Jaffa Gate into
West Jerusalem. Following the armistice, Jerusalem's partition
line was drawn on paper with too thick a pencil, inadvertently
creating a no man's land several yards wide. Mishkenot, then
lying on the very edge of the divided city's border, was exposed
to occasional shelling and the fire of snipers posted on the walls
of the Old City. Reduced to a slum, it was uninhabited for a
time, save for squatters who slipped in here and there. After
the Six-Day War the squatters, impecunious immigrants for the
most part, were settled elsewhere, and Mishkenot was splen-
didly restored.

Among its many amenities, Mishkenot includes a well-
stocked bar in the lobby. On Monday evening, October 12, I
waited there for Sol and Fayge Cohen; they had married in
1946, but I hadn't seen them since 1948. The three of us were
going out to dinner.

Mishkenot's obliging bartender, Bruce Mandel, a stocky, blue-eyed young man out of Morristown, New Jersey, with a neatly trimmed Vandyke beard, bore an uncanny resemblance to the young Richard Dreyfuss. His parents were *ba'alei teshu-vah*, non-observant Jews who had returned to the Orthodox faith. Bruce had quit his yeshiva studies and made *aliyah* in 1982. He served in the Golani Brigade during the war in Lebanon in 1985, put in time as an emergency-room technician in a hospital, then did some security work, and had been at Mishkenot for six months. "I like it here," he said, "but I miss the ambulance work."

I have, on occasion, encountered bartenders who kept a baseball bat or a shillelagh prominently displayed behind the bar, but never before one who wore a revolver in a holster strapped against his right hip. "It's a Glock 17," said Bruce. "I first saw one used in *Die Hard II*. It set me back 1,700 shekels, which is somewhere between eight and nine hundred dollars."

Bruce had taken courses in practical, sports, and combat shooting, and was licensed to run a firing range. "I still do security work. It's my own company. I install alarm systems. In the territories, mostly."

He was an admirer of both the late Menachem Begin and Ariel Sharon. "Land for Peace is not for me. They want everything. I wouldn't even consider negotiations. Rabin is being too generous, too willing to bend. You grant them autonomy and the next thing they'll want is a state, which would only serve as a base for further operations. They want everything. But I've said that already, haven't I? I think your guests have arrived."

I had no trouble recognizing them. Fayge, now the mother of three children, the eldest forty-one years old, had obviously thickened over the years, but she was still pretty, exuding warmth, her smile trusting. Sol, now sixty-seven, was bald with long curly gray sideburns just short of qualifying as muttonchops, and his manner was somewhat mournful. My first thought was that they would not have looked out of place going for an evening stroll on Collins Avenue in Miami, another retired couple — but they were made of sturdier stuff. Sol was a veteran of three wars. He had served with the RCAF from 1943 through 1946. Ten years later, during the Sinai campaign, he was a signals man with the Jerusalem Regiment. In the Six-Day War he fought against the Jordanian army on the Jerusalem front. Fayge was co-ordinating editor of the *Israel Law Review*, an English-language quarterly that tried to sort out an inherited labyrinth of Halakhah, Ottoman, and British Mandatory Law.

Sol, Fayge, and I went to the Minaret, a restaurant run by Israeli Arabs on Emek Refaim Street, in the German Colony. No sooner did we sit down and order drinks than Sol said, "The dream has gone sour," but he didn't elaborate.

To begin with, we talked about the Gulf War.

"You're sitting and listening to the radio," said Sol, "and you're fighting Scuds with Sellotape."

Karen Alkalay-Gut, a child of Holocaust survivors, had written a sequence of poems about those days, which includes the verses:

I think of Rena in Canada,
chewing her nails and screaming
when she recognizes the neighborhood of a hit
in Tel Aviv. Somehow her heart
reaches me, even here, even
hiding under the kitchen table with a quaking dog. . . .

Some differences: we are not an army,
just a bunch of women slapping our babies
into airtight tents, racing to the stores
for masking tape and batteries, wishing —

as we pass a mirror — we didn't look
so much like our mothers.[1]

One of Sol and Fayge's grandchildren, a four-year-old, lives in Tel Aviv. "He still won't go into the room that was sealed during the war," said Fayge.

Sol and Fayge had made *aliyah* in 1950, not to become kibbutzniks, but to settle in Jerusalem. "Our water tank was filled every fifteen days," said Sol. "If you ran out, too bad. But almost everybody you met had been through the siege of Jerusalem or the Holocaust. I was embarrassed. What had we suffered in Canada? Meatless Tuesdays."

Eighteen months after Israel declared independence, its Jewish population of 650,000 had swelled by 350,000. In 1949 alone, 109,000 came from Eastern Europe, 71,000 out of Asia, 31,000 were of Egyptian, Libyan, or North African origin, and some 19,000 emigrated from Western Europe, South Africa, Australia, and North America. A number of East European Holocaust survivors and almost all the North African and Asian Jews had to endure cold rainy months in tents in transit camps, their living conditions dire, even desperate. The disgruntled transit-camp Jews — some of them invalids, others elderly — were an enormous drain on the infant state's still inadequate infrastructure and fragile economy.

Much to their amusement, North American, British, Australian, and South African Jews — many of them only a generation or two out of the *shtetl* — are still referred to in Israel as Anglo-Saxon Jews. Ben-Gurion noted in 1948 that this group, as well as earlier immigrants from Eastern Europe, had been prepared for immigration; they had learned Hebrew and farming on *hakhsharah*s, and most were headed directly to kibbutzim. "Now we shall bring in Jews as they are," he said, "without any advance preparation...because we haven't the time and they haven't the time."[2]

A lack of preparation, however, was only one of many problems.

Israeli agents in Europe had to bribe Communist officials. Jews brought out of Poland, Hungary, Romania, and Bulgaria were paid for in hard currency, sometimes as much as three hundred dollars a head. But once they arrived in the way-station of Vienna, their first experience of the West, there were some who didn't wish to go any farther. And many of those who did proceed to Israel only agreed to it because no other country would take them in. Furthermore, they had no interest in moving into crumbling, isolated villages that had recently been cleared of Arabs, or in starting their new lives in communal farms, but insisted on settling in cities. Reacting to reports that a number of Holocaust survivors had become active in the black market, Ben-Gurion made a typically blunt statement to the Mapai Central Committee on July 22, 1949. "Among the survivors of the German concentration camps," he said, "there were people who would not have survived if they had not been what they were — hard, evil, and selfish people, and what they underwent there served to destroy what good qualities they had left."[3]

Israelis dubbed the new immigrants Avak Adam (human debris). Ben-Gurion once described the Moroccan Jews out of the Atlas Mountains as "savages," and another time compared them to the Africans who had been brought over to the United States as slaves. Ashkenazim were terrified of being overrun, reduced to a minority by the "medieval" Sephardim out of Asia and Africa. In a controversial article published in *Ha'aretz*, Arye Geldblum wrote that the African Jews were a race unlike any the Israelis had ever seen before: "In the [North] African corners of the camps you find filth, gambling, drunkenness and prostitution. Many of them suffer from serious eye diseases, as well as skin and venereal diseases. I have yet to mention robbery and theft. Nothing is safe from this anti-social element, no lock is strong enough. . . ."[4]

"The winter of 1950," said Sol, "was freezing cold, and there were still thousands of immigrants in the transit camps. There was terrible unemployment. Food shortages. Families of six living in one room in a slum in Jaffa counted themselves lucky not to be in a leaky tent. Strangers would stop me on the street and ask, 'Where are you from?' 'Canada,' I'd say. 'Are you crazy?' But we never thought of going home. This was our home. On the other hand, I've got to tell you that of our group that came over here in '50 something like eighty percent returned to the United States or Canada." At different times during his career at the Hebrew University in Jerusalem, Sol has taught adult education, and served as dean of students and as assistant to the president. "You need maybe four to five thousand shekels a month to lead a modest middle-class life here — I'm talking about after taxes, and at least forty percent of our income is gobbled up by taxes. So most professors have to look for additional money in order to support their families — consulting work here and there, mostly."

"All of our children fought in the Yom Kippur War in 1973," said Fayge. Their son Ra'anan, or Ronnie, thirty-seven years old and a computer programmer, is temporarily working on projects in the United States. He served with the Special Services Corps of the Israeli Defense Forces (IDF), and took part in the operations at Ma'alot and Entebbe.

In May 1974, *fedayeen*, Arab terrorists, captured a school bus and kidnapped ninety children at Ma'alot in Galilee. Twenty of the children were killed in the Israeli assault on the school where they were being held. Even as the nation mourned, it was discovered that the outrage had been organized by

Palestinians, hitherto taken to be moderates, who had been meeting with Israeli doves. As for the gallant, brilliantly executed raid on Entebbe on July 3, 1976, it rescued Israelis and others who were confined in a shed at the airport in Uganda after their Air France flight had been hijacked by the PLO.

"When I asked Ronnie about Ma'alot and Entebbe," said Sol, "all I could get out of him was that those are only the operations you hear about."

Sol acknowledged that two percent of Israel's annual budget came from Jews in the Diaspora, most of the money raised by the United Jewish Appeal (UJA) in the United States. "I think those contributions are more important to Jews in the Diaspora," he said, "than they are to us — it's their channel of Jewish involvement. But it's best when the Jews in America are personally involved in a project, say a hospital or a school. And when you also factor in the American government's stake in things here, which comes to billions annually, you have to worry about Israel becoming a beggar-nation. How will we attract investment?"

Sol, who described himself as a secular humanist, is active in a support group for the children of *haredim* who have broken with Orthodox observances. "The *haredim* are very good at picking up runaway kids in Jerusalem, offering them food and shelter, taking them into *yeshivot*, and converting them into *ba'alei teshuvah*. But there was no apparatus to help kids, many of them bewildered, all of them lonely, who were no longer religious and had been shown the door by their parents. They could be found sleeping in bus stations. They had no food, no guidance. So we try to do what we can to help them adjust."

Sol and Fayge both felt that the *haredim* were politically influential beyond their numbers in Israel.

"If my son wanted to marry a divorcée," said Sol, "he couldn't do it here, because he's a Cohen. He would have to be married in a civil ceremony abroad, which the rabbinate here wouldn't recognize as legitimate."

Cohen is the Hebrew word for "priest", and every Jew with that surname (or Cowan, Kahane, Kain, Kagonovitch, or other variations) is supposed to be a descendant of the high priest Aaron. Cohens are prohibited from marrying divorcées, which would put them at risk of being "defiled," and they are not allowed to enter a cemetery unless it is to bury a member of the immediate family. The devout Cohens in Israel avoid the main highway out of Jerusalem to Jericho, since it crosses the Mount of Olives cemetery. A road sign marks a detour, the "Alternative route for Cohens."

Fayge raised another problem. "If a woman is widowed," she said, "but has no children, according to the Halakhah she must marry her late husband's brother, or obtain a release from him. This *chalitzah* ceremony is ugly, obliging the widow to be spat upon or to be hit with a slipper by her brother-in-law. After the war in '73 there were a number of nasty stories. Okay, a brother-in-law would say to a war widow, 'I'll release you, but I want ten thousand dollars.' Or what if the brother-in-law is only five years old? The woman has to wait until he is thirteen to get a rabbinical release, or pay up."

Sol said, "Only when you get out of the country on a trip can you really relax or realize what you are living with here."

It didn't strike me until later that neither Sol nor Fayge had asked me any questions about Canada, or about how Montreal had changed since they had left it forty-two years before. Difficult as it was, I had to accept that in some ways Canada was now the irrelevant Old Country for them, the way Galicia was for my grandparents.

◊ *Eleven* ◊

*A*FTER MY PARENTS DIVORCED IN 1944, MY FATHER continued to support my brother, who was studying at Queen's University in Kingston, Ontario. He also agreed to deliver a monthly check for twenty-eight dollars to provide for my care. My mother, obliged to earn money, rented out the back bedroom and cooked for a refugee who had escaped from Austria immediately before the *Anschluss*. Two years later she placed a small ad in the *Montreal Daily Star* offering "delicious, strictly kosher meals at a reasonable price in a warm, family atmosphere." Eventually Hoppenheim, Putterschnit, and Stein became regulars at our table. Hoppenheim and Putterschnit were bachelors and Stein was a widower. However, the first person to ring our doorbell in response to my mother's ad was an emaciated, soft-spoken, impeccably dressed middle-aged man — a *goy*!

"What do you want here?" my mother demanded.

Mr. Sullivan indicated the folded copy of the *Star* in his hand, my mother's ad circled with a pencil.

"But this is a Jewish home," said my mother, "and we only serve Jewish food."

Mr. Sullivan doffed his pearl-gray fedora and asked, "May I come in, madam?"

"It's eighty cents if it's fish, but a dollar five when I'm serving meat. In both cases, soup and dessert come with."

This seemed agreeable to Mr. Sullivan, but my mother still blocked his path. "And we don't serve liquor here."

Mr. Sullivan, who worked at the City and District Savings Bank at the corner of Park and Fairmount, frequented our table on Tuesdays and Thursdays. It was noted that he ate with his fork upside down, he wore spats, and on evenings when my mother joined the men for dessert he would rise from his chair until she was seated. The others at the table were too intimidated to banter in Yiddish in his presence, and felt obliged, in deference to his manner, to eat without loosening their ties or removing their jackets. Grabbing was also out. "Would you mind passing the bread, sir?" Hoppenheim might say. Or, with just a hint of menace, "Would you care for the last slice of potato *kugel*, sir?"

I served the meals, and Mr. Sullivan unfailingly tucked a dime or fifteen cents, depending on whether it was a fish or meat night, under his tea saucer for me. To begin with, I pocketed the money with exaggerated ceremony for the benefit of Hoppenheim, Putterschnit, and Stein. Unavailingly, as it turned out. Putterschnit explained, "Listen here, you're not a real waiter but by the owner a son, and this isn't even a restaurant."

Mr. Sullivan, who had lost his only son in the battle of the Falaise Gap in 1944, took an interest in me. He brought me City and District Savings Bank blotters, a calendar, and once two baseball tickets that a customer had given him. One night he asked, "Will you be attending university here?"

"That depends. You see, I'm an active Zionist and I could be called up to serve in our army in Palestine any time after my eighteenth birthday."

"Pish pish," said Hoppenheim.

In 1946, following President Truman's "Yom Kippur" speech advocating the partition of Palestine and the creation of a Jewish state, our group leaders in Habonim continued to tutor us in Zionist mythology in the house on Jeanne Mance Street. We also watched inspiring movies and listened to impassioned speakers who fed us anti-Semitic incidents and blatant examples of prejudice, and assured us that we were a form of cultural poison ivy to both the French and the English, and would never be at ease in Canada. But Mr. Sullivan was on our side. "Possibly," he said, "you might consider completing your studies before volunteering to serve."

The next evening, the surprising Mr. Sullivan brought me a novel to read. "Among other delights," he said, "you will find that one of the characters is your namesake."

It was "a Zionist novel" titled *Daniel Deronda*, by somebody called George Eliot, a woman in spite of her name. Daniel Deronda's mentor, the saintly but mortally ill Mordecai, points him on the path to Zion, saying, "There is a store of wisdom among us to found a new Jewish polity, grand, simple, just, like the old.... Then our race shall have an organic centre, a heart and a brain to watch and guide and execute; the outraged Jew shall have a defence in the court of nations, as the outraged Englishman or American. And the world will gain as Israel gains."[1] At the novel's end, Daniel Deronda escorts his bride to Eretz Yisrael, his aim to restore "a political existence to my people, making them a nation again, giving them a national centre, such as the English have, though they too are scattered over the face of the globe."[2]

DURING THE SUMMER my mother rented a large house in Ste. Agathe, in the Laurentian Mountains, and ran it as a strictly kosher boarding house for families who wished to escape the city heat but couldn't afford a proper hotel. She did the cooking, a French Canadian woman was hired to be the chambermaid, and I served the tables, slipping away when business was slow to hitchhike to Camp Kvutza for an overnight stay. There, gathered round a campfire with the other *chaverim*, I learned that in 1895, five months after Theodor Herzl witnessed the humiliation of Alfred Dreyfus, the father of modern Zionism was ensconced in the Hotel de Castille, on the rue Chambron. Then a failed playwright but celebrated journalist, he recorded "idea splinters" for his concept of a Jewish state. During those two febrile weeks in June he was, he wrote, possessed by "thoughts that keep rising like bubbles in a test tube and which, without an outlet, would in the end have burst the vessel."[3] He planned to negotiate with the Czar and the Kaiser, among others, for a mass exodus of the Jews. But beforehand, "In order to get proper respect at the imperial courts, [he] must obtain the highest decorations. English ones first."[4] The state he envisaged would boast "resplendent halls, men in formal black tie, ladies in high fashion."[5] Its constitution would probably be modeled on that of Venice, with a Rothschild as the first Doge — providing the family contributed to the cause. But it also occurred to Herzl that one day he might be crowning his boy "Hans as the Doge and that, in the Temple before the leaders of the nation, [he] would address him as 'Your Highness, my dear Son.'" The new Doge would be led in procession by "Herzl Cavalry." German would probably be the new state's official language, but, he noted, "I need the duel, in order to raise decent officers and to lend an air of French refinement to high society."[6] He had twenty years, he estimated, to "train my boys to be warriors . . . by patriotic songs, the Maccabees, religion, stage plays on heroic themes, honor, etc."[7]

Following a bad migraine attack, on the last and sixteenth day of his creative binge Herzl wrote, "I am leaving a spiritual legacy. To whom? To all people everywhere. I believe I shall rank among mankind's greatest benefactors. Or is this belief already a symptom of megalomania?

"I think life for me has ended and world history begun."[8]

A year later Herzl published *Der Judenstaat*, priming the pump of modern Zionism, and there were many — among them a ten-year-old Ben-Gurion still rooted in a Polish *shtetl* — who regarded him as heaven-sent. A rumor spread that "the Messiah had arrived," Ben-Gurion was quoted as saying to an interviewer in 1966, "a tall handsome man, a learned man of Vienna, a doctor no less — Theodor Herzl."[9]

It was a rumor that Herzl would most likely not have denied. In later life he claimed that he had had a "wonderful dream" as an adolescent, long before his conversion to Zion: "King Messiah came and he was old and glorious. He lifted me in his arms, and he soared with me on the wings of the wind. On one of the clouds, full of splendor, we met the figure of Moses (his appearance was like that of Moses hewn in marble by Michelangelo; from my early childhood I liked to look at the photographs of that statue), and the Messiah called to Moses: 'For this child I have prayed.' Then he turned to me: 'Go and announce to the Jews that I will soon come and perform great miracles for my people and for the whole world.' I woke up and it was only a dream. I kept this dream a secret and didn't dare to tell it to anybody."[10]

Herzl's first journey to Jerusalem, in 1898, happened to coincide with a visit by Kaiser Wilhelm II. On November 2, the Kaiser received Herzl in his imperial tent. The Kaiser, wrote Herzl in his diary, was wearing a gray colonial uniform, veiled helmet on his head, brown gloves, and holding — oddly enough — a riding crop in his right hand. Herzl took advantage of his audience to tell the Kaiser that the Zionists would locate and develop all the water essential to a modernized Palestine. "It will cost billions," he said, "but it will yield billions."

"'Oh well,' said the Kaiser, slapping his boot with his riding crop for emphasis, 'money you've got aplenty. More money than all of us put together.'"[11]

Herzl was disgusted by what he saw of the Old City: "When I remember thee in days to come, O Jerusalem, it will not be with pleasure. The dank sediment of two millennia filled with inhumanity, intolerance, and filth infests the foul-smelling alleys. The amiable dreamer of Nazareth, the one and only human being in all this time ever to pass through here, merely contributed to intensifying the hatred. If we ever get Jerusalem... the first thing I would do is clean it up...clear out the filthy hovels, raze them, burn all non-sacred ruins, and transfer the bazaars elsewhere...."[12]

In *The Labyrinth of Exile: A Life of Theodor Herzl*, Ernst Pawel wrote that Herzl's trip to Palestine was notable for one conspicuous blind spot: "As Amos Elon has pointed out, the trip also took him through at least a dozen Arab villages, and in Jaffa itself, Jews formed only 10 percent — some 3,000 — of the total population. Yet not once does he refer to the natives in his notes, nor do they ever seem to figure in his later reflections. In overlooking, in refusing to acknowledge their presence — and hence their humanity — he both followed and reinforced a trend that was to have tragic consequences for Jews and Arabs alike."[13]

My reward for waiting on tables, at the summer's end, was a week in New York — New York, where I could stay with my uncle Israel and aunt Vera in their apartment in Brighton Beach.

Uncle Israel, Rabbi Rosenberg's eldest son, had been a hero of mine ever since I had been told that, when he was still a young man in Poland, he had turned his back on yeshiva studies and run away with a band of Gypsy players. In the forties he was still in show business, a family figure of incomparable glamor. He and Aunt Vera had a weekly radio program in New York, sponsored by the Manischevitz Company, and by fiddling with the shortwave dial on our RCA Victor I could sometimes catch them on Sunday mornings, the sound washing in and out on waves, riding bursts of static. My aunt, a singer, performed under the stage name Vera Rosanko, and was cherished as "The *Yiddishe Shiksa*" by her fans. Uncle Israel produced, wrote, directed, and often appeared in the comedies that played at his Clinton Theater on the Lower East Side. He was a short, portly man with soft brown eyes and a weary but occasionally teasing manner, and he was a sport. Such a sport. Mornings I would stroll with him as far as the corner, where he would stop to buy five cigars, his daily ration, and then hail a taxi to carry us over the bridge in style to his theater. On the day of my arrival, he would take me to a restaurant on Delancey Street, which he called The Yarmulke, and tell the proprietor, "This is my nephew Mottl, everything's on me." Before we parted each morning he would slip me a fiver.

Menashe Skulnik appeared at the Clinton Theater; so did Molly Picon, and once I saw Aaron Lebedeff, a jaunty song-and-dance man. "[He] would come prancing onto the stage," wrote Irving Howe in *World of Our Fathers*, "to dance and sing with a devil-may-care good nature: what the Russians, and the Jews after them, called a *molodiets*, a lively fellow who performs fine deeds."[14] Uncle Israel's comedies were writ large, just this side of vaudeville, and my tiny aunt Vera, already a grandmother, usually played the ingenue, an innocent child of the *shtetl* abandoned to the fleshpots of New York, rife with *Americanishe gonovim*. I recall that in one play a woman — certainly not my aunt Vera, but another woman entitled to the name *Yiddishe tochter*— reveals to a family gathering that she has been seduced by a *goyisher* fancy man and is going to give birth to an illegitimate child. A bastard! A *mamzer!*

This news was greeted with tears and recriminations onstage and with gasps from the audience. Finally, the stage mother, reviving from her swoon, aghast, asks, "And what will you call the little bastard?"

The disgraced young woman, turning to the audience — beaming — eyes widening — batting unbelievably long false eyelashes — exclaims, "ERNEST BEVIN!"

The theater erupted in cheers.

THE LAST TIME I saw my uncle Israel and aunt Vera, in New York in 1960, they took Florence and me, then newly wed, to dinner at Moskowitz and Lupowitz. Uncle Israel, chewing on a cigar, turned to my beautiful bride, who had given up modeling for Dior and Yves St. Laurent, as well as an offer to play a major role in the London production of *The World of Suzie Wong*, in order to marry me. "How did you manage to catch him?" he asked.

Uncle Israel had lost the Clinton Theater. There was no longer a sufficient audience for Yiddish comedies, and he and Aunt Vera were reduced to playing at the occasional fund-raising banquet. "I should have gone to Hollywood when I had the chance," said Uncle Israel. "Like Muni Weisenfreund and Manny Goldenberg."

Paul Muni and Edward G. Robinson.

❖ *Twelve* ❖

THE JERUSALEM POST WAS DELIVERED TO THE DOOR of our apartment in Mishkenot every morning. At breakfast on October 13, I read that Amatzia Ben-Haim, from Kibbutz Yad Mordechai, had been murdered on Sunday evening in Mei-Tal, an Israeli settlement in the Gaza district. Ben-Haim, a computer expert, had been summoned to the settlement to repair a watering-system computer in a greenhouse. When the owner went off to fetch a functioning computer, a terrorist attacked, bludgeoning Ben-Haim to death with a mattock. Elsewhere, less than five miles from Jericho, two terrorists who had scaled the border fence from Jordan had been shot and killed by an IDF patrol. One of them appeared to be seventeen, the other possibly twenty; they were armed with three knives and carried a Koran in one of their backpacks. The Palestinian inmates in all security prisons except for Nafha had ended their sixteen-day hunger strike after Police Commissioner Gabi Amir agreed to many of their demands: longer family visits, more educational opportunities, ventilators for their cells, and TV antennas capable of picking up Syrian and Jordanian programs.

A page-one story in the *Post* dealt with the previous day's troubles in Gaza. Stone-throwers in Khan Yunis had hit five Israeli soldiers, and seventeen Palestinians had been struck by gunshots. A teenager, Yunis Mahoud Tsaidan, wounded in a clash in the Nuseirat refugee camp on Sunday, had died in Tel Hashomer Hospital. Another teenager, Ziad Mahmoud Dagish, had been shot dead in the same incident. Palestinians claimed that Dagish had been killed by the soldiers, but "the IDF said the cause of death was unclear." Twenty-year-old Riad Farid Zeer was also fatally wounded on Sunday, "apparently by soldiers," after troops in the military outpost of Salfit opened fire on a group pitching stones at them. In another encounter that day, students from a Hebron girls' school heaved stones at soldiers, and a seventeen-year-old girl with a rubber bullet embedded in her leg had to be hospitalized.

That afternoon I caught up with the editor of *The Jerusalem Post*, David Bar-Illan, in his office. Scourge to my friends in the Peace Now movement, Bar-Illan, a former concert pianist, came to journalism in middle age, armed with a full metal jacket of spleen for Israel's traducers, those latter-day Amalekites snickering in the tall grass, sniping at Zion at a time when, according to Bar-Illan, anti-Semitism was "more virulent and ubiquitous than ever."[1] Never mind the Spanish Inquisition, the Black Hundreds, the Holocaust. The worst was now.

Born in Haifa in 1930, Bar-Illan was at the Juilliard School in New York from 1947 through 1950, but his studies were interrupted when he joined the IDF during the Israeli War of Independence. He gave his first piano recital at the Kennedy Center, in Washington, D.C., in 1972, and has performed more than forty times in Carnegie Hall and Avery Fisher Hall in New York. In 1988, he became publisher of *La'Inyan*, a Tel Aviv weekly, and from 1984 to 1989 he was director of the Jonathan Institute, a private foundation dedicated to fighting international terrorism. (The institute was named after Jonathan Netanyahu, the leader of the 1976 commando raid on Entebbe Airport. Jonathan, who was killed in the operation, was the older brother of Binyamin "Bibi" Netanyahu, who would become leader of the Likud Party in 1993.)

Bar-Illan's broadsides have appeared in *The New York Times*, *The Wall Street Journal*, *Commentary*, the London *Daily Telegraph*, and elsewhere. He has also written speeches in English for then Prime Minister Yitzhak Shamir to deliver on visits to the United States. He joined the *Post* as an editorial writer and editor in 1990, a year after Conrad Black bought it from Histadrut, the Mapai Party's trade union bastion, which is also a huge property owner and industrial giant. Black, a pugnacious Canadian newspaper tycoon who now lives in London, is the publisher of the *Daily Telegraph* and the weekly *Spectator*, and the director of Hollinger Inc., a major shareholder in both the Canadian Southam and Australian Fairfax newspaper chains. His purchase of the *Post* for a surprising twenty million dollars (U.S.) made for a sharp editorial turn to the right, and the subsequent resignation of some thirty disgruntled journalists. Under its new management, wrote Bar-Illan in *Commentary*, the paper was no longer a part of the "blame-Israel-first" clique, "providing the foreign press with generous fodder — and an Israeli cover — for its decade-long orgy of Israel-bashing. Correspondents used to quote it with glee. ... After all, no foreigners could be expected to be less vigorous in their excoriation of Israel than Israel's only English daily. Now that the *Post* has the *chutzpah* not only to assert that Israel is more sinned against than sinning, but to suggest that a Palestinian state in the heart of Jerusalem and the suburbs of Tel Aviv, with the inevitable access it would offer to the Saddam Husseins of this world, may not be a good idea after all, some foreign reporters feel orphaned. Let us hope they get over it."[2]

Bar-Illan lives in an apartment on French Hill, a now stylish quarter of Jerusalem that used to be occupied by the Jordanian army. He is married, with five children. A lean, sharp-featured man, charged with nervous energy. We had hardly begun to talk when his phone rang. It was a freelancer calling from Los Angeles. "All we can afford to pay is forty dollars," he said, but then he had to suffer the freelancer's loquacious pitch all the same, unable to get a word in edgewise. Finally he cut in. "This is not a Jewish community newspaper," he said with ill-concealed disdain. "We are an Israeli newspaper." The *Post*, he told me, has a daily circulation of 25,000 to 30,000, its Friday edition sells 55,000 copies, and its overseas weekly 20,000.

"Was there a danger of a schism," I asked, "between Orthodox and non-observant Jews in Israel?"

"The black-suits are resented," he said, "because they do their utmost to avoid military service. 'We're divinity students,' they say, but most of them are in business, diamonds, real estate, and so on." According to the most recent estimate, there are now some 25,000 *haredi* men of army age who have managed to defer their service from year to year.

"There will be no peace until democracy prevails in the Arab countries," said Bar-Illan. "There is hope because Arab mothers value their children as much as Jewish mothers. The people don't want war. Foreign television reporters unfailingly shoot against a background of the most squalid neighborhoods in Gaza. They never show you the affluent Arabs who live in splendid homes. The truth is, the Arabs have never had it so good."

Bar-Illan blames the international media for propagating what he interprets as the world's "anti-Israel venom." They are guilty of misunderstanding the Arab-Israeli conflict. Most of them, he has written in his "Eye on the Media" column, don't see it as a confrontation between a democratic society and the forces of totalitarianism and fundamentalism, or as a drive "spearheaded by the Palestinian Arabs to destroy Israel." Instead, they view it as a "cross between a war of national liberation and a civil rights struggle between Algerians fighting French colonialists and Alabama blacks resisting white sheriffs."[3] His list of willful distorters of the truth is comprehensive. It includes the BBC, the London *Independent* and *Guardian*,[4] ABC-TV news anchor Peter Jennings ("a pioneer in the slanted news business"),[5] the *Chicago Tribune, National Geographic*,[6] the "Macneil-Lehrer News Hour" ("with exemplary impartiality it invites as guests Jews who say Israel is an obstacle to peace, and Arabs who say Israel is an obstacle to peace"),[7] *New York Times* Pulitzer Prize winner Thomas Friedman ("a propagandist for the Palestinian cause"),[8] Seymour Hersh ("an Israeli-basher"),[9] Anthony Lewis,[10] *Paris-Match*, Mary McGrory,[11] *Vogue, Le Monde*, Strobe Talbott ("an old Israeli-basher and Arab apologist"),[12] *The Village Voice* ("one of the most virulently anti-Israel newspapers in America"),[13] Mike Wallace ("In the crowded field of Israel-bashers... [the] star of CBS-TV's *60 Minutes*, stands out. He is unique"),[14] *Washington Post* columnists Rowland Evans and Robert Novak ("the patriarchs of all Israel-bashers"),[15] and Milton Viorst, who has published reports from Israel in both *The New Yorker* and *Tikkun*.

Months before leaving for Israel, I began to subscribe to the *Post*'s international edition, and that's when I first came upon Bar-Illan's "Eye on the Media" column, his weekly jab at the ubiquitous slanderers of Zion. Although I almost never agreed with him, I became a grudging fan of his Dirty Harry stance, and had to admit that he did occasionally punch out a genuine twister. During the Six-Day War, for instance, he noted that a BBC news commentator was equally snide about the Arab claim that Tel Aviv, Beer-Sheba, and Haifa had been destroyed and an Israeli report of an Egyptian rout in the desert. "The truth," said the commentator, "is probably somewhere in the middle. Let us not forget that both combatants are Semites."[16]

Bar-Illan also made a convincing case against the use of anti-Israeli stereotypes by Oliphant, the widely syndicated American political cartoonist. For example, in one Oliphant cartoon he cites Shamir, being stoned by a Palestinian child, crying, "Ve vill let zem freely elect anyone ve approve of, but first zey haff to stop mit zis — ouch!" A second Oliphant cartoon followed hard on then Secretary of State Baker's announcement of the White House telephone number, and a plea for Shamir to call when he was serious about peace. The cartoon showed a Baker who had grown a long beard waiting for the call, while tiny sideline commentators said, "I'll bet he'll call collect, and when he does he'll ask for money."[17]

Bar-Illan's most celebrated and extended quarrel was with Mike Wallace. An "Eye on the Media" column that accused Wallace of producing a *60 Minutes* segment that tailored facts to fit his anti-Israeli bias was reprinted in *Commentary*, and led to a long and vituperative correspondence. The dispute was over exactly what had caused the tragic riot on Jerusalem's the Temple Mount on October 8, 1990, which ended with the killing of seventeen Palestinians. In defense of his point of view, Wallace wrote a letter to *Commentary* denying the Israeli government claim that the seventeen deaths were "the result of an unprovoked attack by a huge mob of rock-throwing Palestinians against thousands of Jewish worshippers at the Western Wall.... Instead, the deaths were a product of panic on the part of the Israeli police, plus years of mutual fear and distrust between Palestinians and Jews."[18]

In the barrage of charges and countercharges that followed, the most pertinent letter to be printed in *Commentary* came from Teddy Kollek, the Mayor of Jerusalem:

After Mike Wallace's report of the events on the Temple Mount on CBS's *60 Minutes*, I wrote a note of protest which was aired the following week. I stand by what I wrote then:

What happened on October 8 was a tragically violent chain of mutual provocations and overreactions. I regret that Mike Wallace deliberately used me to build the credibility of a series of partial truths he presented as final judgement. The situation is delicate enough; it is not served by editing the truth and rushing to assign blame.

Beyond the issue of how accurately the program portrayed what happened on that fateful morning, there is a larger point which was not made by Wallace or any other journalist whose reports I have read. I refer here to the historical context of the events on the Temple Mount which neither explains nor excuses what happened on October 8, but counterpoises an aberration with a policy respected for 23 years.

In June 1967, after an unprovoked war, a victorious army handed its government the greatest prize the Jewish people could dream of: "The Temple Mount is in our hands." This is Zion itself, the core of 2,000 years of longing to return. Yet the Israeli government, out of respect for the shrines of another faith that had been in place for 1,200 years, decided not only to leave the mosques untouched, but also to leave the administration of the site in the hands of Muslim religious authorities. I do not know of any precedent in history for such a gesture.

Certainly there is no precedent in Jerusalem's history. When the crusaders came, they changed mosques into churches. Saladin and his followers did just the opposite. While Jordan occupied Jerusalem's walled city

(1948–67), 58 synagogues were destroyed. Nor were the Jews allowed to pray at the Western Wall, the one remnant of the Temple still extant, despite armistice agreements guaranteeing that privilege. Traditionally every ruler here has destroyed the monuments of his predecessor's rule. Israel's policy on archeology — preserving the remains of all periods and all peoples in Jerusalem's history — like our policy regarding the Temple Mount, is a sign of a very different attitude on our part.

Some of the policies and programs of various Israeli governments have had grave faults which I have not hesitated to criticize, as David Bar-Illan rightly noted, but I do not think our virtues should be taken for granted.[19]

Bar-Illan, sniffing out traitors within the gates, is even more scornful of some of Israel's most talented writers and intellectuals than he is of foreign correspondents. In an October 1991 column, he excoriated Amos Oz, accusing him of peddling intemperate obscenities in a speech he had made about Gush Emunim ("the Bloc of the Faithful"), who believe that their settlement of the West Bank (the biblical Judea and Samaria) is a necessary step in the unfolding process that will lead to the End of Days and the Redemption of Mankind. Gush Emunim, Oz had said, was "A small sect, a cruel and obdurate sect, [that] emerged several years ago from a dark corner of Judaism; and it is threatening to destroy all that is dear to us and holy to us, and to bring down upon us a savage and insane blood cult.... Israel's government of occupation in the territories has become a monster; a monster which has long since crossed the Green Line, removed its masks and even boasts of its monstrosity. Armed gangs sally forth to wreak vengeance upon Arabs, and upon Jews 'who deserve to be shot like Arabs'.... Remember, this cult got the rifles and machine-guns from the State of Israel, from us...."[20]

In April, *The New Yorker* (once the "quintessence of urbanity [but now] a forum for effete armchair liberals") caught it on the chin for publishing "its own in-house Israeli-bashing Israeli, Amos Elon."[21] Elon, in the world according to Bar-Illan, had acquired some of the less fetching characteristics of the Palestinians he so ardently promoted: "He knows that American audiences, even the aging, radical-chic groupies whose innate racism compels them to forgive Third Worlders the most unspeakable enormities, might not cotton to Palestinians who climb roofs to cheer the Scudding of Tel Aviv civilians. For which Elon has a breathtakingly ingenious solution: in a *New Yorker* article about the war, he denies the whole thing ever happened.

"How does he know it did not happen? Simple! He tried to find someone, anyone, who had actually witnessed the dancing and singing... and could not! Ergo, the whole story was a propagandist invention, like the atrocity stories of World War II...."[22]

Bar-Illan's case against Israeli Arabs, reiterated again and again, is based on two premises, both of them shaky, neither of them germane. He is fond of quoting Mark Twain as proof, if it were needed, that before an undoubtedly heroic generation of Zionists came, making the desert bloom, building a modern city where there had been only swampland, dazzling the world with their ingenuity and military triumphs against the odds, Palestine was a "desolate country... [which] sits in sackcloth and ashes... a silent mournful expanse... [which] not even imagination can grace with the pomp of life and action."[23]

There is no denying Jewish accomplishment in Israel, but much of it was achieved on land where another people, however unambitious, was rooted. Their failure to cultivate their gardens does not justify their displacement by a stiff-necked people turning up with a book saying, "This is the turf God Almighty promised me and mine thousands of years ago. We took it by force of arms from the Canaanites in the first place, when Joshua was our main man, and later acquired even more territory, led by King David, in battles against the Jubisites, Philistines, Edomites, Moabites, and Ammonites. Now we're back, what's left of us, so move over or get out."

Bar-Illan, a skilled dialectician but no stranger to sophistry, is fond of protesting that until recently there was no such thing as an Arab Palestinian. He has argued that the only people who traditionally referred to themselves as Palestinians, at least when identifying themselves and their institutions in English, were the Jews, as witness the *Palestine Post*, the Palestine Symphony, the United Palestine Appeal, and so on.[24]

Yes, but the dispute is not about semantics. Palestine is where these people tended their sheep and olive groves for generations. It's true that many had fled the battle zones in 1948, but they fully expected to return in triumph once the Arab armies had driven the Jews into the sea, leaving the remnants ripe for slaughter. Other Palestinian Arabs had certainly been evicted from their villages.

Following the armistice of 1949, Ben-Gurion scandalized Israeli jurists by invoking 150 Emergency Defense Regulations plucked from the book of British Mandatory Laws that had first been brought into play in 1945. These statutes made it legal for the military to quarantine Arab villages and restrict entry and exit to those who had permits. Permits could be arbitrarily denied with no explanation beyond "security considerations."[25] Under Regulation 109, the military government could deport Arabs from their own towns and villages. Regulation 111 allowed for a person to be imprisoned for an unlimited time without trial, under administrative arrest. Violators of these regulations could not appeal a conviction by a military court.

At the time, Dr. Menachem Dunkelmann, a future Supreme Court justice, denounced the regulations as "a violation of elementary concepts of law and justice."[26] Dov Joseph, who would become Minister of Justice in 1950, also objected: "There is no certainty that a citizen may not be imprisoned for the rest of his life without a trial," he wrote. "The license of the administration to exile a citizen at any moment is truly boundless...."[27] But Ben-Gurion was adamant, and his martial law was the plug that enabled him to stem the home-coming tide of Arabs who had fled or been evicted from their traditional villages during the war. The refugees were pronounced "infiltrators," and turned back at the border.

Zionism has had an unexpected triumph. It has created, in Amos Elon's phrase, a mirror-image of itself: Palestinian nationalism — the longing of a dispossessed people for their own state.

◇ *Thirteen* ◇

*T*HAT EVENING FLORENCE AND I STARTED OUT FOR the German Colony, a leisurely fifteen-minute stroll, to join Paul and Helen Workman for dinner in their apartment. Paul, whom I had met years earlier in Canada, now covered the Middle East for CBC Television.

Florence and I climbed the flights of steps from Mishkenot to the Yemin Moshe Windmill, now a museum, emerging on Plummer Blumenfeld Street, which was lined with olive trees. A stout middle-aged Arab woman wearing a babushka, an embroidered blouse, and a long peasant skirt was plucking green olives from a tree, storing them in a sack tied to her waist. Her frisky little boy danced in front of anybody who passed, peddling postcards. We cut through a park where Arab children frolicked in a pool, coming out on King David Street, one of West Jerusalem's main and most pleasant thoroughfares. In the adjoining gardens thin black hoses ran like veins between parched flowerbeds. The day had been excruciatingly hot, but now there was a bit of a breeze. Middle-aged tourist couples, obviously American, passed arm in arm, at ease in Zion. A young, gangly, black-bearded Hasid in shirt-sleeves, trailing *tzi-tzit*, wheeled twins in a double stroller before him, his wife following after with two other small children. An Uzi was strapped to the Hasid's shoulder, which meant that he was most likely a West Bank settler. Suddenly an ambulance, lights flashing, came roaring through the dense traffic. It bore the emblem of the Israeli Red Cross, the Magen David Adom, and a sign on its front door panel proclaimed that the vehicle had been donated by a family in Houston in everlasting memory of Stan. Farther down King David Street, a plaque mounted on an archway leading to a religious school announced that the institution had been restored through the generosity of the Hubberman family of Skokie, Illinois.

Tovia Shlonsky, the young lecturer at the Hebrew University whom I had met in 1962, had been cynical about American Jewish largesse. "Why shouldn't they pay for Israel?" he had said. "Their money is ill-gotten anyway."

Thirty years later, Matti Golan went even further in his diatribe *With Friends Like You: What Israelis Really Think About American Jews*, in which he set up an imaginary book-length dialogue between Israel, a plain-spoken Israeli survivor of wars and terrorism, and Judah, a soft, affluent, American Jewish fund-raiser.

"You're someone with what's known as 'a deep commitment to Israel.' You do all the right things," Israel tells Judah. "You give to the United Jewish Appeal. You visit Israel every couple of years and never forget to bring back a souvenir from the Wailing Wall and a painting from the artists' colony in Safed. You're a member of the board of your Reform synagogue. You attend every meeting, every dinner, and every brunch, not a few of which you host in your own house. You listen with unfailing politeness to the dozens of speakers who come to your community from Israel to tell you for the umpteenth time what you already know by heart. Right now you're the local president of the UJA, having been Jewish National Fund chairman last year.... You are, without a doubt, the salt of the American Jewish earth... [but] in more ways than one, you're my enemy. A more harmful and dangerous one than the PLO.... The Palestinians think I stole their homeland. They want it back. They say they're my enemy and I'm theirs. I know where I stand with them and what I have to do to stop them. They tell the truth, not a lot of tall tales. Whereas you say you're my friend, that you support me, that you love me. But your actual record... is enormously harmful to me...."[1]

Judah protests that he and his kind provide the political support of the United States, and have functioned as Israel's partner since the day it came into existence. "How can there be a partnership," Israel asks, "between someone who sends his son to fight in Lebanon or the Occupied Territories and someone who sends his son to college? Between someone who spends three whole years of his life in the Israeli army, plus an annual month of reserve duty until middle age, and someone who comes as a tourist to Israel now and then? Between someone who pays over 50 percent of his income in taxes to the Israeli government and someone who contributes barely 1 percent of his — and even that, in many cases, because it's partly tax deductible!"

"Why can't I be your junior partner?"[2] Judah asks.

Because, Israel says, you're asking for "the privileges of a senior partner and the obligations of a less than junior one," and then he goes on to say: "The main reason you send money, it seems to me, is that you still don't feel safe in the country that you live in. No matter how much a part of American society you feel, you can't rule out the possibility of unexpected developments. One doesn't have to think of Nazi Germany to imagine situations in which your life could be made difficult, even intolerable. And if that should ever happen, it's good to know there's a safe house you can always escape to. You're relieved to have an option that the Jews of Europe didn't. I'm your insurance company, and you make your payments to me just as you do on your car insurance, your home insurance, your life insurance."[3]

Judah, the author's straw man, doesn't have the good sense to point out, albeit sadly, that the Jews in Israel are more at risk than those who live in North America; and next he is being admonished for working in the annual Israel bond drive, because those bonds, Israel insists, are "the biggest scam in Jewish philanthropy. Here's what happens," he says. "Let's say you buy a million dollars' worth of bonds. You then go and sell them, taking as a tax loss the difference between their dividend on the free market and the dividend of ordinary bonds. With that money you go and buy more bonds. That way you can get up at gala evenings and announce huge purchases of Israel bonds when your only real expense is the difference between the interest borne by them and the interest borne by other bonds, part of which is paid for by the United States Internal Revenue Service.

"So much for what you give."[4]

ACTUALLY, the evidence of American and Canadian Jewish munificence is to be seen everywhere in Jerusalem: just about every park, library, synagogue, operating theater, yeshiva, or gym is tagged in celebration of one family or another. In one sense, Jerusalem is a brilliantly organized panhandler's heaven. The ultimate *Schnorrerville*. The truly affluent Diaspora Jews are expected to endow university chairs, and in return clothing manufacturers, real-estate mavens, and stock market gaons are flattered with honorary degrees and photo ops with the prime minister. No issue of *The Jerusalem Post* is complete without its obligatory photograph of a middle-aged American or Canadian couple beaming in front of their gift: a bloodmobile, Talmud study room, tennis school, or intensive cardiac care ambulance. Even the park bench I came to favor, midway between Mishkenot and the Cinémathèque restaurant, bore a plaque to remind layabouts that it had been donated by the family in memory of John Rubens.

Goyim are dealt with differently. No sooner does a visiting American, European, African, or Asian politician land at Ben-Gurion Airport than he is issued a *kipa*, a tiny knitted skull cap, and whisked off to offer penance at Yad Vashem, the Holocaust Memorial Museum, where he will pose looking soulful. The innocent dead are brandished as counters for securing favorable loans or trade deals. The six million are invoked as equity.

EN ROUTE to the Workmans' apartment, Florence and I stopped for an apéritif at the trendy Café Caffit on Emek Refaim Street. Florence ordered a glass of white wine from a Golan Heights vineyard and I asked for a scotch. This is only worth mentioning because among all the other couples on the crowded terrace — most of them young, animated or absorbed in books or newspapers — we seemed to be the only ones drinking liquor. For the rest, the preferred evening libation was orange or lemonade, Turkish coffee, or soft drinks.

At dinner, Paul offered to take me to a refugee camp. "When we head for the West Bank on assignment," he said, "immediately we cross the Green Line, my cameraman spreads a blanket with PLO colors on the dashboard and sets a large CANADIAN BROADCASTING CORPORATION placard against the rear window. But it doesn't always work. The Palestinians know that Israeli undercover agents, looking into what's going on in the refugee camps, often pretend to be foreign journalists. We've made official protests, but so what? And driving back over the Green Line, the first thing we do is hide the PLO blanket *and* the CBC placard. In Israel, just about every foreign journalist is taken for a Palestinian sympathizer, and angry settlers can also throw stones."

Paul warned me that the German Colony and our neighborhood were both subject to frequent overnight car torchings. Arabs will smash a car window or jimmy open a door and empty a drum of industrial glue onto the seats. Then they will plant long wooden matches upright in the glue, light them, and disappear before the car bursts into flames. Even if the matches are blown out by the wind and the glue fails to ignite, the car is a write-off.

THE NEXT DAY, I turned up early for a lunch with Deborah Harris and Beth Elon on the terrace of the Cinémathèque restaurant. A young film center administrator, leaning against the balustrade, told me about a recent problem he had had to deal with. A brother of a bright young Arab in their employ had been arrested a couple of months back for stabbing a Jew at a bus stop in Jerusalem, shouting, "Allah Akbar!" To everybody's embarrassment, the popular young Arab at the film center had to be closely questioned about his political beliefs. "It turned out there was no reason to fire him," said the administrator, "so he's still here, as quick and obliging as ever, but it just isn't the same any more if you're working late, alone in an office, and he comes by."

Deborah Harris and Beth Elon, both former New Yorkers, are partners in a literary agency that represents many Israeli authors abroad, among them David Grossman, the gifted author of *The Yellow Wind* and *See Under: Love*. Inevitably, we fell to exchanging gossip about publishers and editors and writers we knew in London and New York. Given the drift of our conversation, we could just as easily have been seated in the lobby of the Algonquin Hotel or the bar at Groucho's, or on the terrace of the Café de Flore. Then something happened. There was a loud explosion. Backs stiffened and conversations stopped abruptly on the crowded terrace.

"It came from over there."

"East Jerusalem."

"But there's no smoke."

"It was a jet."

"Are you sure?"

"One of ours, breaking the sound barrier."

"Oh."

Returning to our apartment, I paused by the Arab bread-vendor's cart opposite the Yemin Moshe Windmill to buy a horseshoe-shaped loaf that is sold with a pinch of *za'atar* (hyssop) wrapped in a twist of newspaper. "How much is that?" I asked.

"For Americans," he replied, his manner jovial, "only a hundred bucks." But he accepted five shekels.

My cousin Sam Orbaum, a *Jerusalem Post* reporter, told me that the loaf is called a *beigele* by both Arab and Jew. It is also commonplace, he said, for Arab junk collectors, passing through Jewish neighborhoods on their donkey-drawn wagons, to call out, "*Alte zachen* [old things]," a Yiddish cry familiar to me from my St. Urbain Street boyhood, but one that some Israeli youngsters take to be Arabic. Israeli kids, for their part, frequently borrow from the Arabic, saying *mapsut* for "satisfied" and *yallah* for "let's go" or "come on."

Descending the stone steps to Mishkenot, I met two robed, middle-aged Arab sweepers leaning on their brooms. "*Shalom*," said one, and the other smiled and said, "*Chag sameach*." Happy holiday.

Eight months later, I would read that Bathsheva Hillel, a woman of fifty-seven, had been stabbed five times in the back, apparently by a terrorist, near Mishkenot.

THAT EVENING we met Norman and Tslilla Rose for dinner at the Minaret. Norman, who made *aliyah* from England, is a professor of history at the Hebrew University. He is the author of *Lewis Namier and Zionism* and of a biography of Chaim Weizmann. "I'd be willing to give up the Golan Heights for peace with Syria," he said. And then he added, seemingly unaware of the chilling echo, "We'll be all right here, once we've got a population of six million Jews."

◊ *Fourteen* ◊

*E*ARLY THE NEXT DAY, OCTOBER 15, WE LEARNED
that there had been trouble in other sectors of the city the
previous night. The sixteen-day hunger strike of security prisoners was still in force in three prisons and had now claimed its
first victim. Twenty-six-year-old Hussein Assad, who was being
held in Ashkelon prison, had died of a heart attack in Barzilai
hospital. Once the news reached Jebel Mukaber, the quarter
where he had lived, rioting broke out. Residents burned tires
on the streets and stoned police patrols, and were dispersed with
rubber bullets and tear gas. In another disturbance, this one in
the nearby village of Issawiya, seventeen demonstrators were
arrested.

Overnight, serious trouble had also flared up in the Gaza
Strip, ignited by a report of the death of a Fatah Hawk gunman,
two days earlier. On October 12, the twenty-year-old, armed
with a Kalashnikov automatic rifle, had been killed in a gun-
fight with an IDF patrol in Khan Yunis — but not before he
had critically wounded a young Israeli soldier in the neck.
According to Palestinian sources, the rioting in Khan Yunis had

also claimed the life of eighteen-year-old Tahseen Abu Shabna, and as many as eight were wounded.

The front-page story in the *Post* noted that Fatah Hawk, the armed wing of the PLO, had participated in numerous attacks on IDF patrols, including an August 1 shootout in which Sergeant Doron Darazi had been killed. He had also been wanted for "the murder of those accused of cooperating with the authorities."

In another action on the night of October 14 — this one in Aarabe, near Jenin — a young member of the militant Red Eagles had been captured. It was claimed he had taken part in a skirmish in which an IDF corporal had been killed, and he "had been sought since last May for violent interrogations of alleged cooperators."

Arab and Israeli spokesmen agree that in its first five years the *intifada* has led to the deaths of an estimated 1,100 Palestinians in battle with the IDF, and another 750, accused of being collaborators, have been executed by other Palestinians.

In 1947 there was an equally perfervid atmosphere of long-frustrated expectations, when it was the Jews who were anticipating the creation of their own state. Extremists among them executed — albeit on a much smaller scale — some people "accused of cooperating with the authorities," in this case the British. At the time, the Stern Gang (also known as Lohame Herut Yisrael or Lehi), led by Yitzhak Shamir, issued a document denouncing internal enemies: "Death to the traitor squealer. The underground judges the traitor by the evidence it has. The sentence is executed at the first opportunity available."[1] It has been generally accepted that from 1940 through 1948 the Stern Gang was responsible for forty-two of fifty-nine assassinations or attempted assassinations, half the victims being fellow Jews. On November 6, 1944, Shamir sent two youngsters into Cairo to murder Lord Moyne, the British Minister of State for the Middle East. Afterward, they were caught and hanged, and in 1983, when Shamir was prime minister, postage stamps were issued in their honor. Reminiscing about his underground activities on Israeli army radio in 1991, Shamir said, "Terrorism is a way of fighting that is acceptable under certain conditions and by certain movements." But he made a distinction between Jewish and Arab terrorism. The Jewish actions of the forties, he said, were justified because the Jews were fighting for their homeland. The Palestinians, however, were "fighting for land that was not theirs. This is the land of the people of Israel."

In 1944, the moribund Irgun Zvai Leumi, also known by the Hebrew acronym Etzel, was revived by a new commander-in-chief: Menachem Begin. Begin, who could muster only six hundred trained fighters armed with sixty pistols, a handful of rifles, a few hundred grenades, and two tons of explosives, proclaimed an uprising against British rule. In *The Revolt*, a memoir he published in 1951, Begin wrote: "The very existence of an underground, which oppression, hangings, torture and deportations fail to crush or weaken must, in the end, undermine the prestige of a colonial regime that lives by the legend of its omnipotence. Every attack which it fails to prevent is a blow to its standing. Even if the attack does not succeed, it makes a dent in that prestige, and that dent widens into a crack which is extended with every succeeding attack."[2]

◇ *Fifteen* ◇

W E HAD ARRIVED IN ISRAEL ONLY A DAY BEFORE
Sukkot, the Feast of Tabernacles, the eight-day holi-
day that is one of Judaism's three pilgrimage festivals (*shalosh re-
galim*), the other two being Passover and Shavuot, or Pentecost.
Passover commemorates the Exodus from Egypt, but was possibly derived from an early pagan spring festival; Shavuot, the
giving of the Ten Commandments at Mount Sinai as well as the
first wheat harvest; and Sukkot, the forty-year sentence of
wilderness wanderings imposed on the Israelites before they
were allowed to reach the Promised Land, and the autumn harvest of grapes and olives. For each of these pilgrimage festivals,
the Israelites were supposed to make offerings of thanksgiving
at the Temple.

During the week of Sukkot, observant Jews take their meals
in a tabernacle — a flimsily constructed booth called a sukkah,
its roof made of widely spaced slats overlaid with evergreen
branches. The sukkah is meant to be a reminder of the fragile
nature of the Israelites' shelters on their long journey through
the wilderness, but it also recognizes that it was once necessary

to guard the autumn harvest against robbers, keeping watch in the fields from huts hastily slapped together. Sukkot, a joyful holiday, has been known since Talmudic times as *HaChag*, "*the holiday*". I was not aware until I read Amos Elon's illuminating book *Jerusalem, City of Mirrors* that Arabs use an interchangeable word, *hagg*, to describe the pilgrimage to Mecca.

My brother and I used to help my father set up a sukkah on the balcony of our second-floor, cold-water flat on St. Urbain Street, with bunches of grapes and bananas suspended from the roof slats. We ate our suppers in the sukkah, often in considerable haste, shivering in our overcoats. My unhappily married mother was given to needling my father at the table, intent on diminishing him in the eyes of his children, recalling the lost splendor of *HaChag* in her late, great father's sukkah. Sholem Asch had visited. Rabbi Kook had sent greetings. French Canadian priests had come to pay homage. My grandfather's canary had perched on his finger and sung. The Skaryszewer Illuy, a Ba'al Shem (unlike, need it be said, my father's father, a dealer in scrap metals), had not been interred in an ordinary grave but in one sheltered by a hut. And during the Ten Days of Awe, pious Jews attended the site, sobbing, lighting memorial candles, dropping petitions written in Yiddish on the grave, asking for a favorable response about a loan requested from the City and District Savings Bank, the blessing of fertility for a seemingly barren daughter-in-law, intervention with the Almighty, Blessed be He, for remission from carcinoma. Throughout my mother's recitals my father would sit mute, his eyes lowered but his neck bleeding red. It was left to my cousin Lionel, a son of my mother's sister, to bring me compromising intelligence about the Skaryszewer Illuy. "What they never told us," he said, "is that it was our *zayde* who broke the kosher bakers' strike. He was an arch-reactionary."

Now Jerusalem was not only teeming with Diaspora Jews come to celebrate Sukkot in Eretz Yisrael, but also swelled by the presence of some six thousand gentile fundamentalists enamored of all things Israeli. They were following a long tradition. In 1844, the United States sent its first representative to Palestine, accrediting Warder Cresson as U.S. consul to the Turkish court and "All The Holy Land." Cresson established himself in Jerusalem and a year later embraced Judaism and changed his name to Michael Boaz Israel. In 1847, he founded an agricultural colony, "God's Vineyard," on the outskirts of Jerusalem. Taking the Bible as a text and his own farming experience as a guide, he printed pamphlets and sought *chalutzim* for his project. Within four years, two hundred Americans joined him; fifty-two were Jewish and the others Protestants, or converts to Judaism. Michael Boaz Israel's kibbutz, born before its time, was eventually abandoned, but the gentile lovers of Zion continued to arrive.

In 1962, drifting through the art gallery in the Sheraton Hotel in Tel Aviv, I encountered Brother John, a California millionaire whose holdings included a vast cattle ranch, uranium mines, and chemical plants. The most engaging of tycoons, Brother John had made it his personal mission to replenish the zoos of the Holy Land, flying in once or twice a year with the gift of a giraffe or perhaps an elephant. He had already dropped thousands in zany Israeli investments, but he was not dismayed. "I have just earned my first Israeli dividend," he said. Brother John, a Bible student, had invested in a new chemical plant in an unpromising area because he remembered that Moses said, "Judah will dig riches from the earth here." Banging his gold-tipped walking stick against a chair, Brother John waved a stock certificate at me. "And by George they have," he said, "they sure have."

And now, thirty years later, six thousand fundamentalists had come to Israel for their twelfth annual Feast of Tabernacles. These pilgrims, members of the International Christian Embassy in Jerusalem (ICEJ), originated in eighty countries, including Egypt, Tanzania, Samoa, the Solomon Islands, and Ukraine. They were officially greeted by Prime Minister Rabin, who was cheered when he told them, "Jerusalem must stay united forever under Israeli sovereignty."

Adherents of the "embassy" dismiss Christmas as a pagan feast day appropriated by early Christians. Christ, they allow, was conceived on December 25, but was born in a Bethlehem stable during a Sukkot pilgrimage made by Joseph and Mary. And they believe that during a future Sukkot in Jerusalem they will be able to witness Christ's Second Coming.

Tim King, the ICEJ's financial director, is an American who quit his Toronto insurance agency in 1979 to study at the Institute of Holy Land Studies, and stayed on to become a founder of ICEJ in 1981. ICEJ, he claims, invests five million dollars annually in Israel, donating ambulances to hospitals and helping to establish small businesses, providing they employ immigrants and keep the profits in Israel. They have also financed forty planeloads of immigrants from Russia, in support of Jeremiah's prophecy of the return of Jews "from the north" and the evangelical belief that the ingathering of Russian *olim* (*aliyah*-makers) will hasten the Second Coming.

Fundamentalists, Tim King has said, see Jews as essential to the Redemption, but the Redemption will only become possible after the Jews have accepted Jesus, realizing another of Jeremiah's prophecies (31:31, "Behold, the days come, saith the Lord, that I will make a new covenant with the house of Israel, and with the house of Judah.")

The End of Days, which will herald Christ's Second Coming, is near, according to the fundamentalists, but it is first necessary for the Jews to rebuild the Temple on the Temple Mount, once the site of the Second Temple and, since 691, the setting for the magnificent Dome of the Rock and the al-Aqsa Mosque, known collectively as Haram al-Sharif (the Noble Sanctuary) to Muslims. Then the Third Temple will be destroyed. Christ will return, meet the Antichrist in a nuclear showdown at Armageddon, northwest of Jerusalem, and defeat him and his legions. Two thirds of Jewry will perish in the conflict, and the remainder will embrace Christianity.

An old tale, nourishing the continuing enmity between Arab and Jew, has it that the caliph Omar, who conquered Jerusalem in 638 A.D., asked the Jews where their Temple had stood and then spitefully settled on that place as the only possible site for the Dome of the Rock. Not that the enmity between Arab and Jew was in any need of reinforcement; it already enjoyed the distinction of being the oldest known to mankind. It dates back to the day that Sarah, already a septuagenarian, gave birth to Isaac and obliged Abraham to send Hagar, his concubine, packing, along with her babe, Ishmael. It was compounded when the shifty Jacob swindled Esau out of his inheritance. Ishmael became the progenitor of the Ishmaelites, from whom the Arabs claim descent, and Esau of the Edomites and Amalekites.

The Dome of the Rock was built by the Umayyad caliph Abd al-Malik, on the world's navel, which the Greeks had earlier taken to be located in the Temple of Apollo at Delphi and which the Chinese, no doubt, have pinpointed somewhere in the Middle Kingdom.

The Israeli Ministry of Religious Affairs, honoring a proscription of Maimonides, has posted notices in the Old City declaring that it is forbidden for Jews to visit the Temple Mount. Should we stroll across that broad esplanade, our footsteps might inadvertently violate what was once the Temple's Holy of Holies, the sanctuary that was purported to shelter, in King Solomon's time, the tablets of the law that Moses brought down from Mount Sinai. Only the high priest was entitled to enter the Holy of Holies — and only once a year, on Yom Kippur.

Our guide to the Temple Mount, a bemused, middle-aged Palestinian, pointed out to us a gate variously known as the Golden Gate, the Gate of Mercy, or the Messiah's Gate. According to both Jewish and Christian legend, the Messiah will enter Jerusalem through this gate, proclaiming the Day of Judgment. Taking no chances, the Muslims sealed the gate with cement in the thirteenth century.

Descending steps in the Dome of the Rock, we intruded on robed Muslims at prayer by what is arguably the world's most sacred stone, that long, flat rock that is precious to Jews, Muslims, and Christians. It is, so far as devout Jews are concerned, the Stone of Foundation, humanity's birthplace, the exact spot where Adam was molded from dust. It is on this rock, protruding from the ground, that Cain is supposed to have killed Abel. It is believed to be where Abraham, put to the test by Jehovah, prepared to sacrifice Isaac. Jesus is said to have preached here. And it is also said to be where Mohammed stopped on his *isra*, his celebrated nocturnal flight to heaven, traveling from Mecca to Jerusalem, and ascended to heaven on his horse.

❖ *Sixteen* ❖

O N NOVEMBER 10, 1950, A BOXED ADVERTISEMENT
appeared in *The Jerusalem Post*:

Notice — The meeting of American *olim* to discuss the
problems of absorption and the possibility of setting
up an American office will take place on Sunday November 12, 1950, at 4 p.m. at 40 Yehuda Halevy Street,
Tel Aviv.

The advertisement had been placed in the *Post* by Dr.
Herman Pomrenze, who had made *aliyah* from Chicago, after
he had consulted David Breslau, who had come to Israel in
1949, and another American immigrant, Aviva Skidell. At the
time, all three were dismayed by the large number of North
American *olim* who were returning home, if only because their
dream of a Jewish national home did not embrace *tzenah* (austerity), queuing for two hours in the heat for their ration of de-
hydrated eggs and frozen codfish.

Defending the austerity program in a Knesset debate on August 7, 1950, the Minister of Labor, Golda Meir, argued that the choice was simple: "either ration immigration, or ration food and clothing." And then, invoking the six thousand Jews who had died in the War of Independence, she added, "After all, what is demanded of us? A little less extravagance, so as not to dissipate the inheritance for which our dear ones gave their lives. They did not die for the sake of prosperity, but for the state and a great immigration."[1]

At the start of the debate, Menachem Begin, who had emerged from the underground to become a member of the opposition, had been heard from on November 9, 1949. Austerity, he ventured, was a menace to the state's future security. Hungry children would not grow into able-bodied warriors. "You are bringing up a generation of invalids!" he said.

Recalling those turbulent days on the fortieth anniversary of what was to become the Association of Americans and Canadians in Israel (AACI), David Breslau told *The Jerusalem Post*, "Over 5,000 people came to Israel from the U.S. and Canada during the first few years of statehood. People had great hopes and knew that they were part of a great movement in Jewish history. But these days of great joy were also difficult days. Israel was absorbing thousands of *olim* from the four corners of the earth. Little attention was paid to the small idealistic *aliyah* from North America and other Western countries. Sheer loneliness drove many of them back to the U.S. or Canada with faded dreams."

One hundred and twenty people showed up for the November 12 meeting. "It seemed as though people kept coming and coming," said Breslau. "Crowds came and stood around and talked and talked. The overwhelming majority said that we should form an organization that would take care of the needs of American *olim*. It didn't matter if we were revisionists or

Hashomer Hatza'ir or Habonim. We were united much more by our common, immediate problems than we were separated by our ideological pasts."[2]

Eight months later the organization, initially known as Hitahdut Olei America, opened for business, as it were, in a small room borrowed from the Hebrew Immigrant Aid Society. Members were enjoined to bring their own tea and sugar to meetings.

One afternoon in 1962 I called on Murray Greenfield, who was then director of AACI. Greenfield, an explosively energetic man of thirty-six, had come to Israel in 1947 to serve with Haganah, and in 1962, his work for the association apart, he ran two art galleries and was active in real estate. "Half of the Canadians and Americans who come here leave after two–three years," he said. "If they stay longer they're hooked. Why do they quit? They think it's all going to be orange picking and dancing the hora. They go to a kibbutz and want to dance round a tree after one bushel's been picked. Another reason so many go home is, let's face it, most of them come from middle-class homes and coming here means a big drop in their standard of living. Not everybody can take it. Many others miss their close family ties. Momma."

In recent years, Greenfield pointed out, the annual *aliyah* from North America could be measured in the hundreds.

"I'm a big fish in a small pond," he said, "and I like it. You know, my picture's in the papers here, everybody knows who I am. I'm taking part in something. In America who knows me? Who would care?"

TODAY, the AACI's membership having grown to twenty thousand, the primary function of its twelve full-time counselors is still to ease the trauma of *klita* (absorption). But through its five regional offices — in Tel Aviv, Netanya, Haifa, Beer-Sheba, and Jerusalem — it also offers help with employment and culture shock, therapy, free legal aid, advice on mortgage and rent subsidies, and guidance through the Customs maze.

The national office is at 11 Pinsker Street in west Jerusalem, and that's where I went to talk with the association's no-nonsense director, Olga Rachmilevich, who exudes both warmth and intelligence. Admirably succinct, she immediately pinpointed AACI's raison d'être: "We provide organized *protekzia*." Native-born Israelis, she explained, enjoy the advantage of contacts made from nursery school to military service, but new immigrants are often at a loss. "We supply a network," she said, "showing newcomers which buttons to press."

Since 1948, North America's Jewish population, just short of six million, has yielded a mere seventy-five thousand *olim*. From a peak of 4,267 North American immigrants in 1983, the numbers sank to a nadir of 1,805 in 1989, and some 1,900 in both 1990 and 1991. In 1992, the tally was 2,607.

In the seventies, some three hundred Israeli *shlichim* (recruiters) fanned out through North America, searching for immigrants. But today it costs approximately $90,000 a year to maintain a *shaliach* in the United States or Canada, the community to which he or she is posted traditionally picking up $35,700 of that tab, plus expenses. So now there are only seventy *shlichim* working the territory, but they are more sophisticated than they used to be, according to Yossi Kuchik, executive director of the North American Aliyah Delegation of the World Zionist Organization, and they have moderated their pitch. "We don't use the Holocaust or anti-Semitism as a threat to American Jews," he said in a recent interview. "It doesn't work, and it alienates people."

I asked Olga Rachmilevich how many Americans and Canadians were now living in Israel.

"You mean survivors? About seventy-five thousand. Some forty percent couldn't stick it out. Our twenty thousand adult members actually represent fifty or sixty thousand 'Anglo-Saxons,' when you take in their families." She chuckled. "Many Israelis see our *olim* as refugees and some North American Jews look at us as people who didn't, or couldn't, make it in America. 'Why did you give up the good life?'"

Olga, who could have made it anywhere, is fifty-nine years old, and settled in Israel in 1962. She joined AACI two years later and was appointed national director in 1990. "My husband guides tourists through the Old City," she said. "He has a gun, but he wouldn't know how to shoot it. The bullets are here and the gun is there. We get all sorts here, from naive, generous socialists to born-again ultra-Orthodox Jews, the fierce ones."

The AACI has 350 volunteers in Jerusalem teaching English to Russian immigrants. "They're all *goyim*," said Olga. "Well, a lot of them are *goyim*. But it's rough for them. I know of one couple who were both engineers. Now he's a night watchman and she cleans apartments. There's a good deal of resentment here too. Some Israelis complain about the *olim's* housing being government-subsidized. A neighbor of mine said, 'My son couldn't get into pre-med. The Russians have taken all the places.' Sound familiar?"

The AACI lobbies not only for its own members but also for political change. It was deeply involved in the successful campaign for the reform that means there will be a direct vote for Israel's prime minister in the next general election, rather than the leader of the winning party or coalition automatically filling that office.

"The pre-'67 *aliyah* was made up of socialist types, kibbutzniks," said Olga, "mostly out of Habonim and Hashomer Hatza'ir. And then from '67 to '77 we got the yuppies. Hey, following the Six-Day War we were great! Things were tough in

America. Lots of professionals decided this was a good place to bring up nice Jewish children. Then, after '77, we got the Bible-driven ones, very political. You should know that many Americans came here not to be democrats, not to be pluralists. We make up one percent of the total population but eight percent of the population of West Bank settlements.

"Israelis really believe that all Jews should make *aliyah*," she explained. "Well, not necessarily. But Jews have always taken care of each other. We're part of a family. You do your bit, we'll do our bit. The price we pay is sending our kids to the army and seeing fifty to sixty percent of our income going in taxes. And you people in the Diaspora must pay your price. We need your contributions. Now, there are a couple of Montrealers working in this office, and they'd both like you to say hello."

It came as a pleasant surprise that the typesetting and layout editor of the AACI's bimonthly *Seniors' Spectator*, Frances Neumark, was Morty Pearl's daughter. On the other side of the moon, Morty and I had been Talmud Torah classmates and had played a good deal of street hockey together, resorting to roller skates and a tennis ball once the ice had melted. Morty was connected. In the wartime forties, his postman also worked as an usher in the Montreal Forum during Sunday-afternoon Quebec Senior Hockey League double-headers. And back in those days, when the National Hockey League was limited to six rather than twenty-seven teams, the action provided by the QSHL's Montreal Royals, Quebec Aces, and Ottawa Commandos, among other clubs, was first-rate. The complimentary seats Morty got from his postman were for the high cheap seats in the Forum, but by dint of tossing our caps into the next most desirable section and then clambering over the barrier, we could gradually descend into the choice seats at rinkside. If an usher caught us, we would protest that we had only been trying to retrieve our caps, which had been flung over the barrier by a "bad boy."

Frances was pretty and plump, shy, with a disarming dimpled smile. Her husband, Yehudah, an epidemiologist, was working for his doctorate at the Hadassah School of Public Health. They had made *aliyah* in September 1985, and now had three children. In 1986, the Neumarks had moved to the relatively new settlement of Ma'ale Adumim, on the West Bank, a twenty-minute drive from West Jerusalem. "I used to have to drive past an Arab village to get here," said Frances. "It was calm in the mornings, but afternoons were something else. I've been stoned about four or five times, and after you've been stoned a few times you get angry. Fortunately, the new highway bypasses the Arab village."

"Do you mind if I ask why you made *aliyah?*"

"Because we wanted a better place to bring up kids. Oh, I see," she said, her giggle self-deprecating. "Yeah. But the kids never leave the village. And it's lovely, with parks all around. We are something like fifteen thousand people in the settlement, maybe two thousand of them Russian, who made *aliyah* in the last two or three years. Our babysitter used to be a librarian in Kiev."

The Neumarks' duplex in Ma'ale Adumim cost them $85,000, and Frances estimated that it was now worth at least $220,000. "Okay," she said, "originally we moved to the territories because a house in Jerusalem would have cost us triple that, but after we had settled in we began to feel strongly about never giving it back. The *intifada* is a chronic disease, and there are no easy answers. But I don't think peace will happen just because you give up settlements. Me, I don't believe in giving any of it back, not an inch. If anything, we should be getting more. Let me ask you something. Why don't the Arab countries absorb the refugees the way we took in Jews who had to flee for their lives from their countries, and came here with nothing, mostly? The Arabs don't deserve anything from us. If they'd just go out and get a job. It's hard to help people who won't help themselves. Not many of them are highly educated."

Frances's husband, who comes from an Orthodox family, belongs to Moledet, a party that won only 62,269 votes, or 2.3 percent of the total ballots cast in the last general election, in 1992. Moledet favors an expansion of the settlements in the Golan Heights, and a doubling of the Jewish population of Judea, Samaria, and Gaza over the next four years. Its platform also called for a transfer of Arabs out of the territories, a policy that would be given a jump-start by stopping all incentives for Arab industry and barring Arabs from work within the Green Line.

"Are you also in favor of transfer, Frances?"

"If they had the chance, they'd stab you in the back," she said, and then she giggled and made a sweeping "out of here" gesture with her hand. "I wouldn't be sorry to see them go."

The other Montrealer in the association's national office, Michael Goldstein, was a former vice-president of the Jewish National Fund in Canada. Goldstein, who now attended to fund-raising for the AACI, made *aliyah* with his wife and three children in 1989. "If only I could sell my house in Côte St. Luc," he said, "but show me a Jew who's buying in Montreal these days. I can't tell you how good it is to be here and not have to deal with the nutty language laws and sign laws any more, never mind a referendum on independence or a new constitution every ten years. I feel like a great weight has been lifted from me. Here I never even think about being Jewish. We're all Jewish."

◊ *Seventeen* ◊

*T*HE HEADLINE FOR *THE JERUSALEM POST*'S LEAD
story on Friday, October 16, read: "Massive Manhunt for
Farmer's Killers."

Terrorists had murdered a thirty-five-year-old farmer, Shimon Avraham, slashing him to death in the fields hard by his
home in the moshav of Meitav, south of Afula. The attackers had
fled in a car, which they abandoned near the Arab village of
Mukeibila, within the Green Line. Later, an anonymous caller
told *a-Sinara*, a Nazareth newspaper, that a group called "The
Holy Jihad" was responsible. Elsewhere, the Unified National
Leadership of the Uprising called for a three-day strike in East
Jerusalem and a one-day work stoppage in Palestinian towns, to
mourn the death of Hussein Assad Obeidat, the hunger-striker
who had died of a heart attack.

After breakfast, a taxi driver arrived to take me to Kibbutz
Urim, in the Negev, a ninety-minute drive. Ezra Lifshitz, my
former Habonim group leader, was expecting me.

Taxi drivers, a rough and ready lot who, in my experience,
are mostly of Middle Eastern or North African origin, are regarded with suspicion by Israelis. Prominently displayed signs in

every hotel set out the official rates for intercity travel, and tourists are warned again and again to make sure the driver has turned on his meter before setting out.

Among the twenty-nine parties contesting the general election in Israel had been the Law of Nature Party, the Women's Party, and Al Galgalim ("On Wheels"), the Taxi Drivers' Party. The Kahane Hai Party — its leader Binyamin Kahane, a son of the murdered Rabbi Kahane — had been disqualified, even as the late rabbi's original party, Kach, had been disallowed after being adjudged racist. However, Kahane Hai's petition to be included on the electoral lists had been supported by four of the religious parties: Shas, Tehiya, United Torah, and the National Religious Party. Taken together, these four parties would account for only 14.2 percent of the ballots cast. Another fringe party denied by the Knesset's central elections committee had been Stop Aliyah, if only because its leader had failed to surface with the necessary deposit. A *haredi* party, Medinat Hayehudim, had been turned down as well. Its first two candidates, Robert and Rachel Manning, had been sitting in a Jerusalem slammer, appealing extradition to the United States, where they were wanted on a murder charge; had their party won acceptance and the Mannings been elected by a fluke, they would have gained parliamentary immunity to extradition. The Israel Monarchy Party, which wanted to rebuild the Temple and favored increased tourism and sport, had also been banned, in spite of the plea by its leader, Avraham Badanjo: "The Jewish people has been dreaming of restoring the monarchy for two millennia. I implore you not to spoil that dream now," he said. "It's true that I didn't submit enough signatures of sponsors, and that the particulars of my candidates were awry, but I collected 1,000 additional signatures, which my wife hid from me somewhere in the apartment.... All those who signed are real people.

"On top of that, the Almighty spared my life for this mission when I escaped unhurt on driving into a huge rock on the way home from Meron."[1]

Al Galgalim, my driver said, wanted something done about traffic jams in Jerusalem. The party's platform called for car-parks to be established at entrances to the city, with a supplementary bus service to be run by the taxi drivers, and for government-subsidized rather than expensive privately owned parking lots within the city. Their leader was aware, he said, of the many complaints about price-gouging. Twelve days before the election, the Likud had issued a communiqué claiming that hundreds of taxi drivers had abandoned Al Galgalim, switching their support to Likud. But in the event, Al Galgalim, the political arm of a union with 3,000 members, won 3,355 votes.

My driver, a burly, middle-aged Moroccan, was proficient in slangy English, circa 1951, which he had picked up working on the construction of an American air base in the Atlas Mountains. "So," he said, "you must be a rich guy, come over from Canada to see the forests you paid for. The Wailing Wall. Masada. Floating in the Dead Sea, smoking a big cigar. Where's your video camera?"

"I haven't got one."

"What kind of business are you in over there?"

"Pulp and paper."

"You know the Reichmanns, I suppose?"

"No."

"Why didn't you bring your wife with you to Israel, or maybe you're in Splitsville?"

"She's waiting for me in Jerusalem."

"Young or your age?"

"My age."

"I don't blame her she doesn't want to crash on a kibbutz. Have you taken her to dinner at Ocean yet?"

"Yes."

"That's a week's pay for me. What kind of car do you drive in Montreal?"

"A Ferrari 250 GT Berlinetta."

"Sure. What else? So what do you make of the poor Jews here in Israel? Be frank."

"As a matter of fact, I'm having a delightful time."

"But there's nothing like a return air ticket. You know, they never really wanted guys like me here, Sephardic Jews from Arab countries. It's only because so many Ashkenazim were lost in the Holocaust that they took us in, and that's a proven historical fact. But now they have a new baby. The Russians. Everything is done for them. Duty-free cars, which they sell at a profit. Hard currency only, please. Nice new housing. Cash allowances on arrival. At home you probably contribute to Operation Exodus, because you think if they wear a *kipa* they must be Jews, never mind you take a nice tax write-off."

"Aren't they Jews?"

"Maybe a great-grandmother was or a second cousin somewhere. Let me tell you, in order to get out of Russia there were *goyim* who paid $10,000 to marry a Jewish broad, fat or ugly, who cares? It was a ticket to this paradise. Look at me," he said, glaring into his rearview mirror, "I'm dressed like a *mensh*, yes or no? And I talk to you polite, it's my policy with customers, and I can tell you many things of Jewish historical interest about the sites we pass. Would you like me to do that? I'm licensed. It only costs a little bit more, an operator like you wouldn't even blink. What do you say?"

"No thanks."

"No is no. I wouldn't argue with a customer. But you have already missed out on some outstanding information about the places we passed on the road and I would ask only forty shekels to be your guide, which is less than the official rate. What do you say?"

"No."

"Such a hard nut. Thirty shekels then. How about it?"

"I said no."

"Okay, okay. No hard feelings. I have a family to support, and you know what? I have to compete in Jerusalem with Arab drivers, you better watch out for them. They don't spend to dress like a *mensh* for their customers. *Shmattes* is what they wear. Rags. They have ten children at least, and you know what they eat, those animals? They dump a big plate of hummus on the floor and everybody reaches out with their bare hands. Grab grab grab. They live in filth."

"You know, when I was a kid in Montreal, the man who would become our mayor, Jean Drapeau, once said the same about Jews. He wrote an article complaining that our neighborhood was filthy and that you couldn't pass through our streets without your stomach turning."

"What are you, some kind of anti-Semite?"

"It wasn't my opinion, but the mayor's, when he was a young man back in the forties."

"How could you even say such a thing to me?" he asked, slowing down.

"I was trying to make a point."

"That Jews live in filth?"

"Forget it."

"I fought in two wars, and you come here on a visit and think you can talk to me like that."

"You still don't understand what I'm trying to say."

"Sure, I'm stupid. A poor Arab Jew out of the Atlas Mountains. I'll bet you believe I never even saw a flush toilet before I came here."

"This is ridiculous."

"I think you should apologize," he said, reducing his speed still further.

"For what?"

"I'm offended."

"I'm sorry if I offended you. Now can we get moving again, please?"

"Yes, sir. At your service, boss."

I HAD BEEN to a kibbutz once before, in 1962, and on that occasion my taxi driver had been a grizzly, affable Polish Jew. Before driving with him from Tel Aviv to Kibbutz Gesher Haziv in the Galilee, I had asked him how much the trip would cost.

"Are we married? Do we need a rabbi? We'll settle the fare on the way."

We settled right there for seventeen U.S. dollars.

"In Canada," said the driver, "you must have your own airplane."

"I'm afraid not."

"But many Canadians have private planes. Say, one in ten."

"Not even one in a hundred thousand."

"You think I'd charge more?" His was the usual old, battered De Soto with shattered windows and dented fenders. "Next to Japan," he said, "we have the highest accident rate in the world. And that's without benefit of drunken drivers. Can I pick up other people on the road? We could go partners?"

"No."

Gesher Haziv lay in the foothills of the Galilee, less than a mile from the Mediterranean, about five miles from the Lebanese border. The kibbutz was established on the site of an old British army rest camp in 1949, by Habonim members drawn from Canada and the United States, in association with forty sabras. I arrived on the eve of Passover and was immediately taken to the home of a family of Canadian *olim*, the Shlossbergs. Meyer, who was in charge of the turkey farm, came in, exhausted. "We're expecting more than a hundred guests for the Seder," he said.

The kibbutz movement had been experimenting for years with a more militant Haggadah (Passover text), a revised version that included new Israeli songs and more recent history, but kibbutzniks had found this increasingly unsatisfactory and were gradually returning to the traditional Haggadah. "Some things you can't modernize," an American kibbutznik said. "You know what I miss? I miss my father's jokes."

Gesher Haziv's Seder was conducted by Bill Kofsky, an alumnus of the house on Jeanne Mance Street. A reticent, thoughtful man, then in his mid-thirties, Bill was one of the kibbutz's original settlers. His wife was American and they had two children. In Gesher Haziv, children lived with their families instead of sleeping in dormitories, which was considered a radical departure in kibbutz living in 1962, an experiment that was being closely watched. "Originally," said Bill, "it was felt that we were going to create a new man for a new society and so it was necessary to protect kids from the ghetto mentality of their parents. We might unconsciously taint them. It was best to leave them to their teachers. But somehow it didn't work out. We hadn't counted on Jewish mothers. We found out that after dark many of them were sneaking into the kids' sleeping quarters to hug and slip candies to their very own. So we had to throw in the sponge."

The 120 founders of Gesher Haziv lived in tents for the first year. The next year, while they were still clearing the fields and as yet had no income, they moved into temporary shacks, and the following year they borrowed money to erect their permanent dwellings. "That's how our financial troubles started," said Deborah Shlossberg. "We're still paying interest on these houses."

When the new, unproven kibbutz wanted to borrow money, they had to resort to the black market, where interest rates were as high as thirty percent. Further loans were negotiated to buy farming equipment and to insure against the occasional crop failure. "The result," said Bill, "is that we now put in a fifth of our working day just to pay off the interest."

Debts aside, Gesher Haziv's problems were considerable. "First of all," said Bill, "there's the big turnover in people. Let's say a new guy comes out here with his wife and kids, maybe we build a house for him, we certainly clothe and school his kids. It takes a new guy six months before he's any good in the fields, and all that time we lose the labor of another man, the guy who's training him. Well, okay. But maybe six months later the guy ups and returns to Canada or moves to the city.... Or let's say we decide to go in for cotton. We train a guy, he becomes our cotton expert, and a year later he moves off and we're in trouble with cotton."

Gesher Haziv's socialist practices exacted a toll. As everybody was theoretically equal on the kibbutz, members were elected to offices of authority (secretary, farm supervisor) for a two-year period only. This was supposed to be a safeguard against the development of two classes: workers and bosses. "But the result," said Bill, "is not altogether satisfactory. It takes six months to train a secretary, a year passes, and we have to start training another. We lose a lot in efficiency. Also, in spite of our efforts, we find the same personalities turning up again and again in the bigger, most responsible jobs."

Gesher Haziv, like many other kibbutzim, were unable to make a financial success of agriculture, an activity traditionally dependent on cheap labor at harvest time, and so they reluctantly decided to hire casual labor. They were going to manufacture turkey sausage and they were building a tourist motel. "We are a curiosity," a kibbutznik said to me. "Why shouldn't people come to see how we live?"

A number of the kibbutzniks were distressed by their decline in status. "At one time," said Deborah, "you could walk into town just as you are, and people would point you out with envy and pride. There goes a kibbutznik.... But not today. Now we're looked on as characters. We don't dare go into town without dressing up and putting on make-up."

Bill said, "Once we were considered the elite, today we're looked on as hayseeds. In town they say we've abdicated our worries. You work eight hours a day, they say, you have your food and security, and others worry for you."

Bill had little curiosity about the Canada he had left behind him.

"What's happening in Montreal? It's gotten bigger, that's all," he said. "All my friends are in Israel anyway. I guess we must seem very chauvinistic to you here. We're curious about everything in this country, it's ours and we want to know all there is to know. The names of the different flowers and birds, and all the history."

The day after the Seder, Gesher Haziv celebrated the beginning of the Counting of the Omer, the forty-nine-day countdown to Shavuot. *Chaverim*, guests, and children clambered onto tractor wagons decked out with flowers and started on a bumpy ride that took us through all the fields of the commune. As the group sang rousing songs we wheeled past wheat and cotton fields, the banana plantation, and the cemetery, finally pulling up where the first wheat of the year was to be ceremoniously cut. Members of the Habonim workshop, visiting American students wearing Yemenite shirts and Bermuda shorts, mounted a platform to perform harvest dances to the tune of a solitary flute.

Two young men shared the room next to mine. One of them had given up his American citizenship to become an Israeli.

"Why? Because I'm a Jew," he said. "I feel better here with my brothers, the Yemenites. I have more in common with Iraqi and African Jews than I do with Irishmen in my home town."

"Why didn't you settle on a Yemenite kibbutz, then?"

"I just sort of ended up here. Besides, the Yemenites hardly ever form a kibbutz. They're the sort who like the jingle of money in their pockets."

◇ *Eighteen* ◇

K IBBUTZ URIM LIES IN THE NEGEV, TWENTY-TWO
miles northwest of Beer-Sheba and only eight miles east
of the Gaza Strip. We drove through the gates unchallenged, and
pulled up at the bus station, a cinderblock building painted yellow, where I was supposed to meet Ezra. He hadn't yet arrived,
so I sat down to wait on a bench, grateful for a few moments
alone but uncomfortable in the harsh desert heat.

At first glance, Urim seemed unsightly. Hardly any grass.
The soil dry, caked. Across the road, heavy farming equipment
sat idle in the sun, rusty and flaking. Beyond the apparently
abandoned giant tractors and cultivators, I could make out numerous heifers in long rows of roofed pens. Occasionally kibbutzniks passed on bicycles, with plastic bags hooked to the
handlebars, filled with groceries or laundry.

One of the first American members of Poale Zion to make
aliyah, Pinchas Cruso, came over as a teenager in 1904 and joined
a few dozen boys and girls who had formed a commune in
the village of Petah Tikva. The group hired out as day laborers,

pooling their pay. Cruso recalled that an ideological quarrel soon flared up between liberals and socialist hard-liners as to whether it was morally defensible to nominate somebody to hang back on the *kvutza* doing laundry for the workers in the fields. The hard-liners, led by a young Ben-Gurion, argued that it would be bourgeois exploitation to appoint one of their number a servant, obliging him or her to wash other people's soiled underwear. The liberals prevailed, a laundry was established, and on the first day a sheepish Ben-Gurion turned up with a bundle of dirty laundry.

Urim, which originally lay a couple of miles farther south, was initially settled by a small contingent of refugees from Bulgaria, who were smuggled out of Europe in 1943 and 1944. It was one of the "Tower and Stockade" kibbutzim, stealthily set up overnight, with armed defenders in place by sunrise. The Tower and Stockade policy, which didn't come into play until 1938, was a reaction to the Peel Report of 1937, in which Lord Peel recommended that future Jewish immigration to Palestine be limited to twelve thousand a year and that there be a restriction on the Jewish acquisition of land. In the country's endless continuum of action and reaction, strike and counterstrike, the Peel Report itself was a response to the Arab uprising of 1936, which was prompted by fears of Jewish immigration and land purchases. Forty thousand Jews had come to Palestine in 1934, and sixty-two thousand in 1935. The Peel commissioners allowed that their report offered neither party what it wanted, but "offers each what it wants most, namely freedom and security."[1] It stated:

> An irrepressible conflict has arisen between two national communities within the narrow bounds of one small country.... About 1,000,000 Arabs are in strife, open or latent, with some 400,000 Jews.... But while

neither race can justly rule all Palestine, we see no reason why, if it were practicable, each should not rule part of it. . . . [2]

The Peel commissioners came out in favor of a tripartite solution to the crisis. The Jews would be granted a mini-state made up of Galilee, the Jezreel valley, and the coastal strip that ran from Jaffa to north of Haifa. The Arabs would link the Negev, the Judean hills, and Ephraim to an expanded Transjordan. The British would retain a mandate through an enclave that ran from Lydda and Ramallah to the Holy City of Jerusalem. This, the first of the partition plans, grudgingly accepted by the Jews, would have left the Arabs in control of eighty percent of Palestine, but the Arabs turned it down out of hand, and rebelled again. And it is worth noting that the British, who some forty years later would condemn the Israeli military response to the *intifada*, reacted to the Arab revolt of 1936–39 by sending out planes to strafe Arab villages and interning thousands in concentration camps. An estimated ten thousand Palestinians were killed in the fighting.

Urim was one of eleven Tower and Stockade kibbutzim established in the Negev in 1946 before a new partition plan was drawn up, to take advantage of a British Mandate law that recognized the legality of any building with a roof on it. The kibbutzim were set up on the night when the British least expected such activity: the night of Yom Kippur, October 4.

When the U.N. partition plan was imposed on Palestine, the Jews were left sovereign over fifty — or, according to some, fifty-five — percent of the land. The Arabs rejected this settlement as well, and invaded the morning after Ben-Gurion proclaimed the Jewish state on May 14, 1948. That day an Egyptian airplane passed over Urim, dropping broadsides with a message in both Hebrew and English. The English version read:

IN THE NAME OF GOD,

THE COMPASSIONATE AND MERCIFUL

I address the inhabitants of all colonies in Palestine, proclaiming that we are adhering to the holy words, "If they inclined to peace, so thou shalt."

We now demand that in the benefit of your lives, property, families you should lay down arms. We will not take initiative aggression, unless you insisted on vain resistance, which in no way will last for a long time.

We demand in the name of peace that all inhabitants would yield, and give up all war equipment, arms, ammunition, in their possession collecting them all in one place without destroying them within an hour of receiving this Notice; after which period we will punish obstinate continuators who will be considered as claiming war.

The Lord says, "Maltreat those who maltreat ye in the same manner. Know ye that He is with the pious."

(Holy Koran)

WHEN EZRA FAILED to appear after ten minutes, I walked toward the kibbutz's residential compound in search of the communal dining hall, hoping to find him there. Urim's unprepossessing entry area quickly yielded to a network of sidewalks bordered by olive trees. There were date-palm trees here and there, and an abundance of shrubbery and flowerbeds in well-tended gardens. Patches of moth-eaten lawn struggled in soil that could count on no more than ten inches of rainfall a year. There must have been two hundred people at lunch in the unpleasantly hot dining hall, just about everybody in shirts and shorts and sandals, helping themselves to food out of long metal trolleys. A neighbor of Ezra's, Laizer Blitt, spotted me and said

Ezra had been waiting at the bus stop, had gone off on an errand, but should have returned by now. I went back to the bus stop, and within minutes Ezra was there on his bicycle. I recognized him immediately. He was slightly stooped, but lean and bronzed, his neck seamed, with that endearing smile, totally without guile, that I remembered from years ago. "Hey there, Ezra," I said, "you don't look sixty-six."

"On my last birthday," he said, "I swam sixty-six lengths of the pool without pause. Next year I'll do sixty-seven. Ready for some lunch?"

"Not yet. Thanks."

But we returned to the dining hall all the same, so that Ezra could fill what I took to be his old aluminum army mess kit with some food for me. "The air conditioning in here broke down years ago," he said, "but what with the debt load we're carrying, we would have to think twice before putting in a new system."

As we headed out again, I said, "I thought there'd be a guard posted by the gate. You're only a few miles from Gaza."

"Sure we post guards. At night. But not against the Arabs," he said, laughing. "Against Jewish gangs who work with the Arabs and will steal anything and then sell it in Gaza, where they have nothing. They'll make off with a car, drive it over there, strip it down, and sell the parts. Rabin's full of shit. We should be talking directly to the PLO. If you want to make peace, you've got to make peace with your enemies."

Ezra paused before a bank of mailboxes, unlocked one, and fished out a copy of *Davar*, the Histadrut's daily newspaper. Yanking his short brown hair, he grinned and said, "Look, still brown. A full head and not a hint of gray."

When Ezra had left for the *hakhsharah* in Smithville, Ontario, in 1950, he had spent a year learning to farm. He arrived in Urim in March 1952, joining other Americans and

Canadians already in place, some eighty former members of Habonim among them. To begin with, he shared a room in a barracks with three other kibbutzniks. "We grew field crops. Wheat, hay, oats, barley, potatoes. We were allowed ten pounds a year spending money, maybe worth forty bucks at the time."

"Do you ever yearn for Montreal?"

"If somebody offered me a million bucks I wouldn't go back. I wouldn't know what to do. Here I'm part of something. While I was still there, I always thought this was going to be my home, and the day I arrived I already felt at home."

We stopped at the general store, where Ezra picked up toothpaste, soap, dishwashing liquid, and other essentials, signing for them at the counter. Outside, he indicated the potato fields in the distance. "I had only been here a few months," he said, "and I was out there, harvesting, when somebody came running with the news that my ninety-five-year-old aunt had come over on a visit. I came out of the fields, covered in grime, sweaty, a sack bulging with potatoes tied to my waist. My aunt took one look, rocked her head in her hands, and cried, '*Oy oy oy*, by Pinchas Lifshitz a son has become a picker of potatoes!'"

American *chalutzim* had begun to settle in Israel long before Urim was founded. The first four arrived in 1912 and settled on the kibbutz at Kinneret. Then, in 1921, a small group of American Poale Zion members made *aliyah*. Among them was a couple from Milwaukee, Morris Myerson and his wife, Goldie, later Golda Meir, Israel's fourth prime minister. The Myersons elected to settle on Kibbutz Merhavia, in the Jezreel valley, but were twice rejected because, Golda wrote in *Pioneers from America*, "they could not imagine that an American girl would do the physical work required." However, the Myersons were invited to visit Merhavia and, following a third general meeting of the *kvutza*, they were finally asked to stay.

"I forced myself to eat every kind of food or dish, even if it was hard to look at, let alone swallow," wrote Golda. "The food generally had a most unpleasant taste because of the oil we bought from the Arabs: it was not refined, kept in leather bags and bitter as gall, but it was the base for all our dishes."

Golda introduced a number of refinements to Merhavia: "a white sheet spread as a tablecloth on Friday night, with a vase of wild flowers — that adornment gave us a bad name throughout the Emek. I also insisted on ironing my dress or blouse carefully. This was also viewed as a 'bourgeois' weakness."[3]

In 1932 a number of American Zionist groups coalesced to form the Committee for the Pioneer, Va'ad Lema'an Hechalutz, and sent over twenty-eight *chalutzim* to settle at Degania. But members of Habonim who made *aliyah* in 1939, just before the outbreak of World War Two, weren't able to establish their first kibbutz until late 1943. It was on a swampy hill called Naame, in the Upper Galilee, where malaria was a problem. The kibbutz was named Kfar Blum in honor of Léon Blum, the former socialist premier of France, who was also a Zionist. "We drained the swamps," wrote Shulamit Beitan and Engee Caller in *Builders and Dreamers*, "we cultivated the land; we built factories; we created a way of life."

Hardly any Americans made *aliyah* during World War Two, and then a few days after the U.N. General Assembly voted to partition Palestine, on November 29, 1947, Habonim's national executive committee published a resolution:

> For two thousand years our people dreamed. For two thousand years Jews remembered Zion and prayed for deliverance. In song, in prose, in their hearts and thoughts, Jews kept alive the dream of the Return to Zion — and the dream kept them alive. For two thou-

sand years Jews piously hoped that the Return would take place "quickly in our time."

It has happened and is happening in *our* time. Ours will be the time written of, sung about, talked about as long as the Jewish people will live. Ours will be the generation of the Third Temple.

How fortunate we all are! How happy we all are! ... We call upon all Jewish youth in America, but upon the members of Habonim first and foremost. Let us rise and accept the challenge of history! Ours is the chosen generation! We dare to believe that a new code of ethics will blaze forth from Zion, a new life based on the principles of equality and social justice, the code of the prophets themselves.

The new Eretz Israel calls upon us. Let us go and rebuild Zion. Our help, our support, our selves are needed.

Let us arise and build!⁴

In March 1948, Habonim's national council met in Cleveland and called for a country-wide mobilization. "Recognizing that the Jewish people are at war," it said, "recognizing that our enemies are bent on the destruction of the achievements of the past fifty years of constructive Zionist effort, recognizing that in the last analysis our own strength will be the decisive factor, the national council of Habonim declares a state of emergency in Habonim in order to effectively mobilize the manpower of Habonim for the service of the Jewish people."⁵

All *chaverim* over eighteen were ordered to prepare for immediate *aliyah* or *hakhsharah* training. Within nine months, two hundred *chaverim*, who came to be known as Garin Aleph (settlement group A), left for kibbutzim in Palestine. Ezra was a member of Garin Bet (group B), and by the time he got to

Urim the kibbutz had already moved to its present location, formerly a British police compound and a school for Bedouin children.

Urim's original settlers arrived in 1946 with twenty Holsteins, some chickens, and a good deal of grit. The kibbutz now has a population of six hundred, and some of its members are the children of those who came over with Garin Bet. The dairy cattle herd has grown to four hundred, there are thousands of laying hens, and the field crops include avocado, grapefruit, and oranges. There's a textile plant, and another factory that produces small jewelry boxes. Anybody who wishes to join the kibbutz must survive an interview with the secretary and a secret ballot by the membership. A successful candidate becomes a probationer for a span of six months to a year, after which time the kibbutz votes again; a two-thirds majority is required for the candidate to graduate to full membership. "I don't remember when we ever voted anybody out," said Ezra. However, he did recall the case of an American couple who applied for membership but skedaddled after five days. He laughed. "That night in the dining hall one of the Bulgarians here said, 'Issy come, Issy go.'"

The British police compound was still in place, and Ezra pointed it out as we strolled over to his bungalow. "Things change," he said. "We're all supposed to be equal here, but there are those with private funds. Their parents send them money, or somebody dies and there's an inheritance, or somebody else has had reparations money from Germany. In theory all that money is supposed to go to the kibbutz treasury, but in practice, hardly ever. If you want to phone Canada, go ahead. I don't think I've ever once used up my quota of long-distance calls."

Ezra made coffee, and we sat down at a table in his combination living room, dining room, and kitchenette. There were also two bedrooms and a bathroom.

"There's no mandatory retirement age on a kibbutz, unlike the rest of Israel, but I could be retired now if I wanted to," he said. "Instead, I work in our textile mill from eight to four P.M., and I still do my kitchen duty when it comes up. My bosses in the mill were born here, some used to be my students. Listen, I've reached an age where I don't expect to be prime minister any more. I just want to be useful. I'm happy that at my age I can still do some kind of work."

"How much are you paid here, Ezra?"

"I don't know," he said, scratching his head. "I don't remember. But I'm in the black and that's all that matters to me. Seven or eight thousand shekels."

Ezra, who had studied engineering for five years at McGill, told me that he had always hated it. "When I was a kid, I was dying to learn how to play the violin, but there was never enough money. But here, as Urim became more affluent, we were allowed to develop our hobbies. I said I wanted to study timpani. Let's see, that was in 1964, and at the time I was no longer in charge of construction here, and I was allowed to go to Tel Aviv for two lessons a month. After I had taken twenty lessons, I got this call from somebody I knew in the Israel Philharmonic Orchestra in Tel Aviv, saying, you've got to be here for the concert tomorrow night. But I've already bought tickets for the concert, I said. Which side would I see from with yours? No, no, he said, not in the audience, in the orchestra. We require ten timpanists and we're short one. I told him I was going to need a car if I was to get there in time for rehearsals. Listen, Ezra, he said, you want to play around, don't come to me. I got there all right and we were going to play Berlioz's *Requiem*. The conductor is giving instructions in French and I'm translating for the guys. That night, all of a sudden I get my bassoon cue, my hands are shaking, but I made it. Then in 1969, after I had studied it for a couple of years, I began to teach music here.

"Let me tell you what happened. We hired a music teacher and she ran away after a month. We hired another one and unfortunately she didn't run away. Listen, I was told, why don't you give it a try? So I taught music until two years ago. Once, in the seventies, I got to play with the Israel Symphony Orchestra that was being conducted by Leonard Bernstein. Mahler's Third Symphony. Now I still play, with our kibbutz symphony orchestra. We're mostly amateurs." Ezra shook several pills into a tiny saucer and swallowed them with his coffee. "Once, a few years back," he said, "I was driving to a concert with two women and suddenly I couldn't remember why I was driving or where I was going, but I was making all the right turns all the same. When I told the women with me it certainly frightened them. But it passed in fifteen or twenty minutes. The doctor said I was suffering from attacks of 'transient global memory loss.' The pills are a big help."

"Let's go for a walk."

The trees bordering the sidewalks everywhere turned out to be a nuisance, shedding ripe black olives that squished underfoot no matter how careful you were. Moving on toward the soccer pitch, we passed an incredibly obese old lady riding a tricycle, her slender husband shuffling along beside her. "She can hardly walk any more, she must weigh three hundred pounds, it's terrible," said Ezra. "Her husband watches her like a hawk at mealtimes, but she has to be noshing in secret when he's out. They're Motti Tal's parents. Motti was only in his early twenties, a tank commander, when he was killed in action in the Yom Kippur War. His wife was pregnant at the time."

Ezra was in Paris when the Six-Day War broke out in 1967. "I immediately phoned my unit commander to offer to fly home. Aw, don't bother, he said, it'll be over in three or four days.

"You hear about how efficient our army is. Well, they were really disorganized during the Yom Kippur War. Some guys who served for six months were paid for three days, and vice versa. I was in my forties by that time. The second night, I was on guard duty here when an army truck pulls up. It's midnight. Can we use your ovens, they asked. Sure, why not? We're on the other side of Suez now, they tell me, and all we've got to eat are K-rations. We've got a hundred broilers with us. It turned out the chickens were for Ariel Sharon, you know how that one likes to eat. How will you get them to him, I asked. Don't worry, we've got a helicopter waiting at our base. Worry? If I'd known the chickens were for that bastard, I wouldn't have let them use our ovens."

I asked Ezra what had become of the knife factory I'd heard about.

"Oh, that. It was cutlery. We went partners with another kibbutz — they had the forks, we had the knives. It didn't work out. When the Likud was in office we had high inflation here, four hundred percent annually, and we decided it would be a good idea to borrow and expand, and then pay back in inflated shekels. Then the policy was reversed and we got hit by high interest rates. Now we owe a great deal of money."

In fact Israel's 125,000 kibbutzniks — about three percent of the country's Jewish population, members of 270 kibbutzim — now owe the government and banks a total of ten billion dollars.

"In early days here," said Ezra, "I was in charge of a group laying irrigation pipes in the fields. Arabs on donkeys used to watch us from a distance. As soon as we moved along they would scramble down, say a half-mile back, and steal the pipes we had just laid. Poor bastards have nothing. In Gaza you could probably sell a five-year-old toothbrush, never mind irrigation pipes. I will tell you openly, they have a right to a homeland as much as we do. I don't believe in the land of our forefathers and all that crap. I am for a Palestinian state. The only way to solve the problem."

We drifted past a long, low bungalow. "Over there, that's the workshop for the old people. My mother spent her last years in Urim. We're allowed to bring our aged parents here to live, and we keep them busy with artistic projects. The kibbutz will also pay to send a member's child to university."

Ezra, who was married in 1955 and divorced in 1977, has three sons and an adopted daughter, a Yemenite. One of his sons lives on Urim. Another son, a *ba'al teshuvah*, is now rooted in the Orthodox quarter of Mea Shearim in Jerusalem, where he and his wife run a small business preparing kosher lunches for schools. "When he comes here on a visit," said Ezra, "and he wants to go for a swim, I get him up very early and unlock the pool for him. I'm a lifeguard, I have a key. He's in and out. Fast. Because now he mustn't swim in the presence of women."

◊ *Nineteen* ◊

THE KIBBUTZNIKS OF URIM GOT INTO THEIR FINERY for Friday night dinner, the only meal of the week that was not self-service, their reward for six days of hard physical labor. There was neither wine nor beer. There were plastic water jugs but no napkins on the tables. We were brought chrome-plated containers of chicken soup and noodles, and a ladle that was passed from hand to hand. Then we were served platters of overdone chicken legs and bowls of sticky, overcooked rice.

"Ezra, why don't I take you to lunch in Beer-Sheba tomorrow?"

"We'd have to apply for the use of one of the cars, and everything would be closed because it's Saturday. Another time."

We sat with Ezra's immediate neighbors, the Blitts. Zehara was a former Montrealer. Laizer, a Polish survivor, had seen out World War Two in the forests with his father and a group of partisans. "After the war was over," he said, stroking his beard, "what could my father do to earn money for food? He fermented potatoes and distilled vodka to sell to the Russian soldiers. We applied to come to Palestine, but they didn't want us.

I didn't blame them. I understood. My father was too old and I was a kid. They needed able-bodied men. Soldiers. Eventually we got to Canada, and that country was very good to us and I'll never forget it."

After dinner, Ezra and I went out for another stroll. A couple of hundred people had gathered around a bandstand set up on the grass to listen to an Israeli pop singer, Danny Robas, who was belting out American rock-and-roll numbers in Hebrew.

"We have a few Russian immigrants here, and others who live in Ofakim come to work in our textile factory. They're always looking for angles, ways to beat the system. They don't understand yet that we *are* the system here. These things take time."

I asked Ezra about another Habonim alumnus who had made *aliyah* long ago.

"Oh, he's a real bigshot now. With a house in Beit Shemesh. It's rich, but not really exclusive. I mean, there are Jews all over the place. I'm ready for bed. Oh, I almost forgot, we've got a group of American kids staying here. From the Habonim workshop. They want to talk to you tomorrow afternoon."

"Ezra, what about that lunch? I could order a taxi from Beer-Sheba to pick us up. There must be some restaurants that are open."

"Another time."

Damn.

I AWAKENED early the next morning and slipped out of the bungalow as quietly as possible, to explore. If Urim had been a dust-hole when the members of Garin Bet first arrived, it was evident that over the years they had, by dint of hard work, turned it into a garden suburb of sorts. True, their bungalows, set in rows, were a tight fit, and were furnished no better than motels, but each household had nourished its own little front garden, no two quite the same. There were shade trees, grassy stretches, park benches here and there, a network of cement walks lit at night by streetlamps. There were tennis courts, an Olympic-size swimming pool, and corners brightened by flowering shrubs tended by three kibbutzniks who worked as full-time gardeners. Rounding one corner, I was surprised by a large garden filled with a wide variety of cactus plants, some of them rising to a height of fifteen feet or more — a far cry from my wife's cactus collection, which fits neatly onto a kitchen windowsill. Later, Ezra would explain that the garden had been the loving labor of a schoolteacher who had long since left the kibbutz.

Ezra had showered and shaved by the time I got back, and the two of us started out for the dining hall. For a man who hated engineering, Ezra had certainly paid his dues. En route, he pointed out rows of bungalows whose construction he had supervised. "The ceilings are thin, made of poured concrete, and the roofs are made of asbestos against the heat, with a big air space between," he said. "I also acted as the contractor when we put in the plumbing here. Remember, you're busy this afternoon."

"Yes."

"In the old days, when a Habonim workshop group arrived, the guys all turned out to look over the new girls, but if you think you can get away with having an affair here, you're crazy. It's impossible. Everybody knows where you are all the time."

After breakfast we went to meet Bob and Cynthia Levine, who came from Philadelphia, at the office where Urim's archives were kept. I was shown an aerial photograph of the original Urim; a group photograph of the members of Garin Bet posing before a barn; and other happy-day photographs of youngsters out of North America's inner cities, most of them university-educated, standing in front of tents, proving themselves to the *goyim* by milking cows, riding tractors, laying irrigation pipes, and picking a potato crop by hand. See, we are not money-changers.

Workers in Urim were paid three thousand shekels a year, said Bob, and they were also given a furniture allowance, but they usually needed their parents' help to finance a trip back to America. Kibbutzniks were encouraged to develop their own projects. In Bob's case that meant breeding tropical fish, two hundred thousand angelfish a year. "But the European market is very difficult for us when you factor in the air freight," he said, "and after three years I've yet to show a profit, so I don't know how much longer I'll be allowed to continue. Our biggest problem in Urim is the aging population. Most of us have been doing hard physical labor for thirty years now, and we're tired."

"I've been working in the laundry, on my feet all day, folding clothes, for seventeen years, and my legs can't take it any more," said Cynthia.

"There are some kibbutzim," said Bob, "where all you see now is the older generation and little kids, with nobody in between, but there are committees working on ways to keep youngsters from leaving for the cities, and then there are the Russian immigrants — "

"Don't make me laugh," said Ezra. "The last thing they want is to live on a communal farm."

"And we have begun to attract a few *chalutzim* through the Habonim workshops," said Bob.

"All that is peanuts," said Ezra.

HABONIM HAD undergone a number of sea-changes since Ezra was our leader, the *menahel* of the group that included Jerry Greenfeld, Hershey Bloom, Myer Plotnik, and me, puffing on Sweet Caps, head-manning a dented can in lieu of a puck as we stick-handled through the lane toward the house on Jeanne Mance Street: "He shoots, he scores!" Beginning in the late fifties, Habonim members inevitably became involved in the civil rights and peace movements. In Baltimore, *chaverim* found themselves at odds with some members of the Jewish establishment when they began to join sit-ins and demonstrations against segregated buses. Remembering those days, Meir Ciporen wrote in *Builders and Dreamers*: "Some of the picketing was directed against stores owned by Jewish merchants — including one who had discriminated against Yemenite-Israeli sailors on shore leave, mistaking them for blacks. Habonim took to the streets in protest, but Baltimore Jewry was not sympathetic. 'How does this look,' people in the community asked, 'for a Jewish youth group to be picketing Jews?'"[1]

The increased involvement of Habonim members in American political life led to an ideological quarrel — at the national convention in Camp Kvutza in Lowlands, Ontario, in August 1962 — that threatened to tear the movement apart. There were those who felt that the *chaverim*, committed to *aliyah*, shouldn't bother with the politics of the Diaspora, and there was a radical faction that wanted Habonim to declare its independence from the Mapai Party and the kibbutz movement and deal with the realities that confronted Diaspora Jewry. But the radical candidate for national secretary, Max Langer, a Vancouver-born physician who moved to Brooklyn in 1960 and now lives in Gesher Haziv, was defeated in the election.

In 1965, the Bronx chapter submitted a resolution to the central committee of national Habonim condemning the war in Vietnam, and drawing an analogy between the struggles of the Vietnamese and Zionism. The resolution failed to pass, but during the winter of 1966, when Students for a Democratic Society (SDS) chartered its first two high-school chapters, one in the Bronx, the other in Washington, D.C., both were founded by Habonim members. The following summer, David Twersky recalled in *Builders and Dreamers*, had to be the wildest in the history of Habonim camping. The sixteen-year-old campers, he wrote, were filled with ideas of revolution and students' rights. They wanted free speech and personal autonomy, which, in their case, meant the right to skip swimming lessons and ignore lights-out. Two of their number who refused to stand for the raising of the American flag were expelled from camp.[2]

A year later, Habonim members found themselves adjudged pariahs by both the New Left and the Zionist establishment. As far as the New Left was concerned, Israel was a white-settler colonist state. And then, wrote Twersky, when Israel's triumph in the Six-Day War brought on the occupation of the West Bank and other territories, the case for Palestinian self-determination was made not only by the left, but by Habonim within the Zionist community.

In 1969, the central committee of national Habonim passed the following resolution:

Habonim does not support and will not participate in civilian settlement of the Sinai, Gaza Strip, or the West Bank, because:

1. Arab land is being expropriated for such settlement.

2. Arabs from these areas are not allowed to settle in Israel.

3. The Jews settling in these areas will not be willing to live in an Arab state if return of the territories is necessary as a part of an overall peace settlement satisfactory to the Israeli government and the people of Israel as a whole.

4. Settlement in the territory may block very real peace possibilities with Israel's Arab neighbors.[3]

Members of Habonim workshops, college students and teenagers just out of high school, come to Israel for a year of work and study. The first workshop, made up of forty-two youngsters, arrived in 1951, an austerity year, and learned to get by on variations of eggplant and cauliflower, but it was not until they got to Urim in the spring that they grasped how rich their diet had been. On Urim, their Sabbath treat was a pat of margarine. Conditions had improved enormously by the time the fifteenth workshop made Urim its home in 1965. Two years later, members of the seventeenth workshop, also settled at Urim, learned that hashish could be bought cheaply in the newly acquired streets of East Jerusalem. In an unsigned memoir included in *Builders and Dreamers*, a graduate of the seventeenth workshop wrote: "It would be months before Israel at large noticed the acrid smell wafting out of the volunteers' quarters on kibbutzim all over the country. At that point, and for years to come, Israelis' attitude toward American Jewish youth became one of deeply mixed emotions. There was deep gratitude that so many youthful volunteers were ready to drop everything and come to stand with Israel in its time of trial; at the same time, Israelis were repelled by the American youth culture of long hair and hedonism, of 'drugs and sex and rock 'n' roll.' They wanted American kids, but to a growing degree, they did not want the ones they saw.

"The mutual suspicions generated between Urim and the seventeenth workshop by the presence of drug use among the workshoppers would return to haunt almost every workshop for decades to come."[4]

Accompanied by Ezra, I went to meet members of the Habonim workshop, a seemingly engaging bunch of freshly scrubbed teenage boys and girls, not one of the boys long-haired or one of the girls wearing a nasal ring. There were perhaps twenty of them, sprawled on the grass outside their bungalows. I introduced myself, saying that I had also once been a member of Habonim but had drifted away from the organization years ago, sailing for Europe rather than Israel, and had long since returned to Montreal.

"Are you here because you're going to make *aliyah* now?"

"No."

"Why not?"

"Well, I'm not only Jewish but also Canadian, and Montreal just happens to be my home."

"You actually believe that a Jew can be 'at home' in Canada?"

"Yes, certainly," I said, startled. "I also like it there."

"But not here?"

"I didn't say that."

"Do you like it here?"

"Yes, and I have a number of old friends as well as relatives living here."

"You earn big money writing novels that make fun of the Jews."

"That's not the way I see it."

"Are you a Jewish anti-Semite?"

"Please."

"That's no answer."

"No."

"Is there no anti-Semitism in Canada?"

"Yes. Of course. But if it was once a big problem, that's no longer the case."

"What if there was another Holocaust, this time in America, would you come to live here then?"

"Are you serious?"

"Would you come to live in Israel if there was a Holocaust in America?"

"What you're suggesting is preposterous."

"You haven't answered my question."

"It's a stupid question."

"Would you or would you not come to live in Israel if there was a Holocaust in America?"

"There will be no Holocaust in America."

"'It can't happen here' is what the Jews thought in Germany in 1933."

Rattled, even outraged, as I took my leave with Ezra I heard echoes all the same. I had to admit that the scourge of mindless anti-Semitism had also been perversely nourishing to Jerry, Hershey, Myer, and me during our days in Habonim, proof that the only solution to the "Jewish problem" was an independent Jewish state.

Going into World War Two in September 1939, our country, although the second-largest in the world, was one of the most thinly populated. At the time, approximately 11,300,000 people lived in Canada. But from 1933 to 1948, no more than 5,000 Jewish refugees from Europe were allowed into the country, and grudgingly at that. In 1935, the deputy minister appointed to guard the gates against an anticipated flood of Jews was Frederick Charles Blair. Those who charged him with anti-Semitism, he complained, were the self-serving promoters of an open-door policy. In 1938, he wrote to an associate: "I suggested recently to three Jewish gentlemen with whom I am well acquainted, that it would be a very good thing if they would call a conference and have a day of humiliation and prayer, which might profitably be extended for a week or more, where they would honestly try to answer the question of why they are so unpopular almost everywhere.... I often think that instead of persecution it would be far better if we more often told them frankly why many of them are unpopular. If they would divest themselves of certain of their habits I am sure they could be just as popular in Canada as our Scandinavians.... Just because Jewish people would not understand the frank kind of statements I have made in this letter to you, I have marked it confidential."[5]

In 1946, with the British blockade of Palestine still in place, those of us who met in the house on Jeanne Mance Street on Friday nights hoped for moral pressure from the Conference of the International Refugee Organization then meeting in Geneva. Conor Cruise O'Brien, who was the Irish delegate, wrote in *The Siege: The Saga of Israel and Zionism* that as Irish representative in those days he was supposed to find out what the Vatican thought, so he had lunch with the Vatican representative, a jovial Irish-American monsignor. "The Monsignor was at least not mealy-mouthed. 'I'm not anti-Semitic,' he said. 'I just hate them.' Throughout lunch he talked about the Jews and nothing else. They had done very well out of the war and were now exploiting the real displaced persons in the camps. Selling razor blades. On the black market."[6]

Ernest Bevin, responding to continuing American pressure to allow a hundred thousand Jews into Palestine at once, declared at the British Labour Party conference in Bournemouth in June 1946, that he hoped he would not be misunderstood in America if he said that this was not proposed with the purest motives. They "did not want too many of them [Jews] in New York."[7]

Bevin's riposte resonated in some quarters, if only because those who wished to rid their countries of Jews were among Zionism's earliest and most enthusiastic advocates. In 1848, Colonel Hugh Rose, the British consul-general in Beirut, reported that his Russian counterpart, Constantin Basily, believed "that from hence forward every year some two or three hundred Jews a year will leave Russia for ever for Palestine.... Mr. Basily thinks and hopes that the whole Jewish population in Russia will eventually do the same."[8]

In his biography of Herzl, Ernst Pawel noted that when the father of modern Zionism was still a schoolboy in Budapest, in 1866, his *Der Judenstaat* was anticipated by Gyozo Istoczy, the first deputy to be elected to the Hungarian Diet on a one-plank platform: anti-Semitism. Istoczy surfaced with the then original idea of "the restoration of the ancient Jewish state." This, he claimed, would help revive the faltering Turkish Empire, and enable Jews to function "in a free state of their own, rather than as parasites in Christian Europe." Unfortunately, he added, this plan was being undermined by cosmopolitan Jewish financiers with an appetite for world dominion. "I appeal not to those conniving parasites," he said, "but to the Jewish patriots who have preserved their ancient traditions and love of their ancestral home, to grasp the opportunity for regaining their estate."[9]

An earlier biographer of Herzl, Amos Elon, leaned on the founding father's voluminous diaries for an account of his quest for support in St. Petersburg in 1903. Herzl was granted an interview with the Czar's finance minister, Count Serge Witte. Witte claimed to be a friend of the Jews, in spite of the fact that most of them made a repulsive impression, if only because they were poor and filthy and engaged "in all sorts of ugly pursuits, like pimping and usury." He also complained to Herzl that many of them were active in the revolutionary movement.

Herzl: "To what circumstances do you attribute this?" Witte: "I believe it is the fault of our government. The Jews are too oppressed. I used to say to the late Tsar, Alexander III, 'Majesty, if it were possible to drown the six or seven million Jews in the Black Sea, I would be absolutely in favor of that. But if it is not possible, one must let them live.' What, then, do you want from the Russian government?" Herzl: "Certain encouragements." Witte: "But the Jews are given encouragements — to emigrate. Kicks in the behind, for example."[10]

A framed photograph of Chaim Weizmann, Herzl's successor in the Zionist pantheon, was displayed in the house on Jeanne Mance Street. At the time, we were unaware of the slights the witty, undeniably brilliant, Russian-born Weizmann, a naturalized British subject, endured as he pursued his dream of a Jewish national homeland — a petitioner at the Foreign Office, a supplicant at dinner parties in Mayfair and Belgravia. His opulent home, "Oakwood," at 16 Addison Crescent, fleshed out by a butler, cook, and maids — his chauffeured Rolls-Royce — his suits from Samuel and Son of Savile Row, and his handkerchiefs and silk *caleçons* from Hamboro's — provided him no proof against insult. Miss Jessy Usher, the governess who stayed with the Weizmanns until 1938, taking care of their two sons, wrote: "I felt it my job as a Christian to come into that family and give those boys as far as possible a normal life because Jews are so cruel to their children. Jews have all these customs they impose on them. I wanted to give those Jewish boys as far as possible a normal English life."[11]

Following the Arab riots of 1929 in Palestine, in which 150 Jews had been killed, Beatrice Webb told Weizmann, "I can't understand why the Jews make such a fuss over a few dozen of their people killed in Palestine. As many are killed every week in London in traffic accidents and nobody pays any attention."[12] Nancy Astor, however, seems to have given Weizmann an endorsement of sorts. In *The Impossible Dream*, a memoir Vera Weizmann published after her husband's death, she wrote that Nancy Astor had once glared at Weizmann at a dinner party, and said to the others at the table, "'Don't believe him!... He's a great charmer. He will convert you to his point of view. He is the only decent Jew I have met.'"[13]

More recently, *Time* magazine certified Menachem Begin's conviction that all gentiles were bigots when, on his election as prime minister in 1977, it noted that "Begin rhymes with Fagin."[14]

STROLLING BACK to Ezra's bungalow, we paused to watch a soccer match in progress, one of the games in Urim's annual intramural competition for the Motti Tal Cup. Good-natured onlookers cheered their favorites, while the parents of the fallen tank commander watched from the sidelines, seated at a table shielded from the sun by a canopy. "It means a lot to them," said Ezra.

I picked up my overnight bag, and Ezra accompanied me to the bus stop, where my driver was waiting.

"So," said the driver, as we pulled out of Urim, "what do you think of our kibbutzniks?"

"They're a very dedicated bunch."

"Some socialists. All the hard work is now done by either North African Jews, whom they hire by the day, or Arabs, who cost them even cheaper. Well, you're some lucky guy. She couldn't shop today. It's *Shabbat*."

"My wife?" I asked, baffled.

"Didn't you say you left her in Jerusalem?"

"Yes."

"But who knows how much she spent yesterday? I should worry. You can afford it. Does she have her own car?"

"She doesn't know how to drive. So I had to hire a chauffeur for her. A Sephardic Jew. A very impertinent fellow."

"Ha ha ha. How old are you?"

"Sixty-two."

"If you had a choice, which one of you would you rather have die first?"

"Jesus Christ!"

"Don't be shocked. I know of many people your age, goners already. And I happen to be interested in the psychology of my customers. So answer my question, please."

"You first."

"Her, naturally."

"Obviously, you must adore your wife."

"It's a marriage. Some days we get on, some days we don't. It's a trick question. If a customer answers his wife should die first I know he's an egotist, but if he says him first, what is he? A hypocrite. So what's it to be in your case?"

"Ask me again in thirty years. I haven't given it much thought yet."

"It's time, you know. Sixty-two is sixty-two."

"And now, if you don't mind, I'm going to take a nap."

When we finally arrived at Mishkenot, I handed the driver 150 shekels, the exact price of our outgoing trip, including a fifteen percent tip. "Hey, wait a minute," he said. "That's not enough. It's *Shabbat* today."

"I don't understand."

"There's a twenty-five percent supplement for driving on *Shabbat*."

"But you're not a *haredi*."

"You're damn right I'm not, but it's a government regulation. You want I should break the law?"

"Certainly not," I said, coughing up.

"I could drive you and your wife to Masada tomorrow. We could stop at Qumran, where they found the Dead Sea Scrolls. And on the way I've got a pal who deals in antiquities. No fakes. Everything certified. Good prices."

"No thanks."

"You've got to be careful here. Some drivers, you know."

"I know."

He was already pulling out when I gestured for him to stop.

"You've changed your mind?" he asked, beaming.

"No, but I forgot to wish you a *guten Shabbes*."

Reaching into his glove compartment, he fished out a *kipa*, slipped it onto his head, winked, and drove off at fire-engine speed, as taxi drivers are wont to do in Israel.

"WHAT WAS IT LIKE?" asked Florence.

"I have never been in the presence of so many undemanding *gute neshumes*, good souls," I explained — "or eaten such unspeakably bad food." Then I told her Ezra's last words to me at the bus stop. "I've been here forty years last March," he had said, "and I still believe in it."

❖ *Twenty* ❖

PATRICK MARTIN AND BRONWYN DRAINIE AND THEIR two children were ensconced in an apartment in Yemin Moshe, and we took to dropping in on them for drinks. Patrick was the correspondent for the Toronto *Globe and Mail* and Bronwyn was working on a book about Jerusalem. In my absence, the intrepid Bronwyn and Florence had gone for a ramble through the Old City. A risky business. Palestinians in striped robes, seated on low stools before their hole-in-the-wall shops, proffered brass candlesticks, wooden crucifixes, beaten copper trays, and necklaces and bracelets with Star of David, crucifix, or crescent pendants, take your pick. Bronwyn and Florence were pursued by barefoot urchins selling rolls of film, postcards, and panoramic photographs of the Holy City. The walls here and there, said Florence, were spray-painted with PLO graffiti. A street kid had thrown a stone, nicking Bronwyn on the elbow. They passed the house that the truculent Ariel Sharon had bought in the Arab quarter, his statement that Jews were entitled to move in anywhere they chose in Jerusalem. Five Israeli soldiers lounged about outside, Uzis on their laps.

Sharon hardly ever slept there. And later I learned that the house was in fact a highly sophisticated electronic nerve center, with IDF technicians in attendance, in touch with all of Jerusalem's security stations and ready to propel police to the next trouble spot.

Over the weekend, there had been rioting in Afula. On Friday, the day after Shimon Avraham had been slashed to death in the fields near Moshav Meitav, an estimated three thousand mourners from neighboring settlements had attended his funeral. Later, some of them gathered at a nearby highway turnoff and stoned vehicles with blue territories license plates. Shots were fired at one car, but the driver and passenger weren't hurt. Israeli officials pleaded with the mourners to show restraint and allow the police to get on with the job of catching Avraham's murderers, but the settlers were determined on vengeance. On Saturday, hundreds of them demonstrated outside the Afula police station after two of their number, apprehended carrying cans of gasoline and tires, were arrested.

The *Post* reported that a suspect in the murder of Amatzia Ben-Haim, the computer expert bludgeoned in the greenhouse the previous Sunday, had been taken into custody. The suspect, seventeen-year-old Daya Saluji of Khan Yunis, was not a member of a terrorist group, but had acted on his own. It was alleged that he told investigators "he had been waiting for a convenient opportunity to kill a Jew."

On the *Post*'s editorial page, Moshe Zak, a former senior editor of the daily *Ma'ariv*, charged that the PLO, ostensibly seeking peace with Israel, was double-dealing, its umbrella sheltering terrorists. "Though split over the tactics to be employed in the struggle against Israel," he wrote, "the terrorist organizations see eye to eye perfectly over the need for 'armed struggle' to achieve their final goal, a Palestinian state."[1]

If that was the case, its mirror image was arguably the Zionist faction that was once led by Vladimir Jabotinsky (1880–1940) and his political heirs in the Irgun and Stern Gang.

Jabotinsky, a comrade of Joseph Trumpeldor in many of his exploits — including the formation of both the Zion Mule Corps in 1915 and the Jewish Legion — was an eloquent and enormously influential firebrand. He was a magnificent orator, fluent in six languages, a translator of part of *The Divine Comedy* into Hebrew, who had emerged out of Odessa, like Isaac Babel and Leon Trotsky. Jabotinsky was unwilling to suffer the British management of Jewish immigration to Palestine, or the accommodating Chaim Weizmann, whom he adjudged compromised by the "obsequiousness of his Diaspora mentality."[2] So he formed the World Union of Zionist Revisionists in 1925, its aim to establish a Jewish state on both sides of the Jordan River. Jabotinsky called for illegal immigration, and demanded that Jewish capitalists support a policy of encouraging the largest possible number of Jews to settle on the Yishuv in the shortest possible time. In memory of the fallen Trumpeldor, he named the Revisionists' youth corps Betar, a Hebrew acronym derived from Trumpeldor's name. "With blood and sweat," ran the Betar anthem, "we will create a race, proud and generous and cruel." Betar members learned how to handle weapons and, wrote Avishai Margalit in *The New York Review of Books*, wore neat uniforms with brown shirts and took part in quasi-military drills honoring Jabotinsky as if he were a *Führer*. The central idea of revisionism was the creation of Jewish armies, even in the Diaspora. This was an "orthopedic" thought — to straighten the people's back. But it was also seen as politically necessary — Zionism would be realized in blood and fire. In practice Betar specialized in elaborate martial ceremonies: "Man's superiority over the beast is the ceremony."[3]

Such an elaborate martial ceremony served as a set-piece in *Thieves in the Night*, Arthur Koestler's novel about life on the Yishuv in the late thirties. The novel, published in 1946, was dedicated to the memory of Jabotinsky, who I take it was the inspiration for the underground leader Bauman:

> Bauman read out from a piece of paper the name — which was an alias — of the candidate, and at a sign from him the young officer standing next to the door opened it and gave an order to the sentry in the corridor. The sentry called out the name, and presently a young boy entered through the door, which closed behind him. He saluted and advanced three steps until he stood in front of the table. He must have been told beforehand what to do, for there was no hesitation about him. He might have been about seventeen... [and] gave the impression of being in a trance. Standing rigidly to attention, his wide-open eyes were fixed for a second or two on the flame of the candles, skirted the Bible, and stuck fascinatedly on the revolver.
>
> "Kiss the Bible and touch the gun," said Bauman, rising to his feet followed by the other two behind the desk. The boy did as bidden. It was so still that one could hear the small, damp noise of his lips touching the leather cover of the book.
>
> "Now speak the words after me," said Bauman. "*In the name of the All-present who brought Israel out of the house of bondage in Egypt...*"
>
> "*In the name...*" the boy repeated in a dreamy voice, looking with puckered brows into the candle.
>
> "*...not to rest until the Nation is resurrected as a free and sovereign State within its historic boundaries, from Dan to Beer-Sheba...*"

"*...from Dan to Beer-Sheba.*"

"*To obey blindly my superior officers...*"

"*...officers...*"

"*...not to reveal anything entrusted to me, neither under threats nor bodily torture; and that I shall bear my sufferings in silence.*"

"*...in silence.*"

The candles flickered and one could hear the boy's breathing. In a dreamy, entranced voice he repeated the last words of the oath:

"*If I forget thee, Jerusalem...*"

"*If I forget thee, Jerusalem...*"

"*...as long as my soul resides in my body.*"

"*...in my body. Amen.*"[4]

Menachem Begin joined Betar when he was still a high-school student in the Brest district of Poland. After he left Warsaw University, he became the country's chief organizer for the movement, which by 1939 could claim seven hundred branches and seventy thousand members. "The greatest influence in my life I attribute to Jabotinsky," he told *Ma'ariv* in 1977, "and I learned the doctrine of Zionism from him."[5] According to some, Jabotinsky singled Begin out as his heir, but Begin's biographer could find no evidence to substantiate that claim. Jabotinsky, wrote Eric Silver in *Begin: The Haunted Prophet*, "is whispered to have despised Begin's provincial fanaticism and pietistic emotion."[6]

◆

MY COUSIN Benjy Richler, whom I was meeting for lunch, is the son of my late uncle Joe. My uncles and aunts and most of their children and grandchildren, including Benjy, remain devout

Jews, their year enriched by a stately cycle of cherished holy days. When I was a boy, my uncles used to gather at the dining-room table on Sunday afternoons to study Talmud with my grandfather, Shmariyahu. And to this day many of them loosen the tiny bulb in their refrigerator on Friday afternoons lest, opening the door on Saturday, they inadvertently create light — a violation of the Sabbath.

Max, the most imaginative of my uncles, has paid dearly for his beliefs. Max never finished high school. He was, for a time, a partner in an auto-parts business with four of his brothers. Then he registered for a night-school course in mechanical drawing and started his own business, Atlas Hoist & Body, building heavy-duty mining and dump-truck bodies based on his own original designs. As the business grew, he licensed these designs as far afield as Venezuela, Colombia, South Africa, Australia, and Indonesia, but he was desperately short of money for development. So he was enormously encouraged when he was approached by investment bankers interested in injecting millions into the company and launching a stock issue. They scrutinized his books and were satisfied with what they found, but there was a small stumbling block. Atlas Hoist & Body, they discovered, lost some forty production days a year, not due to labor unrest, but in deference to various Jewish holidays — for which the workers, most of them gentiles, were paid all the same.

"Surely," said one of the potential investors, "this will no longer be the case once the company goes public."

"I couldn't change that," said Max.

But their offer, they pointed out, would make him a rich man.

"It would be against my religious beliefs," said Max.

The investment bankers told Max how much they admired him for his principles, but, unfortunately, they could not go forward under such conditions. "Why don't you take a few days to think it over?"

"There's nothing to think over," said Max.

Benjy had made *aliyah* in 1960. The last time I had seen him, in 1962, he had been teaching school; he had grown into a tall, thin, introverted young man, his knitted *kipa* clasped to his head with a bobby pin. He wore a beard. Why, I asked, had he left Canada?

"I would always think that one day I would have to leave," he said, "all the Jews will have to leave. It's not our country."

In 1962, Benjy took me to a liquor store, where I wanted to buy a bottle of cognac. He interrupted the transaction. "Is this bottle kosher?" he demanded of the shopkeeper.

"Don't worry," said the shopkeeper impatiently. "It's kosher, it's kosher."

At the time Benjy did not agree that Israel's *haredim* were favored with political clout out of proportion to their numbers. "Elsewhere," he said, "I would be for a separation of church and state, but this is Israel. If civil marriage were allowed, there would eventually be two nations."

Now, thirty years on, Benjy and I were to meet at Little Italy, a kosher restuarant with a baffling menu offering, among other dishes, something called "kosher shrimps fettuccine." I arrived early, in need of a scotch, uneasy about getting together with my religious cousin after so long an absence, and still brooding over the many questions I had failed to put to Ezra in Urim. In Ezra's presence, I had been reduced once more to a pimply teenager seated on the floor of the house on Jeanne Mance Street, in awe of the *menahel* who thrilled us with tales of the trials endured by Herzl, Trumpeldor, Weizmann, and other Zionist heroes. Questioning Ezra too closely, it seemed to me, would have been rude. Waiting for Benjy, I was thrust back even further. I was a twelve-year-old again, and the most feared figure in my life was our obdurate, hot-tempered grandfather, Shmariyahu Richler, who had once denounced me before an assembled court of aunts, uncles, and cousins as a *Shabbes goy*, a lout, an *apikoros*, grabbing me by the ear, beating me about the face, and literally throwing me out of his house. I remembered Benjy as a shy, delicate child, ten years younger than me, who was lucky enough to be raised in what I then took to be undeserved affluence. His father, my uncle Joe, was the first Richler to move into Outremont, to a centrally heated apartment in a modern building on Maplewood Avenue. Its wonders included a shower, which he demonstrated for our St. Urbain Street benefit.

When my grandfather died in 1947, my mother insisted that it was only proper I attend his funeral. I arrived at his house to find the coffin set out in the living room, uncles and aunts gathered round. Uncle Joe drove me into a corner. "So here you are," he said.

"So?"

"You hastened his death — you never even spoke to him, though he was sick all those months."

"I didn't bring on his death."

"Well, smart guy, you're the one who is mentioned first in his will."

"Oh."

"You are not a good Jew and you are not to touch his coffin. It says that in his will. Don't you dare touch his coffin."

SINCE I HAD last seen him, Benjy had shaved off his beard, but he was still slender, shy, only slightly stooped, with a tiny knitted *kipa* clasped to his head with a bobby pin. He had not traded on his religious status to evade his military responsibilities but had done his duty, and now had two of his three children, a son and a daughter, serving with the IDF. We both ordered salads, and then Benjy slipped away discreetly to wash his hands, as ritual demanded, before pronouncing his *hamotzi* blessing. He had been to library school since we had last met, and in 1965 had joined the Institute of Microfilmed Hebrew Manuscripts in the Jewish National and University Library in Jerusalem, where he was now the assistant director. For the past twenty-five years he had been kept busy deciphering and cataloguing ancient and medieval Hebrew manuscripts, tracking them down in Egypt, Italy, Germany, England, the United States, and Russia. The Saltykov Shchedrin Library in Leningrad, he said, had 2,000 Hebrew manuscripts and *genizah* fragments, and the Lenin State Library in Moscow some 1,800. A *genizah* is a repository for Hebrew manuscripts adjudged no longer worthy of use: old torn books, documents, personal letters. In most countries, the *genizah* is buried in a local cemetery. But the largest collection of Hebrew manuscripts, an estimated 200,000 leaves, was discovered over a hundred years ago in the attic of the ancient synagogue in Fostat, Cairo. The manuscripts had suffered only minor deterioration in Egypt's dry climate. The existence of that *genizah* had been known for hundreds of years, but according to legend its entrance was guarded by a snake, and those who attempted to explore it were beset by misfortunes. Even so, some nineteenth-century collectors managed to bribe synagogue officials and make off with hundreds of fragments. In 1897, Professor Solomon Schechter of Cambridge University convinced the guardians of the Fostat synagogue to allow him to take about half the remaining contents of the *genizah* to Cambridge, where they can still be found.

Among the Fostat *genizah*'s treasures was a handwritten letter by Yehuda Halevi, the poet and philosopher of Toledo (1085–1140), expressing a longing to visit the Holy Land — a pilgrimage he began but never completed. Halevi's poetry and other writings were George Eliot's source for the impassioned Zionist speeches of my namesake in her novel *Daniel Deronda*.

"For years," said Benjy, "we could get no co-operation from the Lenin State Library in Moscow. Things changed under Gorbachev. Now they blow hot and cold. Everything depends on whether or not the head of the department is an anti-Semitic Pamyat man. In any case, the library people often want a good deal of money to allow us to photocopy manuscripts — money we can't afford. Last time I agreed to leave behind a computer and a micro-camera."

The Vatican's Biblioteca Apostolica, Benjy went on to say, couldn't be more helpful, but, ironically, he could get nowhere with the Lubavitchers of Crown Heights, Brooklyn, custodians of a considerable store of manuscripts. "They will not allow us access," said Benjy, "lest material we microfilm end up being handled by nonbelievers."

The manuscripts microfilmed by Benjy and his associates are largely the work of medieval scribes, who made copies of original works that were sold and circulated before the age of printing. In *Hebrew Manuscripts: A Treasured Legacy*, a beautifully illustrated book that Benjy has written about his work, he noted that several volumes of writings by the great Maimonides (1135–1204) have survived: hundreds of pages from his Arabic commentaries on the Mishnah, a draft from his Mishneh Torah, and a few pages from his *Guide for the Perplexed*.

From the Dead Sea Scrolls to the ninth century, no Hebrew manuscripts have survived. But from circa 1400, manuscripts with compelling colophons have been found:

When I, Chayyim b. Saul Migdoli of blessed memory, also known as Vidal Satori, was in Saragossa at the age of sixty the dear man R. Isaac, son of the venerable R.

Judah b. Dina...beseeched me and my heart was wont to fulfill his wishes, and with Divine assistance and the aid of glass lenses between mine eyes I toiled and wrote these Books of the Bible and I completed them in the month of Shevat in the year 5164 of the Creation [1404]
.... May the Lord who gave me strength to complete this task allow him to study it forever and grant him a long life and male offspring and fulfill the Biblical promise to him and his children "Let not this Book of the Teaching cease from your lips but recite it day and night, so that you may observe faithfully all that is written in it. Only then will you prosper in your undertakings and only then will you be successful."[7]

The epilogue to another colophon, this one more succinct, was the work of a man writing in Soncino, Italy, in 1422, but could just as easily have been composed by many a contemporary Jewish writer: "May the scribe be strengthened and never harmed, neither today nor forever until the day the donkey climbs the ladder about which Jacob dreamt."[8]

Medieval Jewish translators played a crucial role in passing on an important body of Arab scholarship to Europe, for their Hebrew translations antedate the rendering of these works into Latin. Until the thirteenth century, the human figures in illuminated Hebrew manuscripts were depicted with animal heads, lest they become graven images. The paucity of medieval Hebrew manuscripts is partially explained by mass book-burnings — during the Crusades in the eleventh century, in Paris in 1240, and in Italy in the 1550s.

The books buried in European *genizah*s disintegrated in the moist earth hundreds of years ago, but thousands of pages from ancient manuscripts, wrote Benjy, are preserved in a different form of repository: bindings. "Bookbinders in the Middle Ages used parchment pages from discarded books and manuscripts as padding for their bindings. Hebrew books that had been confiscated or stolen during the countless persecutions of Jews in the Middle Ages were salvaged by Christian bookbinders for their 'raw material,' their parchment pages. Notaries found the parchment leaves of large Hebrew books such as Bibles and tomes of the Talmud ideal for use as wrappers for their documents."[9]

Before my cousin went loping off toward King David Street — his long narrow head bobbing — he left me with two gifts. There was a copy of his own *Hebrew Manuscripts: A Treasured Legacy*, inscribed "To Mottl, from Benjy, This is what keeps me going." And, compounding my pleasure, there was a recently published Hebrew edition of my maternal grandfather's puckish tall tales about the legendary Maharal of Prague and the Golem.

◊ *Twenty-one* ◊

HOW THE MAHARAL OF PRAGUE, WITH THE AID OF
THE GOLEM, FOILED A PLOT BY THE EVIL
PRIEST TADISCH TO CONVERT A BEAUTIFUL
JEWISH GIRL TO CHRISTIANITY[1]

By Rabbi Yudel Rosenberg

In the city of Prague, there was a wealthy and influential
vintner named Berger. His only child, a beautiful, modest, sixteen-year-old girl who spoke several languages,
managed the shop for him. Because only the best wines
could be found in his cellars, his shop was patronized by
both army officers and priests. Among them was the
priest Tadisch, a notorious anti-Semite, an expert at en-
trapping Jewish girls in his net and converting them to
Christianity. Tadisch cast his evil eye on the vintner's
only daughter. But the girl's parents were God-fearing
people and, even on Saturdays and holidays, they would
not allow her out of their house. Tadisch devised a plan.
He bought wine on credit. The vintner's only daughter

kept the ledgers, and from time to time sent a servant to the priest's home, where he would be paid in full. A few months passed. Then one day Tadisch complained to the servant that the vintner was claiming payment for ten bottles of wine that he had not received. The servant apologized and explained that it was the vintner's only daughter who had made up the bill.

"Well then," said the priest, "she has made a mistake, and when she comes here with her ledger I'll point it out to her."

The servant reported what the priest had said to the vintner's only daughter. Not suspecting any evil, she took the ledger and, accompanied by the servant, went to the priest's home. Tadisch asked her to present him with an account that was in accordance with what he had entered in his own ledger. She toted up the bill again, but it turned out to be exactly the same as the previous one.

"Oh, yes, now I remember," said Tadisch. "The servant did bring me those ten bottles, but they were like vinegar, and that's why I didn't enter them in my ledger."

The vintner's only daughter was astonished, because she was careful to provide the priest with the best wines. Tadisch ordered the servant to fetch the ten suspect bottles from his cellar, pointing out that he would find them in a special basket. Once the wine was produced, Tadisch said, "Look, I opened only one bottle, and you can see that it's still half full. Let's open any other bottle and taste the wine and you'll see that it's turned to vinegar."

A bottle was uncorked and the servant poured a glass for the vintner's only daughter to taste. Unbeknownst to her, this was in fact sacramental wine, forbidden to a

Jewish girl. She drank the whole glass. "But this wine is fine," she said. "What have you got against it?"

Tadisch, pretending to be surprised, tasted the wine. "Yes, indeed, you're right," he said. "Let's try another bottle."

Another bottle was uncorked, and the vintner's only daughter and the priest both tasted the wine.

"Well, now I see that I was wrong," said Tadisch. "I made a mistake."

Then he began to pay her compliments, and he apologized profusely for suspecting her for no good reason. The vintner's only daughter, who had never allowed her hand to be touched by a man before, was so affected by the sacramental wine that she permitted the priest to take her hand and squeeze it tenderly. That touch burned in her like a snake's poison, and she began to enjoy the priest's attentions. Before departing, she shook hands with him, and he asked her to visit again.

The vintner's only daughter was corrupted. She sent the priest letters whenever his servant came to collect wines, and Tadisch responded with affectionate notes of his own, until she began to visit him secretly. Then one night she didn't return home to sleep. The vintner's only daughter was lost, like a stone in water. This caused a great commotion in the vintner's house. Sobbing and shouting were heard. The distraught Bergers started to search for their only daughter, asking neighbors if they had seen her. Finally they found someone who had noticed her one evening on the narrow street that led to the priest Tadisch's cloister, and this evil news pierced the Bergers' livers. They ran to the priest's cloister, pleading with him to have pity on them and return their only daughter. Tadisch laughed at them, but he was also angry, and claimed to know nothing about the girl. The Bergers returned home, weeping bitter tears, and their friends were sick at heart for the great calamity that had befallen them.

Tadisch kept the vintner's only daughter locked up in a chamber in his cloister, and every day he came to teach her Christian prayers and tried to convert her. Then, when he saw that she was sick, suffering from melancholy, he understood that the only remedy for it was to find a bridegroom worthy of her.

A few miles from Prague there lived an old and very rich duke, who had only one son, a handsome and well-educated eighteen-year-old, and Tadisch decided to make a match between him and the vintner's only daughter. He went to see the duke, and sang the praises of the girl he held captive. Among them, of course, it was a matter of great prestige for somebody to marry a Jewish girl who had been converted. It was decided that the duke and his son would come to Prague on a Sunday to eat lunch with Tadisch, who would present the vintner's only daughter to them, and if they liked her matters would proceed from there.

On the Sunday in question, Tadisch told the vintner's only daughter to dress and make up nicely, because she was going to be presented to a desirable bridegroom. The duke and his son came to Prague and Tadisch threw a feast for them. After they had drunk a good deal and were merry, Tadisch presented the vintner's only daughter to them, and she found such favor in their eyes that they stayed the night the better to be acquainted with her. The next day the priest arranged another big party and placed the vintner's only daughter next to the duke's son, and she sat there happily. After the party, the vintner's only daughter and the duke's son gave their hands to each other, a sign that they were engaged. They decided to marry two months later, on the day that the cardinal would convert her to the Christian faith. The duke's son presented her with a gold ring with a very fine stone, and his initials engraved in it, and then he and his father departed.

Meanwhile, the vintner and his wife did not rest. When nobody in town could help them, they went to visit their relative, the celebrated Rabbi Yakov Ginsberg of Friedburg, to ask him to save their only daughter. The celebrated rabbi replied, "But you have in your city a great and saintly and holy man, the Maharal, and why, therefore, do you come to me? The Maharal can help you more than I can."

Rabbi Ginsberg wrote a letter to the Maharal, asking him to intervene on behalf of the unfortunate parents, and when the Bergers returned to Prague they immediately presented it to the Maharal, and beseeched him to help them in their overwhelming sorrow. The Maharal was deeply concerned, and very sad, but he did not wish to tangle with Tadisch, whom he knew to be an evil man, a real snake, and a rabid Jew-baiter. However, he could not resist a plea from his good friend Rabbi Ginsberg, and he decided to act, but in secrecy. So he proclaimed in a loud voice, in the presence of other supplicants in his house, that he was unable to help the Bergers. But that very night, he sent his faithful old servant, Reb Ranheim, to summon the unfortunate parents, and he assured them that he would try to find a solution to their problem. He was going to manage it in such a way that nobody would know that it was he who had in fact intervened. He instructed the

Bergers to secretly prepare a carriage in the courtyard of their house. The coachmen should be both competent and trustworthy, and two strong and dependable men would also be required. The Bergers, he said, should be ready to escape the town with their only daughter at a moment's notice. Then the Maharal asked, "Do you know of a safe place in another country where you could settle with your only daughter?"

Berger replied that he had a brother in Amsterdam, Reb Chaim, also a vintner, a wealthy and God-fearing man, well versed in the Torah.

Good, said the Maharal, and he instructed the Bergers to fast for three days, beginning the next morning. They were only allowed to eat at night. And on each of their three fast days they must read and finish the Book of Psalms, weeping over it. Before sending the Bergers home, the Maharal urged them not to tell anybody that he was going to help them. The unfortunate parents returned home, their hearts brimming with hope, and for three days they fasted and prayed and wailed, as instructed.

Meanwhile, the vintner's only daughter began to feel homesick. Her parents, she remembered, had been good to her, and she had betrayed them with strangers. She cried all through the night. The next morning Tadisch saw that her eyes were red and swollen, and he asked her what was wrong. She said she wasn't feeling well. Never mind, he said, soon her indisposition would be over.

At that time it just so happened that the Cardinal of Krakow ordered all the priests that were under his jurisdiction to attend a general meeting. The priest Tadisch was also summoned to the meeting, and this was the wondrous thing about it — Tadisch was not directly under the jurisdiction of that particular cardinal. Before Tadisch embarked for Krakow, he warned his servants not to allow anybody in the compound of the cloister.

The Maharal, who heard that Tadisch had gone to Krakow, secretly sent for Yosseleh, the Golem, and told him that a daughter of Israel had fallen into the hands of Tadisch and was imprisoned somewhere in his cloister compound. He ordered the Golem to rescue the vintner's only daughter and to restore her to her unfortunate parents. To this end, the Maharal lent the Golem the famous camel that made him invisible. He also handed him a big bag and a letter for the vintner's only daughter that read: "I am your grandfather who was sent to you by Heaven to save you from here. Now hide yourself in this bag and I shall carry you to your parents."

The Maharal told the Golem that he was to go to the cloister compound in the morning, and to stand by the small iron service door that could only be opened from within, without a key. He was to wait there until somebody left the compound, and then he would be able to slip inside without being seen, as the camel made him invisible. Once inside, he should learn how the door opened without a key and discover where the vintner's only daughter was being held captive. He was to enter her room imperceptibly and to hide there until midnight. After he was certain that everybody was asleep, he was to waken the vintner's only daughter, give her the letter to read, open the bag so that she could slip inside, and then carry her out of the compound to her unfortunate parents. Yosseleh, the Golem, did as he was told, and two o'clock the next morning brought the girl to her father's house.

Who can describe the great joy and weeping in that house when the parents suddenly saw their daughter standing before them? She threw herself at their feet and kissed them, her eyes running with tears, and asked forgiveness for all the villainous things she had done to them. The father and mother embraced her and covered her with hot kisses. But when they asked, "Who brought you here? Who was your savior?" all she could reply was that it was her grandfather from Heaven. The vintner and his wife believed her, and thought that the Maharal had brought the grandfather down from Heaven to save their daughter. Then Berger, remembering what the Maharal had said, told his wife, "This is no time to talk. We have to escape immediately to my brother in Amsterdam," and they got into the carriage waiting in the courtyard and fled, as instructed.

When the priest Tadisch's servant discovered that the girl had escaped, he feared that he would be held responsible. So he hurried down to the cellar of the cloister, unearthed the bones of a dead man, set them in the girl's bed, and started a fire. Before the fire brigade arrived, the room was completely burned. The firefighters found charred human bones and reported that a stranger, who had come to the priest on some matter, had burned to death in the cloister. Later the servant betrayed the priest, and said that he had imprisoned the only daughter of Mechel Berger, fraudulently persuading her to apostasy, holding her prisoner and torturing her until she was tired of life itself, and set fire to herself in the room.

When Tadisch returned from Krakow, he was horrified to learn his servant's story, but he kept quiet, because it was impossible for him to prove that his servant was lying. However, he understood that it was his servant who had set the fire, and he suspected that he had been bribed to allow the vintner's only daughter to escape. Tadisch informed the duke that there had been a fire in his cloister during his absence in Krakow, and that only the bones of the vintner's daughter remained. The duke had to tell his only son that his beloved fiancée had been burned alive, and the son suffered a nervous breakdown.

The duke's son imagined how the fire had burned his beloved while she was sleeping quietly in her bed, and how she must have awakened in pain, but lacked the strength to fight death. He knew no peace. He couldn't eat. He couldn't sleep. The old duke tried to divert his only son with all kinds of pleasures and had marriage brokers seek a suitable partner for him, all to no avail. For no pleasure could satisfy the lad and no girl please him ever since he had seen the beauty and nobility of the Jewish girl. The duke's only son decided that his only consolation would be to find another Jewish girl as delicate and beautiful as his first fiancée. But he understood how difficult it would be to find another girl with these qualities, and that even if he did find one, she most likely wouldn't be willing to become a Christian. So he decided to move to a faraway country to study Torah and convert to Judaism without his father knowing it, and then to seek a Jewish girl who was to his liking. He told his father that as long as he remained so close to Prague he would continue to brood about his lost fiancée, and it would only be a question of time before he lost his mind. So he suggested to his father that he study at the university in Venice for a number of years, and afterward return to the duke's house and contract a new marriage. It was extremely difficult for the old duke to separate himself from his beloved only son, but he saw no other solution to the lad's consuming sorrow. He gave his son a great deal of money and sent him to Venice.

The duke's only son rented a room in Venice, paying a year's rent in advance, and told the landlord that he was a merchant who traveled a lot, and that he would only be using his quarters occasionally. The landlord was to collect his mail from the post office and leave the letters in his room, thus enabling him to eventually get his father's letters and reply to them.

Now, in those days the celebrated Rabbi Yakov Ginsberg, the Gaon of Friedburg, was world famous, the second most renowned rabbi after the Maharal. He spoke many languages, and was knowledgeable in all the sciences, and he was the one the duke's only son picked to teach him Torah and convert him to Judaism. The Gaon took to the duke's only son immediately. He converted him to Judaism and gave him the name Abraham Yisharon. The duke's son proved to be a brilliant student, but the Gaon was also president of Friedburg's rabbinical court, he was awfully busy, his study time limited, and so he told his convert that he would now have to pursue his studies at the yeshiva in Amsterdam. He advised Abraham not to reveal that he was a convert, and he gave him a letter commending him to the head of the yeshiva in Amsterdam, saying that Abraham was a relative of the Gaon of Friedburg from the Yisharon family in Bucharest. The Gaon blessed Abraham and promised him that God would provide him with a worthy bride in Amsterdam. "When they offer you a bride, and tell you she's from a good family," said the Gaon, "from the family of the Gaon of Friedburg, only then will you know that it is a suitable match."

So Abraham left for Amsterdam, where the head of the yeshiva received him warmly, and he studied Torah with such application and intelligence that he earned a reputation as a great rabbinical scholar and soon became known as "the genius of Bucharest." Even as he continued with his studies, Abraham would slip away to Venice from time to time to collect the old duke's letters and reply to them from there, maintaining the pretense that he was a student in that city. Two years passed. Then the head of the yeshiva in Amsterdam instructed Abraham to return to his native city to find a wife. Abraham protested that he wished to settle in Amsterdam and find his bride there, because all the inhabitants were God-fearing, which wasn't the case in Bucharest. He also let it be known that he was the son of a very rich man, capable of paying any amount required for a suitable marriage, and this news spread quickly through the city. Soon enough marriage brokers were besieging him with propositions. Abraham rejected all of them until a certain marriage broker suggested that he consider a young girl who lived in the house of Chaim Berger. The rumor in Amsterdam was that the girl was an orphan, the daughter of Chaim's brother, and that she had a great inheritance. Among her other qualities, said the broker, was an illustrious family connection: she was a relative of the celebrated Gaon of Friedburg. When Abraham heard this he understood that this match was inspired by the Holy Spirit, and this was clearly the bride for him. So he told the broker to proceed. Clearly, the marriage broker didn't have a difficult task, given a bride and groom of such quality. But neither the groom nor the bride was truthful with the other. The duke's only son didn't want people to know that he was a convert. And the vintner's only daughter didn't want everybody in Amsterdam to know that she had a bad reputation in Prague, where she had almost become a Christian. The match was satisfactorily concluded, all conditions agreed upon, and the bride and groom were enormously pleased, neither suspecting the truth about the other.

A few weeks after the engagement Abraham brought the vintner's only daughter some expensive gifts, among them two gold rings with precious stones. But in order to put on the new rings, the vintner's only daughter had to remove the one she always wore on her finger. When she set it on the table, Abraham saw his former initials engraved on it, and recognized that this was the ring he had given the bride who had burned to death in Tadisch's cloisters. He fainted, falling to the floor, which caused a great commotion. When he was revived, he looked closely at his bride and realized that this was in fact his original bride from Prague. He pleaded with her to tell him who she really was and how she had come by his ring. She had nothing to be afraid of, he said. And now it was the vintner's only daughter who swooned, falling to the floor. When she was revived she felt compelled to reveal everything. Abraham wept and said, "You should know, my dear, that I am your first bridegroom. I am the only son of the old duke. But now I am Jewish, and Providence made me go through all these trials, and brought me back to you."

They both wept, and held each other, happy in their new love. Abraham next revealed his secret to the head of the yeshiva and to the bride's uncle, Chaim

Berger. Both men were overjoyed to hear the blessing of the Gaon of Friedburg, who had told Abraham that it was in Amsterdam that he would find his true love. The head of the yeshiva said, "Now it is absolutely clear that this union was planned in Heaven, and whatever Satan wished to bring about in transgression of the law was turned around by Providence so that things could be done in accordance with the law."

The marriage of the vintner's only daughter and the duke's only son was celebrated with considerable pomp and circumstance in Amsterdam. That very year the old duke died, leaving all his money and properties to Abraham. And by the time Abraham and his wife settled on his late father's estate, the priest Tadisch was no longer in Prague. He had been convicted, and condemned to hard labor, for the murder of his servant's child in a failed plot to manufacture an accusation of ritual murder against the Jews, but I will go into this matter in my next story.

Once established in their palace in a village only a few miles from Prague, Abraham and his wife threw a great ball. Reb Mechel Berger and his wife came, and a luxurious carriage was sent to fetch the Maharal, who at last revealed his role in the rescue of the vintner's only daughter. "As I was recently helped by Providence to get rid of my evil opponent, the priest Tadisch, I am no longer afraid to tell the truth," said the Maharal. "You should know that it was not her grandfather who descended from Heaven to save the vintner's only daughter, but me. I was the one who sent her a man with a letter and a big bag."

All the guests applauded and thanked God Almighty for the miracles that were performed, and they gave presents to the Maharal, including the luxurious carriage and horses that had been sent to bring him to the ball. The Maharal also collected a good deal of money for charity to be dispensed in Prague.

A number of years later Reb Mechel Berger and his wife both died. Rather than inherit his father-in-law's estate, Abraham gave the house to the yeshiva, and went on to perform many good deeds in Prague. And he and his wife lived happily together for many years.

◇ *Twenty-two* ◇

MONDAY, OCTOBER 19, WAS SIMCHAT TORAH, THE eighth day of Sukkot.

The Torah is divided into weekly portions, one of which is read in the synagogue every Saturday morning. In the Young Israel Synagogue of my childhood, on Park Avenue near St. Viateur, only the aged or truly devout members of the congregation remained seated for the reading of the weekly portion. The others, my father among them, would wait it out in the back room, retiring there to gossip, catch up on things, and possibly plot an evening of steam baths, smoked-meat sandwiches, and poker at our neighborhood *shvitz*, the Colonial Baths — or a Saturday night stag party to catch the stripper at the Gayety Theater. Peaches. Ann Curio. Georgia. The legendary Lili St. Cyr. Following the Torah reading, the men would remain in the back room, kibitzing, until our earnest rabbi finished his sermon, a blight that was tolerated for the sake of the wives, who sat in a separate section of the synagogue, rapt, and were thrilled when the rabbi came to speak at one of their Ladies' Auxiliary meetings. Our rabbi, it should be noted, was no pale, round-shouldered Hasid. He was cleanshaven. He preached in English. He belonged to the Book-of-the-Month Club. And he had survived the scandal that arose after it was discovered that he submitted to a manicure from the saucy Miss O'Hagan, given to wearing sweaters a size too small, whenever he went to have his hair cut at Jack and Moe's.

If a bar-mitzvah boy, coached for months by Mr. Yalofsky, was reading the weekly portion, usually in a voice that was still girlish or cracking, the men could count on a kiddush after services were done: little squares of honeycake, schnapps in shot glasses, maybe slices of *lokshen kugel* with raisins — if the parents weren't pikers like the Finestones, who my father swore had watered the schnapps, never threw out a piece of string, and soaked their streetcar tickets in hot water and then peeled them apart, making two out of one.

On Simchat Torah the annual cycle of Torah readings ends. The last poignant verses of Deuteronomy are read aloud to the congregation:

> And Moses was a hundred and twenty years old when he died; his eye was not dim, nor his natural force abated.
>
> And the children of Israel wept for Moses in the plains of Moab thirty days; so the days of weeping and the mourning for Moses were ended.
>
> And Joshua the son of Nun was full of the spirit of wisdom; for Moses had laid his hands upon him; and the children of Israel hearkened unto him, and did as the Lord commanded Moses.
>
> And there hath not risen a prophet since in Israel like unto Moses, whom the Lord knew face to face,

In all the signs and the wonders, which the Lord
sent him to do in the land of Egypt, to Pharaoh, and to
all his servants, and to all his land,
And in all that mighty hand, and in all the great terror, which Moses wrought in the sight of all Israel.

Then the reader begins the cycle again, chanting the first five
verses of Genesis, proof that the study of the Torah never ends:

In the beginning God created the heaven and the earth.
And the earth was without form, and void, and
darkness was upon the face of the deep; and the spirit of
God moved upon the face of the waters.
And God said, "Let there be light." And there was
light.
And God saw the light, that it was good; and God
divided the light from the darkness.
And God called the light Day, and the darkness he
called Night. And the evening and the morning were
the first day.

On the evening of Simchat Torah, the Sefer Torahs are removed from the ark and members of the congregation, children
included, take turns parading about the synagogue carrying
them, their silver bells jingling, to the accompaniment of a good
deal of singing and hand-clapping. It was an evening of terror
for me when I was a nine-year-old. The twin scrolls of a Sefer
Torah are dauntingly heavy. Dropping one is a sin — in my case,
a sin compounded by the fact that the Sefer Torah I was given
the honor of carrying had been the work of my grandfather
Rabbi Yudel Rosenberg, who was also a scribe, or *sofer*. My
grandfather would have written his Sefer Torah with the quill of

a turkey feather on parchment manufactured from the hide of a kosher animal, the hair removed after it had been soaked in limewater for nine days. Before beginning, he would have been obliged to test his quill and ink by writing the name "Amalek" and crossing it out, symbolically blotting out Amalek, as it is written (Deuteronomy 25:19): "Therefore it shall be, when the Lord thy God hath given thee rest from all thine enemies round about, in the land which the Lord thy God giveth thee for an inheritance to possess it, thou shalt blot out the remembrance of Amalek from under heaven; thou shalt not forget it."

Amalek was the grandson of Esau and ancestor of the Amalekites, nomads in the land between Egypt and Canaan, many of whose descendants can no doubt now be found organizing for Hamas in the Palestinian camps of Khan Yunis, Rafa, Jabalia, and Gaza Town.

With Amalek's name blotted out, the Skaryszewer Illuy would have next pronounced aloud the declaration "I am writing the Torah in the name of its sanctity and the name of God in its sanctity." Before daring to write the name of God he would have said aloud, "I am writing the name of God for the holiness of His name." Mistakes he made could be erased with a knife and pumice stone, but none of the names of God may ever be corrected or erased. A faulty Sefer Torah, or one beyond repair, must be buried in an earthenware urn in a cemetery.

STROLLING ON Jerusalem's King David Street, early on Simchat Torah morning — another scorcher — I passed young women in their finery, clasping prayer books, drifting toward their synagogues in groups of five or six. The men trailing after, enduring the heat in black fedoras, white shirts, ties, and dark suits, carried their prayer books and prayer shawls in small velvet bags. Briefly, I envied them their sense of community, their festive spirit.

But that night it was the menacing, dark side of religion, Jerusalem's curse, that seemed to be rampant in more than one sector of the Holy City. Crowding barriers erected outside Prime Minister Rabin's official residence, God-crazed settlers wearing prayer shawls and phylacteries, Uzis protruding from their belts, had gathered to protest terrorism in the occupied territories, invoking Jehovah's name in their call for vengeance. And elsewhere, no doubt, equally fervent Hamas youngsters were sharpening their daggers in praise of Allah. Some of them were said to be equipped with plastic keys to ensure their entry into heaven should they be wasted in an IDF fusillade.

Jerusalem enjoys (or, more properly, suffers) not one but three successive Sabbaths, on Friday, Saturday, and Sunday. Friday mornings the muezzin, chanting into an amplifier, attracts shoals of the Muslim faithful out of the warrens of the Old City to the Dome of the Rock. Late in the afternoon, shortly before sunset, sirens proclaim the coming of the Jewish Sabbath: all public transportation ceases until sundown Saturday, and on Saturday morning devout Jews repair to more than a thousand synagogues. The next morning, Jerusalem wakens to the pealing of church bells calling each to each. Alas, this overwhelming religious presence has not made for Isaiah's dream of a peaceable kingdom "where the wolf shall dwell with the lamb, and the leopard will lie down with the kid."

The muezzin sometimes slips a nugget out of the Koran's social pages into his prayer: "The Lord has not begotten a son." And some Christians, in the same ecumenical spirit, have named Mohammed the false prophet, Satan's firstborn son. On the other hand, since 1917, Greek Orthodox and Armenian patriarchs have no longer led their congregants in an Easter chant that began:

O Jews! O Jews!
Your feast is the feast of devils,
Our feast is the feast of Christ.

Fridays, even as Muslims gather on the esplanade of the Dome of the Rock, it is possible — as it has been since the fourteenth century — for Christian pilgrims to follow Franciscans bearing a wooden cross along the Via Dolorosa, believed to be the path Jesus took to his crucifixion at Golgotha. Each of the fourteen Stations of the Cross is blessed with its own tawdry souvenir shop.

Long before the Jews had returned to rule over Jerusalem, Muslims and Christians were regularly defiling each other's sacred places. In 1860, an awning had to be built over the open cupola of Christ's tomb, to protect against Muslims emptying their slops into it. Earlier, Crusaders made a point of pissing in the prayer niche of the al-Aqsa Mosque, and at least one pilgrim, a German nobleman, shat through a hole in the mosque's vaulted roof. Never mind. Now there are ultra-Orthodox Jews who claim that the Muslims are intruders at the Dome of the Rock, trespassing on Jewish-owned property; evidence of King David's purchase of the site from Araunah the Jebusite is to be found in 2 Samuel (24:24): "And the king said unto Araunah, Nay; but I will surely buy it of thee at a price: neither will I offer burnt offerings unto the Lord my God of that which cost me nothing. So David bought the threshing floor and the oxen for fifty shekels of silver."

Biblical testimony that in fact all of Samaria and Judea belongs to the children of Israel, God-given to Abraham, can be found in Genesis (17:8): "And I will give unto thee, and to thy seed after thee, the land wherein thou art a stranger, all the land of Canaan, for an everlasting possession; and I will be their God."

Shortly thereafter, however, Jehovah did point out to Abraham that Ishmael, albeit a wild man with every man's hand against him, was also his seed (Genesis 21:13): "And also of the son of the bondwoman will I make a nation, because he is thy seed."

Arguably, even the biblical title to Israel is clouded.

ON THE EVENING of Simchat Torah, Liberty Bell Park swelled with *haredim*, the bearded men lugging Uzis, their wives with babes in arms. Pale young men danced and sang, hoisting Sefer Torahs high, and stamped their feet on a specially erected platform, sidecurls flying. Ecstasy floated on the hot evening breeze. And all at once these followers of Menachem Mendel Schneerson, the ninety-year-old Lubavitcher rebbe (and they believed, possibly, just possibly, also the long-awaited Messiah), began to chant, "*Moshiach! Moshiach! Moshiach!*" Everybody else joined in the delirium.

Montreal has its own Lubavitcher Yeshiva, one of 1,350 worldwide, and until recently a billboard on the route in from the airport proclaimed BIENVENUE LE MESHIACH, providing a telephone number for those who wanted, as a frequent newspaper ad put it, to "BE A PART OF IT." The Lubavitcher movement — which claims two hundred thousand adherents, some as far-flung as Tanzania, and millions of sympathizers — is also known as Habad, an acronym of the Hebrew words for wisdom, understanding, and knowledge. The seventh Lubavitcher rebbe presided over his flock from his headquarters at 770 Eastern

Parkway, in Crown Heights, Brooklyn. Before he was rendered speechless by a stroke, he heard supplicants daily, handing each one a dollar that was supposed to be passed on to charity. "Many of his visitors, however," wrote Michael Specter in *The New York Times Magazine*, "bypass the charity box mounted on a nearby wall and instead race to the street, where enterprising Russian immigrants wait to laminate them, melting the rebbe's stern, fatherly portrait over the benign face of George Washington."[1]

Shops in the surrounding streets sell garishly colored, framed photographs of the rebbe, as well as posters, calendars, zippered cases, and wallet-size cards, all embossed with his image; and no Lubavitcher hearth is complete without its portrait of the rebbe. A violation, I should have thought, of the Second Commandment, which enjoins Jews "not to make unto thee any graven image."

There were children in Crown Heights who laid out their best clothes before retiring for the night, just in case the Messiah would waken them the next morning. Followers of the rebbe in Israel, convinced that he was indeed the Messiah, built an exact replica of 770 Eastern Parkway in Kfar Habad, a small settlement near Ben-Gurion Airport. Some of them reportedly never ventured far without their electronic beepers, lest the rebbe declare himself the Messiah in their absence.

The Lubavitcher rebbe, who had never been to Israel, did pronounce on its politics with considerable influence. In the winter of 1992 he sent the then prime minister, Yitzhak Shamir, a warning against trading land for peace. "It would be an abomination," he said, "even to think about discussing autonomy for the Palestinians."[2]

Mind you, the Lubavitcher rebbe seems a benign figure when set beside another rabbi, the pistol-toting Moshe Levinger, who founded Kiryat Arba in defiance of the Israeli government in 1968. Kiryat Arba, crowding the Arab town of Hebron, was the first of the West Bank settlements.

Born into a family of German Jewish Hasidim in Jerusalem in 1935, Levinger, the father of the settlement movement, has been adjudged one of the "true heroes of our generation" by Ariel Sharon, but dubbed "Israel's foremost religious fascist" by *The New Republic*. He believes that Israel is a holy nation that must be governed according to Halakhah and can tolerate no possible accommodation with Arab sojourners on the land. Levinger, who now lives in Hebron, was sentenced to four months in prison in 1991 for beating up an Arab woman and breaking the arm of her nine-year-old son because her daughter had teased his daughter. At the time, he told reporters, "I won't behave like Jews in the *galut* [the Diaspora] who say it's raining when a *goy* spits on a Jew."[3] He once informed an interviewer from *Ha'aretz*, "The Arab is interested in his rug and his house. National sovereignty for the Palestinian people is a Jewish invention...." He went on to tell the writer Robert Friedman, "This land does not belong to the Palestinian people. In all its history, it has belonged to the Jewish people. And because it is our place, we have to build more settlements and bring more Jews to live in *Eretz Yisrael*. The Arabs don't understand that our connection to Hebron is no less strong than it is to Tel Aviv. If diaspora Jews think Hebron is part of the 'occupied territories,' they won't move there. And if the Arabs don't stop the *intifada*, they will be transferred."[4]

Levinger won only 3,700 votes when he ran for the Knesset in 1992. He may have been undone by his notorious TV commercial, which showed him, back to the camera, "firing a pistol at a paper target, and then swirling around to confront the camera, raising his gun and exclaiming, 'Only force will end the *intifada*!'"[5]

AN ISRAELI psychologist once lamented that some visitors to Jerusalem are subject to a peculiar kind of madness, and become dangerously God-crazed.

In 1951, Mustapha Shukri Ashu, a devout member of an organization called Holy Jihad, assassinated King Abdullah of Jordan on the Temple Mount because the king was trying to make peace with the Israelis.

In August 1969, Denis Michael Rohan, an Australian tourist and a Protestant, set fire to the al-Aqsa Mosque in order to hasten the coming of the millennium; he wanted to facilitate the rebuilding of the Jewish temple "for sweet Jesus to return and pray in it."

The day before Mustapha Shukri Ashu murdered the king, wrote Amos Elon in *Jerusalem, City of Mirrors*, he wandered about the city "drunk with Koranic lore" — even as Rohan, before he set his fire, drifted through the city obsessed "with biblical texts and their heavenly revelations."[6]

In April 1982, Alan Harry Goodman, an American armed with an M-16 automatic rifle, shot his way into the Dome of the Rock, killing one man and wounding three others. He climbed the Stone of Foundation, brandishing his gun, but then surrendered quietly to police. His aim, he said, had been to liberate the Temple Mount from alien Muslim control and become king of the Jews.

In 1984, sixteen Jewish moon worshippers, members of a kabbalistic sect, were caught with explosives; their intention was to blow up the mosques on the Temple Mount.

A year later, twenty-eight well-known West Bank settlers, members of a fundamentalist terrorist group, were caught by the police while they conspired to blow up the mosques on the Temple Mount. "Four were caught red-handed," Amos Elon wrote, "as they were placing explosive charges under Arab buses. Two more were arrested soon after, on their way from the booby-trapped buses to pray and give thanks at the Western Wall. Twenty-two accomplices were arrested at their homes. The explosive charges had been set to go off under the Arab buses during rush-hour traffic. They would have killed and wounded hundreds of innocent people."[7]

Through the ages, it's probable that more deadly sins have been committed in the exalted names of Jehovah, Christ, and Allah than were ever perpetrated in the service of pride, covetousness, lust, anger, gluttony, envy, and sloth.

◇ *Twenty-three* ◇

ONE MORNING, ACCOMPANIED BY PAUL WORKMAN and Azur Mizrachi, his affable cameraman, I set out for Dheisheh, a Palestinian refugee camp. Our first stop was to be the field office of the United Nations Relief and Works Agency for Palestine Refugees (UNRWA) at Sheikh Jarrah, in Jerusalem. En route, we geared down to creep necessarily slowly through the teeming market square opposite the Damascus Gate, a hodge-podge of rickety wagons laden with vegetables or junk, ancient trucks with panting engines, bicycles and donkey-carts, and lined with hole-in-the-wall cafés, bakeries, and butcher shops, the signs in Arabic. Arab workers out of Gaza congregate here, waiting to be picked up by Israeli contractors who will provide a day's work on one building site or another. At UNRWA we were directed to the office of Public Information Officer, where we were confronted by an insufferably elegant Sandro Tucci. "Whom do you wish to talk to in Dheisheh?" he asked.

I failed to respond immediately, nonplussed by his manner of a bored maître d' of human suffering. He smiled tightly and began to recite specialties that were not listed on the menu. "I can offer a young man who had part of his jaw shot off, a recent widow, a boy who came out of prison crippled."

I was tempted to ask if he took AmEx? Visa? Instead, I said, "If possible, I'd like to talk to people who haven't already been interviewed again and again."

Turning to his assistant, Marina Barham, he said, "Take him to the homes of Nihad 'Odeh and Mohammed Abu 'Aker."

Miss Barham, an intelligent young Palestinian Christian who spoke fluent English, was to serve as my guide and translator.

Dheisheh lies on the main road out of Jerusalem, through Bethlehem to Hebron, with its overhanging settlers' suburb of Kiryat Arba. Israelis tooling past the camp usually accelerate lest they be stoned, their cars readily identifiable by their yellow license plates. So setting out from the UNRWA field depot, Azur took the usual precautions: he laid a CANADIAN BROADCAST-ING CORPORATION placard against the rear windscreen and spread a blanket with PLO colors on the dashboard.

As we drove through the Jerusalem quarter of Talpiot, Miss Barham pointed out a sizable detached stone house. "That was our family house until '67," she said, "and every time we pass, I see it. My grandfather still keeps a key to the front door."

I remember that Spanish Jews expelled by the edict of the Catholic monarchs in 1492 also held on to their front-door keys, sometimes passing them down through the generations.

Miss Barham did not have an Israeli or a Jordanian passport, but only a *laissez-passer* issued by the Israeli government. "Two months after I applied for a passport," she said, "I was invited to meet with an Israeli intelligence officer in a room in the King Solomon Hotel. He told me not to tell my parents that I was seeing him. He knew everything about me. It was a pleasure, he said, to talk to such a well-educated young woman. He offered me immunity. Privileges. Money. A diplomatic passport. If only I would agree to inform on Palestinians abroad. Don't worry, he said, I wouldn't have to inform on my friends. But if there was a conference somewhere, I would just have to say who was there, and where they were staying. Little things like that. No harm in it. He attempted to recruit me three times, but each time I said no. Finally, after a three-month wait, I got my *laissez-passer*."

In June 1991, UNRWA estimated that there were 430,083 registered refugees rooted on the West Bank, of which 114,763 lived in twenty different camps. Dheisheh, its official population 8,048, was surrounded by a twenty-foot-high fence, with entry and exit possible through a narrow turnstile.

"At least," said Azur, "Rabin ordered the ugly aluminum support screens taken down. Then you couldn't even see out."

There were two Israeli Defense Force bases opposite Dheisheh, and four observation posts mounted on roofs within the camp, and the narrow hilly streets were regularly monitored by three patrols of six to eight soldiers each. Established as a tent city in 1949, Dheisheh had its first houses constructed in 1954. Now its residents, making a political statement, would not allow any renovations, and neither would they agree to be moved, unless it was back to the villages they had fled or been evicted from in 1948. Hussein Shahen, a camp official, said, "We get no services from the Israeli government, but if anybody here refuses to pay his income tax, he can have his property seized. Say his carpentry shop, if that's what he does for a living."

Climbing the dirt road to Nihad 'Odeh's flat, we passed fly-ridden mounds of decaying refuse, cannibalized hulks of rusting cars, abandoned mattresses bleeding stuffing, and piles of rubble. An aged, robed Arab sat on a low stool outside a poky shop displaying boxes of fruits and vegetables and a couple of shelves of canned goods. Another old Arab, intent on his Koran, squatted before opened cartons of Marlboros and packages of razor blades.

"I want you to know," said Paul Workman, "that compared to the conditions that prevail in Gaza, this is Westmount. It's Park Avenue."

Nihad 'Odeh, a pretty widow of thirty-four attired in an embroidered green càftan, had been warned in advance of our visit. She invited us to sit down in her living room, and went to prepare Turkish coffee. Her flat, part of a cinderblock row, was made up of a tiny kitchen with a tiled floor, two bedrooms, and two sitting rooms. The furnishings were wretched. Framed verses from the Koran hung on one wall. A plaster-of-Paris model of the Dome of the Rock that sat on a side table was inscribed "If you support God, God will support you." Photographs of Nihad's late husband were everywhere. The most conspicuous was crudely colored and had a purple paper valentine pasted on it. Nihad joined us, poured the coffee, and sat down to tell her tale.

"My husband worked in construction in Saudi Arabia. On May 9, 1988, he was here on vacation at a time when I was six months pregnant. There were clashes in the camp. A disturbance. The soldiers were here. I had gone to the kitchen to prepare some food when I heard shots. My husband also heard the shots and he went to the window to see what was happening. He was shot through the head by a soldier. Look," she said, indicating the hole in a windowpane that had never been replaced, "the bullet hole." Then she swept a pillow from a tattered sofa. "And look, the blood. His blood. That's Ibrahim's blood. He was dead by the time they got him to the hospital and I would not allow an autopsy because the Jews use the body parts."

Marina, responding to my skeptical look, said, "It is a very true suspicion."

At least, I thought, we no longer poisoned wells or required the blood of Christian babes for our Passover matzohs, but I kept quiet.

Nihad was the mother of four sons and four daughters. "Ibrahim was only thirty-eight years old when he was murdered," she said. "He was the camp's first martyr of the *intifada*."

Marina explained that, following the death of a martyr, the PLO provides the widow with a pension of $100 a month — but she must go to Jordan to collect it.

"The military told me that only close relatives could come to Ibrahim's funeral," said Nihad. "Twenty to forty people at the most was all they would allow. There was a curfew — soldiers — but more than four hundred people came. Helicopters flew overhead. There was a clash with the soldiers and seventy people were injured. Eighty were arrested. Afterward, I would wake up in the morning and I would find food on my doorstep. My husband was shot for no reason. I complained to a human rights organization. I asked for compensation. The military governor came to see me. 'Maybe a neighbor shot your husband,' he said. Then there was an investigation and six days later he was here again. 'We are very sorry,' he said. 'Please accept our apologies.' And then he pointed at my swollen belly and said, 'I hope you have a boy and you call him Ibrahim.'"

Ibrahim's and Nihad's family had both fled their village in 1948, fearful of the approaching Israeli army. "Later," she said, "we regretted it. I've been here for many years and I expect nothing."

But did she not hope, I asked, that one day there would be a peace settlement?

"We will never give up Jerusalem. Jerusalem is sacred to all Muslims. It is our second-holiest site."

I didn't correct her, but I did venture that Jerusalem was also sacred to Jews.

"The Jews haven't suffered as we have. We fight with stones. They have guns. Many of our children have lost their fathers."

Outside, I trailed behind Paul and Marina with Azur, a Jew whose family had been obliged to flee Syrian oppression. He spoke fluent Arabic. "Is Marina translating everything correctly," I asked, "or is she doing a number on me?"

"She's doing an honest job," he said, "but widows get more than one hundred dollars a month from the PLO and they don't have to go to Jordan to collect it. On the other hand, since the Gulf War, the PLO has been cut off by Saudi Arabia and others, and Palestinian workers have been deported from Kuwait, another loss of income, so now I don't know."

We moved on through an alley strewn with rubble to the house of Mohammed Abu 'Aker and Aba Nidal Abu 'Aker. It was, I could see at once, considerably more prosperous, if only on the Dheisheh scale. There was a large new TV set in evidence. A Sony ghetto-blaster. A telephone. Electric fans. A decent sofa and armchairs. We had come on a day of mourning, the second anniversary of the death of their nineteen-year-old son, Mohammed. The living room's centerpiece was an idealized but crudely drawn portrait of Mohammed, underneath which was written:

YOUR HEART IS BEATING,
INTIFADA IS VERY STRONG.

A family group awaited us: Mohammed's ancient, shriveled grandmother, his grieving parents, his two brothers, and a sister. The right arm of one of the brothers was freshly bandaged right up to the elbow. Mohammed's mother, Aba Nidal, wore a scarf with PLO colors. A plump, excitable matriarch of substance, black eyes smoldering, she was the one chosen to recite the family's tale, and such was her puissance that no sooner did she start than the living room was transformed into a theater. When

Mohammed was only fifteen, she said, he was already active in the *intifada*. One of the stone-throwers. "He was arrested and held in prison, where he was tortured. He was confined in a cell where there wasn't enough room for him to lie down or stand properly. They placed a black sack over his head. They beat him. They made him suffer electric shocks. From time to time they would waken him out of a deep sleep and serve him soup in a dirty bowl. He was released by the courts after three months, but when he was sixteen he was imprisoned again, this time for a month. He hadn't been out for very long when the soldiers came for him another time. But he was in hiding. My two other sons, who were both in prison then, saw my picture in an Israeli newspaper, and read how the reporter wrote that I had been beaten with sticks when the soldiers came to search our house. They searched my house every night, but Mohammed was staying with his grandmother and only came home for a bath. One night the soldiers came when he was here, but he escaped, the soldiers running after him. And now they knew he came home to bathe in the evening, and they hid, waiting for him. The next day he was to be here at eight in the evening and there was to be a demonstration at ten. We heard two shots, very close to the house, and then a girl came running. 'Mohammed's been shot,' she said. He was shot with a dum-dum bullet, which exploded in his abdomen. These bullets are against the law. Mohammed was taken to the hospital, where the doctors were surprised that he was still alive. We went to a human rights organization and Mohammed was allowed to fly to the United States for treatment. My husband accompanied him to a hospital in Boston. Mohammed lived on life-sustaining machines for two years after he was shot."

She nodded, and her husband passed me photographs of their wasting son lying on a hospital bed.

"His weight dropped from sixty-five kilos to thirty kilos," she said. "He was only nineteen years old when he died, two years ago today."

Outside, a muezzin called the faithful to prayer. Mohammed Abu 'Aker, responding to a nod from his wife, said he suffered from a debilitating heart condition and worked in a gas station in the Jewish settlement of Zar Hadas. "We come from a village near Jerusalem," he said, "where I used to own eight thousand *dunams* of land."

Before we left the house, we were each handed an envelope with an invitation to that afternoon's memorial service, "on the second anniversary of the death of the legendary martyr Mohammed Abu 'Aker in Bethlehem."

DESCENDING A SLOPE to our car, which we had left outside Dheisheh's fence, we were careful to avoid patches made slippery by rotting garbage. "How can he afford that house," I asked Marina, "the TV set, the radio, on a gasoline-station worker's salary?"

"He is probably helped by relatives who work in the oil fields or maybe even America."

Paul drove back to the UNRWA camp with Marina, and Azur and I proceeded to Kiryat Arba, where we were scheduled to meet with the West Bank settlers' most eloquent advocate, the ferocious Eliyakim Ha'etzni. "You won't care for what he has to say. Neither do I," said Azur. "But he is nobody's fool."

"Do you think Abu 'Aker really owned all that much land and had it taken from him?" I asked.

"Where do you start here and where do you stop? How far back can we go in making amends? Sure, many Palestinians were evicted from their villages. Land was appropriated. But my family had to leave millions behind when they fled Syria. Other Jews came out of Yemen, Libya, and Egypt with nothing but what they could carry. One of our problems is that most foreigners, and even some Jews who have never been here, think you have to hike for a mile or cross a river or climb over a mountain to reach the West Bank. They don't realize it's just around the corner. It begins across the street. It's right here."

Feigning sleep, I brooded over Nihad 'Odeh's heartfelt declaration, torn from the rock of her misery: *The Jews haven't suffered as we have. We fight with stones. They have guns. Many of our children have lost their fathers.*

And once again, in my mind's eye, I was cutting through the lane to the Habonim meeting house on Jeanne Mance Street, horsing around with Jerry, Hershey, and Myer. Then we passed the home of my obdurate grandfather, who sat on the balcony, catching the evening breeze, *Der Kanader Adler* on his lap. Was he, I now wondered, sitting out there pondering the fate of those Reichlers left behind in Rawa Ruska?

Once, my grandfather raised the shutters of his rolltop desk and showed me the revolver that had been his when he had served in the army of the Emperor Franz Joseph. According to a family legend, a story that still gives me the chills, a great-uncle on my mother's side smashed one of his testicles on a blacksmith's anvil to avoid being conscripted into the army of the Czar. From 1825 to 1855, during the reign of Czar Nicholas I, Jewish children between the ages of twelve and eighteen were taken from their parents in the Pale of Settlement and pressganged into the army for periods of up to twenty-five years. The merciful Alexander II reduced their period of obligatory military service to five years. In 1899, following a pogrom in Jassy, Romania, organized by the city's police chief, the *fus-*

geyer (hiker) movement was born. Bands of able-bodied young Jewish men, marching in double-file, knapsacks on their backs, tramped hundreds of miles to the port of Hamburg, and from there sailed steerage to America. On the road, they sang the "Song of the *Fusgeyer*":

Geyt, yidelekh, in der vayter velt;
in kanade vet ir ferdinen gelt.

Go, little Jews, into the wide world;
in Canada you will earn a living.[1]

I ran through this heritage of outrages and endurance in my head, not forgetting the 1903 pogrom in Kishinev, when the murder of a mere forty-nine Jews qualified as a "massacre." Or the Black Hundreds, the notorious Russian nationalist movement, perpetrators of innumerable pogroms, that emerged in 1904. Or Kristallnacht (the Night of Broken Glass), when the Nazis, in November 1938, set fire to 191 synagogues and looted thousands of Jewish shops in Germany and Austria. Or Vichy France's Pierre Laval rounding up thirteen thousand Parisian Jews on July 16, 1942 — three thousand children among them — and locking them up in the Winter Velodrome until they could be retrieved by the Gestapo. Or the conference at Wannsee that led to the Final Solution. But, even sending buckets down the well of my Jewish provenance, I still had to allow that Nihad 'Odeh and Aba Nidal Abu 'Aker were not culpable. They could not be blamed. Big-bellied, black-eyed Aba Nidal Abu 'Aker — endlessly rocking, keening, but also relishing the importance that injustice had bestowed on her, rendering her the mother of a martyr, was unnervingly reminiscent of the St. Urbain Street grandmothers of my boyhood, spinning their sorrowful tales of the Old Country. Instead of drunken Cossacks wielding swords, it was IDF delinquents with dum-dum bullets. Even as I luxuriated in guilt, I had to acknowledge a deeper feeling, one that I hadn't plucked out of my liberal convenience store. I was grateful that, for once in our history, we were the ones with the guns and they were the ones with the stones. But, taking it a step further, I also found myself hoping that if Jerry, Hershey, Myer, and I had been born and bred in the squalor of Dheisheh rather than the warmth of St. Urbain, we would have had the courage to be among the stone-throwers.

EN ROUTE to Eliyakim Ha'etzni's house, we stopped for a beer at a street-corner canteen in Kiryat Arba. It was a kosher canteen run by a good-natured young *haredi* with corkscrew sidecurls, a follower of the Lubavitcher rebbe.

"So," said Azur, teasing, his manner affectionate, "when is the Moshiach coming?"

"Soon, soon."

"Is it the rebbe?" I asked.

"If the rebbe is not the Moshiach," he said, "then surely he is the one who will proclaim him."

Kiryat Arba was established on a rock-strewn slope in 1968 by Rabbi Moshe Levinger and forty *haredi* families, and was officially recognized by the government a year later. Today, although ringed by barbed wire and watchtowers, it is a pretty, prosperous town, home to some five thousand settlers surrounded by hostile Arabs. No settler is more visible than the lawyer Eliyakim Ha'etzni. Ha'etzni, a former member of the Knesset, belongs to the Tehiya ("Survival") Party, which is fiercely dedicated to saving Judea and Samaria from those treacherous doves who would swap land for peace. They are particularly opposed to the dastardly Yitzhak Rabin, who might yet enter history, Ha'etzni once wrote, "as a second Rehoboam, who had helped fatally divide his people and his land," and might even add his Jewish name "to those of Nebuchadnezzar and Titus, who exiled the Jews from Bethlehem, Shilo, Beit El and Hebron."

Hebron, soaring three thousand feet up in the Judean hills, is now a largely working-class Arab city with a population of eighty-five thousand. It is a veritable hotbed of Muslim fundamentalism, but it remains truly sacred to Jews also. According to the Pentateuch — the first five books of the Old Testament, and an oral tradition for something like a thousand years, transcribed only after the Exile — Hebron was the site of the Israelites' first known acquisition of land in Canaan. After the death of Sarah, Abraham bought the Cave of Machpelah, saying to Ephron (Genesis 23:4), "I am a stranger and a sojourner with you: give me possession of a burying place with you, that I may bury my dead out of my sight." He paid Ephron the Hittite four hundred shekels of silver (Genesis 23:17) for "the field of Ephron, which was in Machpelah, which was before Mamre, the field, and the cave which was therein, and all the trees that were in the field, that were in all the borders round about...."

Jewish tradition has it that this is where the Tombs of the Patriarchs are to be found. Not only Sarah was buried here, but also Abraham, his son Isaac, and Isaac's wife, Rebecca, and Abraham's grandson Jacob, and one of Jacob's wives, Leah. Their resting places are also sacred to Muslims. But Yigael Yadin, among others, was dubious. Yadin, the archeologist who supervised the excavations at Masada, once had the temerity to venture that these tombstones where Jews had come to pray for centuries were actually where the bones of a few long-forgotten

Arab sheikhs were interred — a suggestion that managed to outrage both Jews and Muslims. The burial place of Moses, or Nabi Musa, as he is celebrated in the Muslim pantheon, is also a matter of dispute. According to the Pentateuch, Moses was interred in Moab and "no man knoweth of his sepulchre to this day." However, Muslims believe that Moses so disliked it in Moab that he rolled underground to a tomb in Jericho; the exact spot is marked by a shrine built by Saladin.

After David returned from his slaughter of the Amalekites, it was to Hebron (2 Samuel 2:4) "the men of Judah came, and there they anointed David king over the house of Judah." And later all the tribes of Israel came unto David in Hebron (2 Samuel 5:3) "and king David made a league with them in Hebron before the Lord: and they anointed David king over Israel."

Hebron, wrote Paul Johnson in his *History of the Jews*, has been in turn a Hebrew shrine, a synagogue, a Byzantine basilica, a mosque, a Crusader church, and then a mosque again. "From 1266 the Jews were forbidden to enter the Cave to pray. They were permitted only to ascend seven steps by the side of the eastern wall. On the fourth step they inserted their petitions to God in a hole bored 6 feet 6 inches through the stone. Sticks were used to push the bits of paper through until they fell into the Cave. Even so, the petitioners were in danger. In 1518 there was a fearful Ottoman massacre of the Hebron Jews."[2]

On May 2, 1980, a group of *haredim* from the settlement of Beit Hadassah gathered to worship in the Cave on a Friday night. Afterward, they were attacked by four Palestinian terrorists armed with assault rifles and grenades. Six yeshiva students were killed and sixteen wounded. This brutal ambush led to the formation of a Jewish underground terrorist group that, exactly a month later, planted a bomb under the car of Bassam Shaka, who was the mayor of Nablus and an ardent PLO advocate. The bomb blew off both Shaka's legs.

MY COUSIN Sam Orbaum had provided me with *The Jerusalem Post* file on the truculent Eliyakim Ha'etzni.

In August 1992, Ha'etzni filed a complaint against the Israeli Broadcasting Authority for allowing the Palestinian spokesman Faisal Husseini to present his case on an interview program. "The government is going to have a very hard time," Ha'etzni said, "legitimizing the presentation of the PLO's chief leader inside this country."[3]

The same month, in a *Post* op-ed piece that anticipated the forthcoming meeting between Prime Minister Rabin and then President Bush, Ha'etzni warned against granting the Palestinians even limited autonomy — a license, he wrote, for an Arab police force made up of former "masked, hatchet-bearing murderers."[4] He also complained that "Today, owing to American pressure, Arabs are allowed to build freely whenever they wish, while Jews [on the West Bank] cannot build even privately financed homes. Will this new American definition of 'civil rights' and 'nondiscrimination,' this new racism directed against Jews, prevail during the five years of 'Autonomy'? Will the Arabs have free access to state-owned land, while the Jews remain cooped up in their chicken-pens waiting for slaughter?"[5]

In another op-ed piece published in the *Post*, Ha'etzni noted that by freezing funds for the settlers, "The State of Israel has achieved normalcy. At last it has its 'Jews,' its scapegoats, the ever-guilty, the chosen-and-rejected, those who always make news. The settlers are the Jewish State's Jews."[6]

AZUR AND I HAD A TWO P.M. appointment to meet Eliyakim Ha'etzni at his house in Kiryat Arba. We arrived right on time, but either he had forgotten about us, or his after-lunch snooze had lasted longer than he intended. We had to ring the doorbell several times before a sleepy-eyed Ha'etzni greeted us in his undershirt. His displeasure obvious, he grudgingly showed us into his living room, and then excused himself to retrieve his shirt. Born in Kiel, in Schleswig-Holstein, in 1926, Ha'etzni had come to Israel in 1938. He was tall, big-featured, lanky, with a shock of gray hair, steel-rimmed glasses, and huge protruding ears; a man who clearly had no time for idle chitchat or an exchange of civilities. Before he even sat down, he pointed at the sculpture of an unwinding black snake on the top of his TV set, glared at me, and said, "The media belongs to the left. That snake you see coming out of my TV is not there by accident."

I mentioned that we had spent the morning at Dheisheh.

"The real goal of the Arabs is to drive the Jews into the sea," he said. "They only discovered that they were Palestinians after the Zionists built a state here. We have already given up three quarters of Palestine, which they call Jordan, and where the so-called Palestinians make up seventy percent of the population. Look outside," he said, indicating a large picture window, "and you will see the Judean hills. Our historical land, our political entitlement coming from the Bible. Why should I give it up? Why should I be exiled to live in the Diaspora, in Tel Aviv, on the Philistine plains?"

Ha'etzni spoke effortless English with a pronounced German accent. But he had the disconcerting and intimidating habit of shouting at the two of us, his voice often flirting with hysteria, as if, in his mind's eye, he was poised on a balcony, hectoring the multitudes below. In fact, at one point I was tempted to shout back, "Ha'etzni! Ha'etzni!" just to see if he would acknowledge the chant by raising his arms aloft.

"We are not for transfer," he said. "But we should take the families of those children who throw stones and send them into exile. After ten such cases there would be no more stone-throwing. This is the advice I got from the Arabs themselves," he said, watchful, his eyes taunting. "They probably told you in Dheisheh about the policy of home demolition where arms were found or terrorists were hidden. What they didn't tell you is that immediately a home is demolished, they get money from the PLO to build another one. The Arabs are different from us for three reasons. One, they have no regard for human life — human life is cheap for them. Two, they will kill anybody, not necessarily the perpetrator. Three, they are terrorists who favor indiscriminate killings of innocent civilians."

In Dheisheh, I said, I had heard complaints about torture.

"A certain amount of physical pressure is permitted in dealing with terrorists. But yes, there is police brutality in Tel Aviv. A state is a machinery for oppression, even a Jewish state. Some of the new conscripts in the army suffer from sadism. Look here, what a Jewish state is all about is to enable us to be the same as everybody else. Why must we prove to be better? We were rewarded for that with Auschwitz. So I needn't excel any more. I don't have to show how good I am."

Ha'etzni pointed out that he often acted for the Arabs in Hebron, defending them in court. "They are not trash. They shouldn't be humiliated, having to wait by the roadside to be picked up for construction jobs. Arabs have a saying that a hungry cat is a tiger. I am in favor of equal pay for equal work. We should have raised dramatically the health standards of the Arabs. Unfortunately, as things stand, there is a very big difference between Jewish hospitals and Arab hospitals."

I asked Ha'etzni if he was in favor of returning the Golan Heights to Syria.

"Even with the Golan, every one of our kibbutzim is fenced in. There are fences around all the Jewish settlements, because we are the object of attacks. Labor didn't win a majority of the Jewish votes. To give back the Golan is suicide. It is putting a bullet to our heads. Suckers that we are, we are sick in our minds. In '67 the Arabs said, let the sword judge between us. So now you have it! We have filled the graveyards with our children, and they must pay. Tell me," he added, his voice rising, "why a Jewish war should be different from others, and why we should return our territorial gains? Will the Americans give back New Mexico? Texas? California?"

But what if Rabin did trade land for peace, I asked, and the West Bank settlements had to be abandoned?

"Then," he said, "there will be civil war. Let's see if our children will come to kill me."

◇ *Twenty-four* ◇

T HE LAST TIME I'D SEEN GDALYAH WISEMAN, IN 1947, he had dropped out of McGill engineering in his third year, at the age of twenty-one, and married Esther, a Torontonian, and the two of them had left for the *hakhsharah* camp in Smithville. I caught up with him again early in November in the Wisemans' modest three-bedroom house high in the corkscrew Haifa hills. Sixty-six years old now, stocky, bald except for a fringe of curly gray hair, and given to self-deprecating laughter, he said, "I'm a Jewish nationalist, that's why I made *aliyah*. I never felt pushed out or uncomfortable in Montreal, but neither was I committed. From the age of fifteen I knew that I wasn't going to stay. But when I came here in '48 I never dreamed that we would be at war eight years later, or that I would be serving in the army until I was fifty-eight years old."

Gdalyah put in a brief stint on a kibbutz in 1948, and a year later completed his engineering studies at the Technion Institute, where he was now a professor. "My favorite joke used to be that we had come to a country the size of Toronto," he said.

"There wasn't much to eat. Bread, spaghetti, cottage cheese. Starches, mostly. The meat ration was so small it didn't pay to stand in line for it. We used to keep a carp in the basin under the shower, and every time we showered in the evening we had to lift out the basin with the carp. By the time it was killed by the end of the week I felt I had done in a friend."

Gdalyah served with the IDF from 1950 to 1952. He wasn't drafted in '56, but he served with an engineering unit attached to the air force during the Six-Day War, in charge of earth-moving equipment. "Following that war," he said, "the euphoria lasted for a long time. We didn't grasp the limitations of military might. There was also a feeling that there was no way we had to worry about what other people thought. I couldn't survive on my university salary, never mind pay for our children's education. I do consulting work for private corporations. But this is a small country, and as in any small country, talented people are hard put to find sufficient scope for work in their fields. When engineers abroad hear of the projects I've been involved in they are amazed. Look, I would have made a hell of a lot more money if I lived elsewhere. In fact, I'd be a wealthy man today."

Gdalyah had no contact whatsoever with Arabs. "But we simply can't afford to have the whole world angry with us. I'd like to see us get out of the West Bank. The question is, can the Palestinians get their act together? I don't think the moderates can carry the people with them."

I mentioned that, according to a chart published in *Ha'aretz*, Arabs were more heavily taxed than Israelis, caught in the net at a much lower pay scale.

"But they have to be taxed more," said Gdalyah, "because they earn less."

The Arabs had fled their villages in '48, he said, they hadn't been evicted. Then he corrected himself. "Well, maybe here and there we gave them a little bit of encouragement," he said, "rolling lighted dynamite sticks down the hills toward their villages."

EVENTUALLY FLORENCE and I had to quit Mishkenot, with its impeccable hospitality, and move on to hotels in Haifa and Tel Aviv. In my experience, the staffs in Israeli hotels are unique. They are unobliging at best and, given any opportunity, downright rude. The Dan Hotel, on the Tel Aviv waterfront, also proved to be garish, the food bland and unappetizing. But that's where I met my cousin Shaindel, née Richler, and her husband, Julius Orbaum, for lunch. They are Sam Orbaum's parents. Julius is employed in the workshop of the Caterpillar Tractor Company and Shaindel has a job in the Tel Aviv offices of the Association of Americans and Canadians in Israel. Since 1982, they have lived in an apartment block in Petah Tikva, hard by Tel Aviv. Julius was apprehensive about the peace negotiations. "Where we live," he said, "on one side you can see the West Bank, and on the other side the sea. The Arabs can't be trusted. Whatever you give them, they will want more."

"They aren't all bad," said Shaindel.

"Well, some aren't. Maybe. During the Gulf War," Julius recalled, "when the Scuds were coming in, one of my customers, an Arab contractor from the West Bank, used to phone every morning to see if we'd made it through the night."

Shaindel used to live just down the street from us on St. Urbain. We played together as kids. I always look forward to these infrequent family reunions, anticipating that they will yield insights, unlock memories, but I am usually disappointed. Although Shaindel and I both tried to keep the conversation flowing, we now had hardly anything to say to each other, and

I was soon smoking and drinking too much. Finally, Shaindel asked, "What do you remember about me back then?"

"When you were possibly twelve years old, a pretty girl, more than somewhat saucy, your father threw you out of the house after he caught you wearing lipstick."

"Oh, that. What else?"

"Milk bottles."

"What?"

"I had never seen so many empty milk bottles lined up in a dark, long entry hall."

"In our house, you mean?"

"Yes."

"Oh."

Shaindel had three brothers. Shmulick, the eldest, born again Shmul Shimshoni — the locksmith I had visited on my previous trip — was now a grave-digger in Hadera, doing God's work, he said. Their father, Shimshon Herscovitch, had been an erratic provider. One night I had stumbled on Shaindel's mother and mine seated together at our kitchen table, busy with scissors, rolls of absorbent cotton, gauze, and sewing needles.

"What are you making?" I asked.

"You are not to come in here," my mother said, "and shut the door after you."

"Bandages?"

"I said *out*, and I mean right now."

My older brother took me aside in the living room. "Don't you know anything yet, you little *putz*?"

"Go ahead and punch me, just once, and I'll tell Ma that you drink beer now."

"They're making Kotex in there."

"Come on!"

"She can't afford to buy them in a store."

AFTER THE INCOMPARABLE beauty of Jerusalem, grubby Tel Aviv — redeemed from swampland, out there on the Philistine plain — was something of a letdown. Dizengoff and Ben Yehudah streets were crammed with shops displaying trashy religious artifacts and souvenirs. Chanukah candelabra lit by batteries. Country-fair-quality models of David's Tower, the Jaffa Gate, or the Wailing Wall. Clunky necklaces. Masada lampstands. Poorly crafted silver ceremonial wine cups. Fake scrolls. Insufferably ornate sterling silver or brass trays. Overpriced and hideous paintings of *haredim* at prayer, or mawkish Safed street scenes more appropriate to a jigsaw puzzle than framed canvas.

Wedged between these tourist traps were camera-supply shops, fruit stands, sandwich bars, cheap clothing stores, and car rental and tour agencies. There were also shops, with signs in Russian, offering immigrants the best prices for jewelery or icons or musical instruments. But, to be fair, these tacky streets did also pulsate with down-and-dirty energy, a liberation from Jerusalem's sublime but crippling heritage. Look at it this way. A prankster God didn't tempt Abraham to commit infanticide on a rock on Magen David Square. Christ didn't preach to passersby on a corner of the Allenby Road. Mohammed didn't stop for a travel voucher at Egged Tours before galloping off to heaven. In Tel Aviv I could unknowingly wait for a traffic light to change on the very street corner where Arthur Koestler used to run his lemonade stand, but I couldn't — anywhere in town — inadvertently trample on the site of what was once a temple's Holy of Holies. Before 1909, there was nothing but mosquitoes here.

Deborah Harris, the literary agent from New York who had once lived in Tel Aviv, had recommended an agreeably sleazy watering hole, the Bonanza, on a street named after Joseph

Trumpeldor, my boyhood hero. The attractive young barmaid was a recent Russian immigrant.

"Is it difficult for you here?" I asked.

"It is difficult, yes."

"Will you stay?"

"For three thousand dollars a lawyer here says he can get you into Canada, but you are not allowed to work."

A number of impecunious young Russian girls have been reduced to working as hookers in Tel Aviv, reportedly turning tricks for as little as four bucks, one fifth the going rate for a quickie with a Moroccan-born whore. There were fistfights before the competing groups worked out a modus vivendi. Now the streets belong to the Moroccans and the Russian newcomers are confined to massage parlors.

One day, stopping on the terrace of a café on Ben Yehuda Street to order a beer and a pita pocket stuffed with lamb and trimmings, I was approached by a likable young Canadian who was with UNRWA. He was accompanied by a charming young Palestinian girl. He told me that it had taken him three months of haggling with officious Israeli bureaucrats before he had acquired a passport for the girl, which would enable her to accept a scholarship to study at Western University in London, Ontario. Obviously the young man saw Israelis as colonial oppressors, intruders in Palestine, and the Palestinians themselves as innocents, sweet-natured victims harassed by IDF bully boys who took pleasure in shooting at them with rubber bullets or worse. Given a chance, I'm sure he could have quoted Amnesty International statistics at me about what Eliyakim Ha'etzni had described as "permissible physical pressure." And I had no reason to suspect the veracity of the Amnesty International reports, or to deny the shame implicit in them. But I also had no doubt that, forty-six years earlier, this young man would have been an equally staunch supporter of those intrepid Habonim alumni who were herding dazed concentration-camp survivors into leaky tubs in Naples, running the British blockade, and, if successful, releasing their desperate cargo onto the beaches of Haifa and Tel Aviv. I told him that some six thousand Jews, many of them even younger than he was, had died in an unnecessary war, after five Arab armies invaded Israel in 1948. The Palestinians had been undone again and again, not by the courage and panache of the Israelis, or by the machinations of international Jewry, but by the mind-boggling stupidity of their own leaders. They had, in Abba Eban's enduring phrase, never missed an opportunity to miss an opportunity. Had they only had the wit to accept the findings of the Peel Commission in 1937, they would now possess eighty percent of the land that then constituted Palestine. Had they agreed to the U.N. partition plan in 1947, they would soon be celebrating the fiftieth anniversary of their own state, made up of half of Palestine, as it then was, and including the Old City of Jerusalem. Had they not been pledged to the destruction of the "Zionist entity," random terrorism, and a determination to drive the Jews into the sea, they could have prospered in a land that belonged to the progeny of both Sarah and Hagar.

"Look here," he said, "the Palestinians weren't responsible for the Holocaust and shouldn't be asked to pay for it. And what you so glibly call terrorists, they think of as freedom fighters."

ANOTHER DAY, Florence and I went to lunch with Bubbi Zerwanitzer, a documentary filmmaker in his sixties. Bubbi was an immediately familiar and endearing type. A cultivated man. A *mensh* who hadn't shucked what too many smart-ass Israelis disdain as "ghetto hang-ups," and what others, myself included, cherish as *neshuma*, soul. A melancholy Jew, Bubbi had a heart laden with guilt, some of it his, still more harvested. He was the one who gave me the *Ha'aretz* chart that showed how Arabs were more heavily taxed than Jews.

"The Arabs were here for a thousand years," he said, "more, and we moved many of them out. Morally, they are in the right."

I told him about my meeting with Ha'etzni.

"There are crazies on both sides," he said. "Enough. More than enough. But, unfortunately, he is right about one thing. The biblical land of Israel *is* the West Bank."

The insensitivity of some of the recent Russian immigrants troubled him, but so did their plight. "There are Russians," he said, "who are only off the plane for an hour and they want to know, what are so many Arabs doing in our land? We must have something like ten thousand musicians here now, most of them second-class, and reduced to playing their violins or singing on street corners, because how many teaching jobs are available in such a small country? The man who delivers my groceries was a doctor in Leningrad. Do I tip him? I tip him. Yes, I tip him. But I can't look him in the eye. I lower my eyes, I am so ashamed for him."

Sifting through my notebooks in the bar of the Dan Hotel that evening, I was suddenly overcome by homesickness for my nearly empty, unspeakably rich, sinfully misgoverned country. Suffering from a surfeit of Israel's seemingly insoluble dilemmas, I longed for the familiar nursery-school name-calling between English and French — *our* two founding races, so to speak — the progeny, not of Sarah and Hagar, but of dispossessed Highland sheep farmers and peasants out of Brittany and Normandy. I yearned for some Canadian homebrew farce rather than the daily death toll of Arab and Jew.

October 25. Five IDF soldiers were killed, and three seriously wounded, in a Hizbullah roadside bomb attack against an IDF convoy inside the eastern sector of the security zone in south Lebanon. And Arab workers, waiting to enter Israel from Gaza at the Erez checkpoint, rioted, heaving rocks. Three buses were partially burned, fifteen Arabs were injured, and a daylong commercial strike was declared in Gaza.

October 27. Attacks by Palestinian gunmen with grenades in Jenin, and another attack by knife- and ax-wielders in Gaza wounded two Israelis. A Gazan in Khan Yunis, and another in Gaza City, were both shot dead by other Palestinians, apparently for co-operating with the authorities. A Katyusha rocket fired into Kiryat Shmona killed fourteen-year-old Vadim Shuchman, whose family had emigrated from Russia two years earlier. A neighbor, also a new Russian immigrant, told a *Post* reporter, "I never thought that in the Jewish State we would need to hide like mice. We have a strong army and we should bombard the terrorists with at least a hundred shells for every one of their Katyusha rockets."

All at once, I was fed up with the tensions that have long been Israel's daily bread. I resented the need to stiffen every time an Arab came striding toward me. I was weary of the West Bank's loopy, God-crazed *yeshiva buchers* toting Uzis on the streets of Jerusalem and Tel Aviv. Ironically, the American-bred *olim* among them, playing latter-day gunslingers, actually owed more to their TV heritage of "Maverick" and "Rawhide" than they did to the teachings of Hillel, the great sage of the Second Temple period, or Rabbi Akiva ben Joseph (c. 50–137 A.D.), the legendary biblical scholar. I also didn't want to encounter any more appealing boys and girls in uniform, lugging submachine guns rather than briefcases stuffed with textbooks.

I was raised to proffer apologies because my ostensibly boring country was so short of history, but now, after five weeks in a land choked by the clinging vines of its past, a victim of its contrary mythologies, I considered the watery soup of my Canadian provenance a blessing. After traveling through the Rockies, Rupert Brooke had complained that he missed "the voices of the dead." Me, I was grateful at last for their absence.

THAT NIGHT I finished rereading Arthur Koestler's *Thieves in the Night* in bed. When the novel first appeared in 1946 it was greeted with scorn by my *chaverim* in the meeting house on Jeanne Mance Street. Joseph, the protagonist, was the son of a Russian Jewish pianist and a gentile, English mother whose family had never approved of the union. Joseph's father died early in the marriage and, at age eleven, Joseph accepted that his name was rarely mentioned. Like Daniel Deronda before him, Joseph hardly suspected that he was a Jew, or at least half of one. (Actually, he wouldn't have qualified under Halakhah for, according to our suspicious rabbis, only the son of a Jewish mother is entitled to call himself a member of the faith.)

Raised in a large country house in Oxfordshire, Joseph learned to play cricket and tennis, ride a horse, and attend church. Passing for a *goy*, he fell for Lily, whom he met at a tennis tournament during the summer vacation of his second term at Oxford, in the early thirties. Lily was the quintessential *shiksa*: "blonde, slim, pretty and divorced."[1] Alas, she was also an enthusiast "for a new political movement which organized demonstrations through the London East End, and whose members wore black shirts and had fights with policemen."[2]

Following a chaste two-year courtship, the two of them drank too much champers at a hunt ball. "She asked him in a whisper where his room was, and told him how to find hers."[3] After they had made love in her room, she switched the bedside lamp on to look for a cigarette:

The sudden light had revealed their nudity, and with it the sign of the Covenant on his body, the stigma of the race incised into his flesh. The horror in her face made him at first think that she had discovered in him some repulsive disease; then, in a voice icy with contempt she had accused him of infamy and deception, cross-examined him about his ancestry, ordered him to get dressed and clear out of her room.[4]

As a consequence, the course of Joseph's life was changed. He broke with his mother's family. He became a Zionist. He made *aliyah*. And in 1937 he found himself in a convoy setting out to found Ezra's Tower, a Tower and Stockade kibbutz in the Galilee. He had become "a thief in the night."

At our Habonim meeting house we were outraged that Joseph had been driven to join our noble cause only because the rich bitch Fascist *shiksa* he had bonked had humiliated him, revolted by his shorn dick. After the fact, as it were. This, I recall, prompted a heated late-night seminar at Ben Ash's Delicatessen.

"'The sudden light,' my ass. How dark could it have been in her room in the first place?"

"Yeah. Right."

"And anyway she had to know first, because, hey, guys, they help you put it in — your boner, I mean."

"G'wan."

"How in the hell would you know that, Mr. Expert?"

"He read it somewhere."

"Like fuck I did."

"Yeah yeah yeah. But it's true they like to handle it first, and she would have felt the crown and known he was a Hebe even before they screwed."

"What if she was, like, too shy to touch his schlong first?"

"Boy, you don't know anything, do you?"

"Oh yeah. You're forgetting that she was British, for Christ's sake."

"Sure, British. But a divorcée, you *shmock.*"

We were also insulted by Koestler's attitude toward sabras. In his diary, Joseph mused that this young generation of Israeli-born Jews was being brought up in a language that suffered from a loss of memory,

> with only the sketchiest knowledge of world literature and European history, and only a very dim idea of what everything was about since the day when the Ninth Legion under Titus captured David's Citadel. They speak no European language except a little English on the Berlitz-school level.... As against this, they know all about fertilisers and irrigation and rotation of crops; they know the names of birds and plants and flowers; they know how to shoot, and fear neither Arab nor devil.
>
> In other words, they have ceased to be Jews and become Hebrew peasants.
>
> This of course is exactly what our philosophy and propaganda aims at. To return to the Land, and within the Land to the soil; to cure that nervous overstrungness of exile and dispersion; to liquidate the racial inferiority complex and breed a healthy, normal, earthbound race of peasants. These Hebrew Tarzans are what we have bargained for. So why am I frightened of them?[5]

At sunrise, after Ezra's Tower has been established on a hill overlooking an Arab village, Bauman, the savvy underground leader, surveys the surrounding terrain with a telescope and observes, "All quiet.... Too quiet for my liking,"[6] just as Joel McCrea or John Wayne, anticipating an Indian raid, said in so many westerns of blessed memory.

Time will forgive the brilliant author of *Darkness at Noon* for this badly flawed but well-intentioned book. But there is a first-rate intelligence at play here, and *Thieves in the Night* is worth rereading for its insights into British Mandate official-dom, as well as Arab and Jew. There is a particularly apt, if sting-ing, portrait of a member of the Zionist Executive in Jerusalem, the tiresome Mr. Glickstein, who is seldom without his "propa-ganda smile." Matthews, the American foreign correspondent, ever at odds with Glickstein, has to admit that he is usually right,

> and that all these admirable guys were doing an ad-mirable job about this National Home of theirs. But he wished to God Glickstein would talk less about it, and with less of that intensity which sprayed the moisture from his lips into one's face, and that all these clever and admirable guys would relax sometimes and offer a guy a drink instead of statistics and heroics, and would get drunk sometimes themselves.[7]

Unhappily, the driver who was to take us to Masada turned out to be a direct spiritual descendant of Mr. Glickstein. From the moment he picked us up at Mishkenot (where we were still staying at the time), through the two-hour drive to Masada, our visit to that astonishing site, and the trip back, he never stopped nattering, overwhelming us with statistics, pointing out every Israeli miracle on either side of the road, watching closely for our reactions in his rearview mirror. We tooled past green-houses where resourceful farmers, exposing their plants to twenty-four hours of artificial light a day, grew tomatoes from seed to fruition in six weeks. "Imagine that, Mr. Richler." Yes, but I had purchased some of those sickly pink tomatoes in a Montreal supermarket and they had tasted of nothing more than water and pulp. He slowed down to show us where there would be a pipeline one day, pumping desalinated sea water into the desert to make it bloom. We stopped at another place where, once the money was available, waste from Israeli toilets would be chemically treated to heat a city yet to be built.

"Tell me," I asked, "have you guys ever thought of bottling Israeli piss and marketing it abroad as perfume?"

"My husband was only joking," said Florence.

"Sabra cologne. Essence of Dizengoff cooking oil. Gaza Strip aftershave. Scent of *haredim*."

Next we came upon a trailer camp baking in the desert, where Russian immigrants were temporarily housed, probably hitchhiking to Tel Aviv once a week to present their papers at the American and Canadian embassies:

Geyt, yidelekh, in der vayter velt;
in kanade vet ir ferdinen gelt.

In January 1992, Hillel Halkin, an American-born writer and translator who made *aliyah* in 1970, appealed in *The Jerusalem Report* for more North American *olim*: "to this day relatively few Jews who have come to live [in Israel] have done so because they really wanted to. Most, like the Russian Jews arriving now, simply had nowhere else to go."[8]

One evening a week before flying to Israel, Florence and I were joined for dinner at a restaurant in Frankfurt by several Canadians who were with our embassy in Bonn. One of them told me, "We get a lot of applications from suspect Germans these days. 'Why do you want to come to Canada?' I ask. 'We're tired,' they say, 'of seeing our income tax being spent on Gypsies and Jews.' Of course we don't accept such people." And then, asking me not to quote him by name, he went on to say, "I was really surprised when we were visited by a bigwig from the Canadian Jewish Congress who explicitly requested that we should not admit any more Russian Jews to Canada, or as few as possible, but make sure that they went to Israel."

The first Gorbachev-era Russian immigrants were welcomed by singing and dancing at Ben-Gurion Airport. Israelis overwhelmed them with gifts of old furniture and clothing, and invitations to dine in their homes. Joy was unconfined. In a time when *aliyah* by West European and North American Jews had been reduced to a trickle, they were seen as a twofold blessing: a bulwark against the threat of an eventual Arab majority in "Greater Israel," and, for secular descendants of Ashkenazi Jews, a safeguard against being outnumbered by a proliferation of notably fecund *haredim*, Yemenite, North African, and Ethiopian Jews. But, come September 1992, a headline in the daily *Ma'ariv* proclaimed "The Russian Demon Has Been Let Out Of The Bottle", and the writer went on to say, "The Russian *aliyah* is the most criminal wave of immigration that Israel has ever seen." Responding in *The Jerusalem Report*, the most celebrated of the Russian immigrants, Natan Sharansky, allowed that crime had risen on the fringes of this *aliyah*. There had been murders, he wrote, assaults, fraud, forgery, and prostitution. This was not only because of the inherent difficulties of the immigrants in a new society, he argued, but also because they were from a country where the law was hostile and the system evil, where some felt morality had died.

Sharansky complained in his column that, if the symbol of the Russian *aliyah* had once been the physics professor cleaning the streets with a broom, it was now the cheap blond hooker working the streets. A linguistics expert he knew had been working as a room-service waitress in a luxury hotel. "She told me that of all the hardships of her new life, the most difficult was the way the hotel's clients treat her. The moment they find out she is a new immigrant from Russia, they act as if services of a different nature automatically come with the room service. Thousands of immigrant women suffer such indignities every day."[9]

Quoting police statistics, Sharansky noted that although members of this "criminal" *aliyah* now accounted for ten percent of the Israeli population, they had been involved in only two to three percent of police reports. He offered reasons for Israeli disillusionment with the Russian *olim*: "The immigrants began to be perceived not as pitiful refugees, but as strong competitors with aggressive demands, who at the same time are distant from the life of this country, from Jewish traditions and identity; who see the Jewish State as just one of their alternatives, along with the United States, Europe and South Africa, or even staying in Russia; who advise relatives back home to wait, if they can, before coming here."[10]

This being Israel, there is also a religious problem.

According to a survey commissioned by the Reform Movement's Religious Action Center, just short of a third of the couples who came over from the former Soviet Union are tainted, in that either the husband or the wife is a gentile. The survey also showed a percentage who claim to be Jewish but couldn't prove it by the Interior Ministry's exacting standard. Perusing the iffy origins of many of the Russians, Rabbi Uri Regev, director of the center, anticipated a real problem for the children of such couples, which is to say, many of them may never be able to legally marry in Israel. The American Union of Hebrew Congregations wants Israel to relax the stringent marriage qualifications for 150,000 Russian immigrants.

The dilemma of the Russian *olim* is rich in ironies on both sides of the globe. Their sudden ability to acquire much-coveted exit visas from the former Soviet Union has proven, to the satisfaction of Pamyat members and other indigenous anti-Semites, that there *is* an international Jewish conspiracy. Otherwise, how come only the Yids are free to leave? Something else: the sour truth is that many, possibly even a majority, of the Russian *olim* would prefer to settle in America or Western Europe rather than Israel. Stripped of its romanticism, Operation Exodus, the rescue of Soviet Jewry, has its unattractive underside. It appears that fat-cat Diaspora Zionists, who would not wish to make *aliyah* themselves, have ordained it good enough for their less fortunate East European brethren; they have collaborated with Israelis to create a situation wherein Jews are holding other Jews hostage.

◇ *Twenty-five* ◇

*L*ATE ONE AFTERNOON I SAT IN THE BAR OF THE
Dan Hotel in Tel Aviv, waiting for Hillel Halkin. I had
been unable to find a copy of his out-of-print book, *Letters to
an American Jewish Friend: A Zionist Polemic*, published in the
seventies, but I was familiar with the argument at its core: it
was "that for any Jew in this day and age who cares seriously
about being Jewish, the only honest place to live is Israel."[1] My
God, here was a writer who in one sentence managed to im-
pugn the honor of nearly seven million Jews who feel at home
in North America, never mind the others at ease in the United
Kingdom, Australia, France, and elsewhere. And in the same
sentence he also managed to dismiss as uncaring about their
Jewish heritage, and necessarily dishonest, a far from uninterest-
ing bunch — say, Saul Bellow, Cynthia Ozick, Philip Roth, Norman Mailer, Arthur Miller, Alfred Kazin, Susan Sontag, Joseph
Heller, Woody Allen, Anita Brookner, Bernice Rubens, Allen
Ginsberg, Dan Jacobson, Frederic Raphael, Harold Pinter, and
the late Irving Howe, Bernard Malamud, and Isaac Bashevis
Singer, among many others.

Ruminating over why so many American Jews had failed to make *aliyah*, Halkin wrote in a *Jerusalem Report* column, "Jews are no different from other people in putting their own comfort and economic welfare first — they are only different in feeling so embarrassed about it that they will resort to almost any myth or rationalization before admitting their true motives. They have, in a word, just enough idealism to lie to themselves systematically, which is why preaching Zionism to them is a waste of time."[2]

Waiting for the presumptuous author of such a self-serving *pensée* to appear, I anticipated a fierce quarrel. Obviously Halkin was a stranger to self-doubt, but could he really believe that I lived in Canada only because I was a slacker and a sybarite, and not because it was my home and therefore a country I cared about deeply — more deeply than Israel, for that matter?

Halkin turned out to be a gentle, soft-spoken man. It was with the most disarming smile, albeit tainted by condescension, that he said to me, "Jews have a choice. They can either make *aliyah* or assimilate."

"Either/or? Nothing but?"

"Yes. However, I have no quarrel with those who have chosen assimilation."

Halkin's assumption that it was impossible to lead a full Jewish life in American was unnerving. Zionist zealots and anti-Semites, those most unlikely of bedfellows, share an undeniably racist article of faith — the odious notion that Jews born and bred in North America or other Western countries can never be bona fide citizens of their homelands. In *With Friends Like You*, Matti Golan argued for "the importance of Israel not as a Jewish home, but as a *home*, period. The difference between our two mentalities is the difference between someone who lives at home and someone who lives in a rented room. The family you rent from may be the kindest and nicest you could wish for, but you still have to behave yourself and stay in its good graces if you don't want to be out of a room."[3] In Golan's book-length dialogue between a righteous Israeli (Israel) and a wimpy American Jew (Judah), Israel says that before an American Jew dares formulate an opinion "you ask yourself how it will sound to your non-Jewish neighbors. You're very anxious to get across the message that you aren't us: that you don't think like us, that you wouldn't behave like us, that they shouldn't resent you because of us."[4]

Golan's insatiable appetite for Diaspora financing, his sense of Israeli entitlement, is equaled only by his scorn for American Jewry. In *With Friends Like You*, Israel, who obviously couldn't have done his homework, says,

> There are today in America over 300,000 Jewish households with an annual income of more than $1 million. [That is to say, one out of every ten American Jews is a multi-millionaire.] Only a third of them — one out of three! — gives over a thousand dollars annually to the UJA. The rest contribute less or nothing at all. And yet at the same time, huge and steadily growing amounts of Jewish money are donated annually for non-Jewish purposes. In 1981 Walter Annenberg alone donated $150 million to the Corporation for Public Broadcasting. This past year he gave $15 million for the absorption of Soviet refugees in Israel and $50 million to some purely American institution. When Jack Linsky died in 1982, do you know whom he willed $50 million to? The UJA? A new hospital in Israel? No, sir. He gave that little boodle to the Metropolitan Museum of Art. In 1986 Milton Petrie donated $10 million for cancer research.[5]

No allowance is made for the fact that Annenberg and Petrie are not only Jewish but also American, as was Linsky; that their *shtetl* progenitors probably sailed steerage to that country; that they were able to rise out of penury to immense wealth, and just might be grateful to the society that made it possible. Furthermore, I should have thought that, far from being reprehensible, such huge contributions to the Corporation for Public Broadcasting, the Metropolitan Museum, and cancer research were a tribute to Jewish munificence.

During our sojourn in Jerusalem, Tel Aviv, and Haifa, as we ambled down the high streets or eavesdropped in cafés, the delight that Diaspora Jews took in the existence of a Jewish state was in evidence everywhere. On my first trip to Israel, in 1962, I flew in on El Al. Descending over Lod Airport, as it then was, we broke into song, belting out *"Sholem Aleichem"* and *"Lomir alle zingen."* We clapped hands. Some wept. It was a *mechaieh*, a joy, an instant *simcha*, but the truth is, our interests and those of Israelis are sometimes in direct conflict. In America, for instance, the B'nai Brith's Anti-Defamation League (ADL) is quick to denounce any anti-Semitic act, no matter how piffling, but there are Israelis schooled in realpolitik who welcome every such incident as proof that Diaspora Jews live in "rented rooms," and as a possible prod to both big donors and much-sought-after "Anglo-Saxon" *aliyah*.

Actually, anti-Semitism is on the decline in America. Meeting in New York in December 1992, the Anti-Defamation League presented its latest poll, showing that one in five Americans held pronounced anti-Semitic views. However, amid all the reports and statistics, wrote J. J. Goldberg in *The New Republic*, one fact received only cursory attention: that by nearly every available measure, anti-Semitism was a diminishing problem:

> Discrimination in housing, jobs and schooling, once endemic, has all but disappeared. State-sponsored anti-Semitism, long a defining fact of European life, is virtually

unknown here. Hostility toward Jews, measured in public opinion polls, has been declining steadily for two generations. Events that seemed sure to provoke broad anti-Semitism, from the Arab oil boycott to the arrests of Israeli spy Jonathan Pollard and Wall Street cheat Ivan Boesky, came and went without a blip.

Only one common measure of anti-Semitism has gone up of late: "anti-Semitic incidents." This includes not only graffiti but increasingly arson and assault as well. (Even this indicator declined last year — for the first time in a decade — dipping 8 percent according to ADL figures.) Still, it's not a key test to most experts. The ADL's 1991 total of 1,879 incidents, the all-time high, amounted to just five a day — mostly epithets hurled and swastikas daubed — in a nation of 250 million people.[6]

While not dismissing the likes of David Duke, the former Klansman who ran for the Senate in Louisiana, or Louis Farrakhan, the anti-Semitic black preacher, or the 1991 riot in Crown Heights, which left a young Australian Hasid murdered, Goldberg noted that the ADL's 20 percent figure for anti-Semitic views actually represented a one-third drop from 1964, when 29 percent of those polled were counted as prejudiced. "What's more," he wrote, "someone who says Jews are 'too powerful' is not necessarily anti-Semitic. American Jews *are* powerful. Over the last quarter-century, bodies such as the ADL and the two AJCs (Committee and Congress), together with the American Israel Public Affairs Committee, the pro-Israel lobby, have become a serious force in Washington."[7]

Too powerful, therefore, could be a judgment call. "Jews make up 2.5 percent of the population and 10 percent of the Senate.... In private," he discovered, "some Jewish agency staffers insist that the alarmist tone set by a few national Jewish agencies, mainly for fund-raising purposes, is a key cause of Jewish anxiety." And he concluded: "Of course, the tactics of a few bureaucrats in New York or Los Angeles hardly explain the nationwide fear gripping American Jews, many of whom are barely aware of the ADL's existence. More likely, the masses are driving the leadership. Maybe it's time for the leadership to start leading, and tell their public the truth."[8]

One form of anti-Semitism never monitored by the ADL, at least so far as I know, is the Israeli variety, expressed in a disdain for North American Jews. In *With Friends Like You*, Israel (that is to say, Matti Golan, who was once Minister of Information at the Israeli Embassy in Canada) recalls a train trip he took from Montreal to Ottawa twenty years ago. He shared a table in the dining car with an elegantly dressed businessman in his fifties.

> "He was a cultured person ... who asked many questions about Israel, about life there, and about our wars. . . . Eventually the conversation shifted to Canada. And then to the Jews. Perfectly naturally, without the slightest hint of embarrassment, he observed that most of them were involved in finance, the clear implication being that he thought you all shylocks. I don't remember the details, but the bottom line was that he did not have a particularly high opinion of you. I began to feel a bit uncomfortable."

> "That's all?" asks Judah. "A *bit* uncomfortable?"
> Israel replies, "I wasn't sure I understood him. I told him that though he might not be aware of it, most Israelis, including myself, were Jews, too. How could I think that he wasn't aware of it, he replied. Of course he

was! 'But it's not the same thing,' he explained straightforwardly. 'You Israelis aren't like Jews at all.' When I asked him what the difference was, he thought for a moment and answered, 'That's obvious. You have a home.'"

"Which made you feel good," says Judah.

"Perhaps it did a bit."

"Well, I have news for you. Your dinner partner was an ordinary anti-Semite."

"Then so am I. Because I notice the same difference he did."[9]

I first stumbled on this widely held Israeli contempt for Diaspora Jews at a cocktail party in Tel Aviv, back in 1962, when I fell in with a man called Migdal. Migdal, thin and severe, in his sixties, came of a French Jewish family. A graduate in engineering, he had arrived in Palestine with the Foreign Legion in the twenties, then quit the Legion and swiftly established himself as a consultant engineer and agent for British firms in Palestine, Transjordan, and Syria. He returned to France in 1939, fought first with the French army and then with the British as a colonel. Still later he commanded a sector of Jerusalem during the siege. "This country," he said, "restored Jewish pride with the defense of Jerusalem. You'll find we're a new kind of Jew here. We don't cringe."

"The Jews in Canada didn't cringe either," I said, "when it was time to go to war."

I asked Migdal if it was possible that the concept of a nation-state, with all it entailed, was contrary to what had evolved as the Jewish tradition.

"If you mean," he said, "that we have compromised our lousy Jewish souls here, then you're right. This state deals, lies, and cheats, just like any other. But we have restored Jewish pride. It's worth it."

On my initial trip to Israel, when I was staying at the Hotel Eilat, the bartender, a Jew from Tangier, said, "One day I served a Spaniard here. A rich man. He told me that in Madrid he was an anti-Semite. He said, I didn't believe these Jews could ever build a country so I thought I'd see for myself. Well, now I've seen the country, he said, and it's marvelous. It wouldn't surprise me if you people had the atom bomb in five years and took over the Middle East in ten. But you're not Jews; you're different. You've fought for your land, you've spilled blood for it, and you have pride. The Jews in Spain only fight for their families and their businesses. You're different here, he said."

Not until I wakened at three A.M. did I surface with a satisfactory riposte: "Why didn't you tell that bastard that just about half of the Americans who fought for *his* country in the Abraham Lincoln Battalion in *their* civil war just happened to be Jewish?"

But the next time I ran into the perverse need of some Israelis to be flattered by the endorsements of anti-Semites, I was prepared. It was at the Ocean Restaurant in Jerusalem, where Florence and I had gone to dinner. Seated at the next table was a muscle-bound, middle-aged man wearing wrap-around sunglasses, a Ralph Lauren shirt — the first three buttons undone to reveal his gold necklace — a Philippe Patek wristwatch, designer jeans, and leather sandals. His wife, her helmet of raven-black hair lacquered, her diamond earrings clashing with her necklace and rings of jade and onyx, cuddled a white toy poodle against her groin, whispering endearments as she fed it tidbits from her plate. "Where are you from?" the man asked.

"Canada. Montreal."

"Ah, yes. The Bronfmans. David Azrielli. The Ritz. Money, money, money. You'll find we're different here, the Israelis."

"But you can't be an Israeli."

"Of course I am."

"Surely, if you were really an Israeli, there would be a plaque banged into your forehead, saying you had been donated in everlasting memory of Zipporah Rappaport of Saskatoon by her adoring grandchildren, Vanessa, Sean, and Nanette."

TO BE FAIR, our American Jewish clothesline is also tarnished by some dirty laundry. Or, put another way, the ADL has also been remiss, in failing to measure the countervailing prejudice of a surprising number of "Anglo-Saxon" Jews against Israelis. In the weeks before leaving for Israel, I was astonished by the reaction of some Jews to our forthcoming trip.

"You'd certainly never get me to go there," said one, "because the truth is, I've never met an Israeli I liked."

Somebody else said, "They're the pushiest lot I've ever come across. Always leading with the elbows. So deliver a message for me and mine, please. We don't owe them a living."

The most literate of my companions at Grumpy's, the Montreal watering hole that I favor, reminded me of something in Isaac Babel's play *Sunset*: "Remember what Mendel Krick says? 'Put a Jew on a horse and he's no longer a Jew.' *Gut gezukt*, I'd say. And now let me tell you something else. I was over there in '66, and I had to go to a bank to cash some traveller's cheques. There was a sweet, elderly lady ahead of me in line, and she asked the teller something in Yiddish. The teller, an unpleasant young woman, actually shouted at her. 'We don't speak Yiddish here. That's the language of the ghetto.' To this day, I wake up some time in the middle of the night, furious with myself, because I didn't reach over the cage and slap that arrogant, mindless little bitch hard."

❖ Twenty-six ❖

*A*FTER I.F. STONE VISITED PALESTINE IN THE WIN-
ter of 1945, he wrote, "I understand why the Palestinian
Arab, to whom Palestine is also home, who has fully as much
right there as the Jew, does not wish to live as a minority in a
Jewish nation. No one likes to be ruled by an alien people...."[1]
But Stone was understandably impressed by what the *chalutzim*
had accomplished: "In the once malarial marshes of the Emeck,
the Jews have done and are doing what seemed to reasonable
men the impossible. Nowhere in the world have human beings
surpassed what the Jewish colonists have accomplished in Palestine and the consciousness of achievement, the sense of things
growing, the exhilarating atmosphere of a great common effort
infuses the daily life of the Yishuv."[2]

Today, no doubt, he would be even more impressed by
what Israeli ingenuity has wrought. Typical, I take it, were the
date-palm plantations we passed on our drive back from
Masada. Each tree was equipped with its own computer, mea-
suring both its individual yield and the intake of water it

needed. Irreverent, street-smart Israelis, recipients of the most sophisticated fighter aircraft that American engineering could devise, have tinkered with them in their own workshops, raising their efficiency more than a notch. Mind you, they are the progeny of a people one of whom, years ago, published a legendary edition of Shakespeare in Yiddish, with the audacious credit *"fartaiched und farbestert"* — "translated and improved".... Israel is the home of a far from inconsiderable microchip industry and it's no longer a secret that it is also a nuclear power. But if this tiny country is easily the most technologically advanced in the Middle East, it is, for that very reason, also the most vulnerable. During the Gulf War, one of Saddam Hussein's crude Scud missiles, aimed at Tel Aviv, landed within a mile of the defense ministry, its tall, vital tower bristling with electronic dishes. Another Scud exploded only three quarters of a mile from Haifa's oil refineries. Given that now Hussein probably has more advanced missiles, purchased from either North Korea or China, it seems to me, although I am hardly an expert in such matters, that he could just about paralyze the country with a dozen that were well aimed.

Not the least of Israel's achievements, as Arthur Koestler noted in 1946, has been "the revival of Hebrew from its holy petrification to serve again as the living tongue of a nation." In *Thieves in the Night*, Joseph writes in his diary: "But this miracle involves a heavy sacrifice. Our children are brought up in a language which has not developed since the beginnings of the Christian era. It has no records, no memories, hardly any trace of what happened to mankind since the destruction of the Temple. Imagine the development of English having stopped with 'Beowulf' — and even 'Beowulf' is a thousand years nearer to us! Our Classics are the books of the Old Testament; our lyrics stopped with the Song of Songs, our short stories with Job."[3] But since 1946 a number of Hebrew writers of stature have emerged, revivifying the language, molding a modern idiom — among them, Yehuda Amichai, A.B. Yehoshua, Amos Oz, and David Grossman.

Incongruously, medievalism still flourishes side by side with Israel's technological and cultural triumphs. One day I read in *The Jerusalem Post* that a conclave of the country's most devout rabbis had ordained that if a Jewish woman was to submit to artificial insemination, the sperm, of necessity, had to be certified as of gentile origin: otherwise, the woman ran the risk of being guilty of incest. At dinner that night with Janet Aviad, the Elons, Avishai Margalit, and others active in the Peace Now movement, this led to a good deal of irreverent, priapic speculation. Another day rabbis solemnly protested the cartoon of a dinosaur embossed on kosher yogurt cartons. The dinosaur, never mentioned in the Pentateuch, didn't exist so far as they were concerned. It was an atheist heresy.

BRAGGADOCIO IS commonplace in Israel, part of the necessary armor, perhaps, of a tiny nation that has been at risk ever since its foundation — a land surrounded by enemies pledged to its extinction since day one, its pre-1967 waistline unhealthily narrow — just over five miles — rendering it vulnerable to being cut in two by a surprise attack. All the same, the boasting grates: "We have restored Jewish pride here." Certainly Israel is *a* source of Jewish pride, but hardly the only one. For generations, long before Israel was born again, a majority of Diaspora Jews, both Orthodox and secular, took pride in being members of our faith without necessarily brandishing it like a baseball bat. In North America, only a minority denied their heritage, like Walter Lippmann, or anglicized their names, but all of us were also shaped by the society in which we were rooted.

I am a Canadian, born and bred, brought up not only on Hillel, Rabbi Akiba, and Rashi, but also on blizzards, Andrew Allan's CBC Radio "Stage" series, a crazed Maurice Richard skating in over the blue line, Leacock's *Literary Lapses*, wild blueberries out of the Lac St. Jean country in August, Mackenzie King's procrastinations, the Dieppe raid, Jackie Robinson breaking into organized baseball with the Triple A Montreal Royals, *Northern Review*, Molson's ale, the Dionne quintuplets, the novels of Hugh MacLennan and Gabrielle Roy, Morley Callaghan's short stories, the Stanley Cup playoffs, my father betting on doomed penny stocks plucked from *Northern Miner*, Johnny Greco losing to Beau Jack in Madison Square Garden, Eaton's catalogue, the RCMP's legendary Sam Steele taming Sitting Bull in Manitoba without firing a shot after the Sioux chief gave Custer what for at Little Big Horn, *les Canadiens sont là*, fools going over Niagara's Horseshoe Falls in a barrel or crossing it on a high wire, and midnight swims in cool mountain lakes during our short hot summers.

Staying at the Hotel Eilat in 1962, I discovered that the manager, Harvey Goodman, had been brought up right around the corner from where I used to live on St. Urbain Street. Goodman, thirty-one years old at the time, had been in Israel for ten years. "All Jews should come here," he said. "We're hated everywhere."

"Nonsense," I said.

"Come on. How can you feel comfortable in Canada — among them? They don't want us. Me, I'm always nervous in their company. Fuck 'em!"

But since Goodman quit Canada in 1952, Jews have served in our federal Cabinet, as provincial premiers, leaders of mainstream federal and provincial political parties, chief justices of both the Canadian and Quebec Supreme Courts, and members of Parliament, without provoking riots. Of course we also endure international Jewish conspiracy freaks, skinheads who daub swastikas on synagogue walls, those who deny that the Holocaust ever happened, and other nutters, but they are on the fringe. "Respectable" anti-Semites, like the one Matti Golan warmed to on his train ride from Montreal to Ottawa, are still out there, like weeds. But they are now no more plentiful than those Jews, only a couple of generations out of the *shtetl*, who would rather our government cut back on immigration from Hong Kong, India, Pakistan, Haiti, the West Indies, and Central America, because (whisper it) these newcomers stick together rather than mix; they tend to work for a pittance in the needle trade or, if they are Chinese, to be driven by a need to excel; they think they can continue to wear turbans in Canada, or build mosques in decent neighborhoods, or even run for Parliament. Put plainly, they suffer from *chutzpah*.

Hillel Halkin, among others, professed to be weary of "feeling Jewish" in America. "Here I never have to think about it. I am at home."

But many of us, unapologetically Jewish, do feel at home in North America, the most open of societies, and even harbor a sneaking, subversive sympathy for gentiles, who must find a number of our apparatchiks exasperating and endlessly kvetchy. For if we once rebuked the *goyim* for supporting quotas on Jewish students at universities, as well as maintaining country clubs, hotels, and neighborhoods that were *judenrein*, there are those Jews who now mourn the passing of most of these restrictions, and complain that it is by dint of having become so acceptable that we are menaced today. Ostensibly proud, these Jews take our rich heritage to be so fragile that it can only survive in adversity. Or, put another way, better a pogrom than a mixed marriage. A bemused Leonard Fein, editor and publisher of *Moment* magazine, once said, "It is seduction, not rape, [American Jews] fear most."[4] Another observer of the American scene, Professor Jacob Neusner of Brown University, has written, "The central issue facing Judaism in our day is whether a long-beleaguered faith can endure the conclusion of its perilous siege."[5] But the end, wrote Charles E. Silberman in *A Certain People: American Jews and Their Lives Today*, is *not* at hand, for all the talk about intermarriage and assimilation. "It is true that an open society makes it easier for Jews to abandon their Jewishness, but it also reduces the temptation to try, for Jewishness is no longer perceived as a burden, still less as an embarrassment, as it was in my youth. Then, young Jews often rebelled against their Jewishness, and a considerable number sought to abandon it in the hope of gaining acceptance in the non-Jewish world. Today, by contrast, young Jews are comfortable with their Jewishness, whether they express it in religious or secular terms."[6]

Looked at closely, the interests of Diaspora and Israeli Jews are seriously at odds. Our continued well-being in North America and other Western countries is dependent on a strict separation of church and state, but in Israel church and state are in bed together, obdurate Orthodox rabbis wielding enormous influence through political parties that usually hold the balance of power. In Israel, *haredim* retain exclusive control over the laws governing marriage, divorce, and conversion. To their minds, wrote David Landau in *Piety and Power*, the rules of Reform marriage and divorce, accepted in America, propagate halakhic bastardy: it could lead to a schism, the emergence of two peoples, should the Orthodox rabbinate refuse to sanction the marriage of their adherents, a minority, to either Conservative, Reform, or secular Jews, who make up the majority. The historical precedent the *haredim* cite is the schism between Judaism and Christianity during the century after Christ. Rabbi Norman Lamm, president of Yeshiva University in New York, has said, "In fact, the halakhic divide is deeper now than it was then."

Landau dismissed the Orthodox warning of a possible schism as rhetorical — or fanatical — hyperbole, arguing that there was too much that united Jews. But he also noted that, "In 1988–89, with the *haredim* in Israel politically more powerful than ever before, their demand that the State recognize only Orthodox conversion strained the ties between Israel and the Diaspora almost to breaking-point. Jewish representatives from the United States and Europe baldly threatened the Israeli leaders: If you give in to the *haredim* on this — we will turn our backs on you. The 'centrality of Israel' in Jewish life, which is the bedrock of Zionism, will be destroyed.

"The threat worked; Orthodoxy suffered a stinging defeat. But the conflict is bound to break out again, since neither side has shifted its basic position."[7]

◇ *Twenty-seven* ◇

I LIED.
When somebody called from Whitehorse, in 1984, to say
that Jerry Greenfeld had died of a heart attack and would I
come to the funeral, I protested that I hadn't seen or heard from
him in forty years. But late one summer afternoon in 1981, just
as I was settling in for a nap on the sofa, Jerry phoned. "Mordy,
you old turkey you, how goes the battle?"

"Jerry?"

"Yowza."

"Where are you calling from?"

"Wilensky's. Where else? I had to have me a 'Special,' if only
for old times' sake. But I could like hop into a taxi and be at
your place in fifteen minutes."

I told him that I was just about to leave for the Montreal
Press Club, and asked him to meet me there for drinks.

Jerry's hair, steel-gray now, was brushcut. He wore horn-
rimmed glasses and had cultivated a handlebar mustache. He
didn't, as I had anticipated, bounce a mock punch off my shoulder. Instead, we shook hands, Jerry squeezing hard. "Jeez,

you've got palms soft as a baby's ass," he said, "and that's some gut you've got there."

Jerry was still trim, broad-shouldered as ever, with the natural grace of an athlete. His sharkskin windbreaker had been displaced by a biker's studded black leather jacket, zippers everywhere. His jacket squeaked when he reached for his drink — a boilermaker. Leaning across our table to clink glasses, he said, "*Skol. L'chaim.* It's good to see you, old *chaver* of mine."

"It's good to see you too. I should have brought my mitt."

"You remember those days?"

"Damn right I do."

He had been demobilized five years earlier, he said, and now lived in Edmonton with his second wife, Marylou, a real beaut. "Built? You better believe it," Jerry said. He hung out with Wayne Gretzky, Mark Messier, Paul Coffey, and the rest of the Oilers. Peachy guys. But they never went out boozing the night before a game. "We're going to win the Stanley Cup next year, you bet your sweet ass we are!"

"What do you do in Edmonton?"

"I've got me a garage and body shop, four guys on my payroll, not one of them a frog, because I won't put up with their shit."

"They don't like putting up with ours either, and would you mind lowering your voice, please?"

"Don't tell me you're scared of that bunch."

"No, but a number of my frog friends just happen to be sitting at the bar right now."

"Roger. Got the message. Hey, it's a good place to bring up children."

"Edmonton?"

"Yeah, and it's only an hour into real mountains, not the worn-out little hills you've got here."

"How many children have you got?"

"Two left at home. Marylou's and mine. I love them. But I had to kick out the eldest, Bruce, from my first marriage, after he came home one night with an earring in his left ear," said Jerry, wetting his little finger and passing it over his eyebrows. "Hey, am I upsetting you?"

"No."

"You got some of *them* sitting at the bar too?"

I laughed and ordered another round.

"Maybe you think I phoned because I want to borrow money?"

"No. Honestly."

"I own three cars, two of them vintage. A '64 Mustang and an MG TD, both worth plenty if I wanted to sell, which I don't need to. You heard of Peter Pocklington?"

"Yes. Certainly."

"I handle his cars, and any time I feel like taking in a game, I phone him, and I sit with Peter and his wife. We've gone fishing together on the Great Slave Lake."

"Why did you join the army, Jerry?"

"What do you do in Edmonton? How many kids you got? Why did you join the army? Is this like some kind of interview?"

"No."

"No. Yes. Haven't *you* got anything to say?"

"Sure."

"Go ahead, then. I'm listening."

"How about another round?"

"I thought you'd never ask. Hey, I read a hundred and four books last year, two a week, most of them in hard covers. What do you think of Follett, *The Key to Rebecca?*"

"Sorry, but I haven't read it."

"What if I wanted to write up my experiences in life, all the crazy characters I met in Germany and elsewhere, the hard knocks I took, the broads I've had, the funny things my kids say, would you be willing to give it a gander if I sent it to you? I mean, like with your connections I could get a publisher and maybe even a movie sale."

"I saw Myer in London."

"Don't look now, Millicent, but he's changing the subject on me."

"He manages a group called The Highlanders. He's doing awfully well."

"Big fucking deal, The Highlanders. A zillion Chinese never heard of them. Hey, let's face it, we were such a bunch of little pricks back then. Dancing the hora at Camp Kvutza. Watching all those boring documentaries. Pretending we were going to make *aliyah* one day. Aw."

"Ezra made *aliyah*. So did Sol and Fayge Cohen."

"Let me tell you something, old friend, I've been around, and Canada's the greatest country in the world, and I'm proud to have served in its armed forces overseas, on the Western world's front line against the Communist menace, with the greatest bunch of guys you could ever meet, real friends," he said, his eyes shiny, the drink getting to him, "*loyal*, not the sort to turn on you, taking you for a crook."

"Are you going to look up Hershey while you're here?" I asked, fishing.

"What for? So he can give me a tour of his Westmount mansion again, letting me see his collection of first editions that cost him a small fortune? Or some fuckin' plaque saying he's Man of the Century for what he gave to UJA? Or show me photographs of the cottage he keeps in Vermont, just in case he has to pull out of Montreal, P.Q., or Piss Quick, as we used to say? Well, let me tell you something, if it comes to independence or sovereignty association or whatever they're calling it this week, it's guys like me you'll come crying to, and I'll have to re-enlist to protect you, and you can tell those friends of yours at the bar to go shit in their hats if they don't like it. Oh, big bloody successes, you, Myer, Hershey. Always sticking it to me. Rolling in *mezuma*. Well, there are more important things than money, let me tell you. Maybe I never finished high school, but at night Marylou and I listen to symphonic music together. I've got my pride, you know. I can remember when I had all the girls and the three of you were glad to be seen with me after what I did in a basketball game against Montreal High or Westmount. Remember Rifka Seligman?"

"Sure I do."

"I happen to know you took her out umpteen times and never got to first base with her, but she used to like nothing better than licking my dick, kiddo. Friday nights. After our meetings. So, looking for a trip down memory lane, I phone her last Friday night, she's married to Manny Fishbein, a doctor yet, and a maid answers and says, it's the Sabbath, the Fishbeins don't take phone calls. Is there any message? Tell her Jerry Greenfeld called, and I leave a number. But she never calls back. I'm bad news, eh? Do they cash checks here?"

"Only for members."

"Shit. This should be my round, but I got to the bank too late."

"Don't worry. I'll get it," I said, ordering.

"I want to know what Hershey told you about the time I stayed with him."

"He never mentioned it."

"Bullshit."

"Okay, okay. He says he put you up, and you were gone early the next morning, and so was a pearl necklace belonging to his wife, and a few other things."

"Well, I've got to hand it to him," he said, shaking his head, chuckling.

"It isn't true?"

"*Emmes* is what you want, you got it. The truth. It must have been back in the Swinging Sixties, I was in a jam, just in from Calgary, I'd had too much to drink and I got mugged. I asked Hershey, that old *chaver* of mine, could he put me up for the night. He hemmed, he hawed. But he had to say yes, didn't he," said Jerry, leaning closer, "because of what he knew I knew and didn't want his stuck-up wife to hear. Hanna Rosen, I knew her before her nose job. Boy, what a pair! I don't mean hers. I mean them. Hershey and Hanna. He grudgingly pours me a drink. 'This isn't ordinary scotch, I'd like you to know. It's a single malt.' Glen *tuchis-lecker* or whatever. 'Twenty-one years old.' And she quickly slips a coaster under my glass, I might leave a watermark on her antique table, for two cents I'd piss all over it. Sure, I'm allowed to sleep there, but before I'm shown to a tiny bedroom, just enough room for me and their laundry, he makes a big ceremony of locking his liquor cabinet and the glass bookcase with his precious first editions. Tell me, what is this first editions horseshit? Isn't the story exactly word for word in a second or third edition of a book?"

"You're absolutely right, but people also fork out thousands for old baseball cards or movie posters. Collectors are a special breed."

"I didn't steal anything, but I was so angry that before I split I took her pearl necklace, broke the strand, and scattered the pearls on the floor. And yes, I also grabbed a sterling silver tray, got out my Swiss Army knife, scratched FUCK YOU into it, and dumped it on their lawn. Don't you understand anything? He used me to put in a whacking big insurance claim. He probably came out a few thousand bucks ahead on my overnight visit. Couldn't you countersign a check for me and get them to cash it?"

"Forget it. I'll order you another drink," I said, signaling the bartender.

"What about you?"

"I think I'll pass on this round."

"Ha ha. So much for your rep as a boozer. You can't even keep up with your old *chaver*."

"Okay, I'll have another one as well," I said.

"Only two weeks ago, Marylou put it to me. Either you give up drinking, she said, or I'm leaving. Hey, I said, I'm sure going to miss you."

"Oh."

"Do you only laugh at your own jokes?"

"Tell me what you meant by, Hershey knew what you knew and didn't want his wife to hear."

"Ixnay. I'm not the kind to say anything behind Hershey's back." His eyes charged with rancor, Jerry simulated an inner struggle. He stroked his handlebar mustache. He chewed his lip. "All right, then tell me something, you have such a good memory. Friday nights we all went to Habonim together. Affirmative or negative?"

"Yes. So?"

"If nobody answered the front doorbell, because my father was out or snoozing maybe, and I was playing records in the back room, how did you guys get in?"

"We climbed over the front balcony and in through the living-room window."

"What I can never forgive Hershey is that he made me suspect my beloved father of having stolen our money. My father, may he rest in peace, who had to bring me up without the help of a wife."

"But you detested your father."

Jerry, bracing himself against the table, slid back in his chair. "You can say anything you like about me," he said, "but insult my father's memory and I'll have to flatten you right here."

"My God, are you really trying to tell me that Hershey broke into your place and took the money?"

"Negative. I said no such thing. I just explained how he could have got into my bedroom."

"But any of us could have got in that way. Me included."

"Elementary, my dear Watson. Only you never would have had the guts."

"Why would Hershey have done such a thing?"

"Question, why? Answer, because he had assumed that Rifka was going to make him host at her Sweet Sixteen party, he had already paid for her corsage in advance, the prick, but it was me she picked."

"So he stole the money we had collected for Israel?"

"Knowing that I would get the blame."

"You're crazy, Jerry."

"Like a fox."

"How do you know it was Hershey?"

"I know it in here," he said, tapping his forehead. Then all at once he began to cough. Beads of sweat slid down his forehead. "Excuse me," he said, unzipping a breast pocket, fishing out a little aspirin tin, and swallowing an oblong colored pill with his drink.

"What's that?" I asked.

"Digitalis. For my angina. I was discharged from the army because of my bum ticker. The medics give me two years to live. So this is my last trip ever to good old Montreal, Piss Quick. One for the road, eh?"

"Jerry, I don't believe Hershey stole the money. You never had a stepbrother fighting the Japs in the Pacific. Rifka Seligman never gave you a blowjob. You don't know Wayne Gretzky and you can't phone Peter Pocklington for hockey tickets. And I'm willing to bet those pills you're popping are either vitamins or tranquilizers. There's nothing wrong with your heart. In fact, you look to be in great shape. But you are also the world's greatest bullshit artist."

"You finished?"

"Yeah," I said, laughing.

"I don't believe the second one is mine," he said, beginning to sniffle. "What am I supposed to do?"

"What are you talking about now?"

"Little Darlene. The youngest. She doesn't look like me. Marylou works at a club. She's an exotic dancer."

"A stripper?"

"Slip her ten bucks, and she'll dance on your table and pick up a silver dollar with her coozy. You can buy them at the bar. The silver dollars."

"Oh my God, Jerry, what are you going to do?"

"Look," he said. And he stood up and turned his trouser pockets inside out to show me that they were empty. "I'm not going back to her. I'm heading for North of Sixty. I've got my plane tickets for tomorrow and the offer of a good job in Yellowknife."

"What about your garage?"

"Never mind. That's my business. But I've spent my last buck and I've got nowhere to sleep tonight," he said, smiling at me, waiting.

I lit a cigarillo, taking my time.

"Yeah, I thought as much," he said. "You would never put me up. I'm contaminated."

I pulled money out of my pocket and counted it. "I've got two hundred and twelve bucks here. Take it."

"But like it's a loan," he said.

"Sure thing."

"Boy, I'll bet you're pleased to humiliate me like this. I made your day, eh?"

"Oh, calm down, Jerry. Have one more drink."

"Not with you I won't," he said, getting out of his chair, stumbling. "You know how many times you looked at your watch since I sat down with you?"

"No."

"Eight. I counted. So thanks for the loan and up yours," he said, moving unsteadily toward the door.

◇ *Afterword* ◇

*E*ZRA LIFSHITZ HAD SAID, "WE SHOULD BE TALKING directly to the PLO. If you want to make peace, you've got to make peace with your enemies."

Almost a year later, after protracted secret negotiations in Norway, Israel did make a tentative peace with the PLO; and on September 13, 1993, Prime Minister Rabin and Chairman Arafat met and shook hands on the White House lawn. It wasn't a case of love suddenly blooming on the desert, the progeny of Isaac and Ishmael finally grasping that they were both Semites with a heritage that had to be shared. On one side, the blundering PLO was confronted not only by Hamas devouring its support in Gaza and the West Bank, but also by an empty cashbox, the price paid for Arafat's foolish endorsement of Saddam Hussein during the Gulf War. On the other side, Rabin was also intimidated by burgeoning Muslim fanaticism in the occupied territories and, a military strategist above all, he understood that missiles smarter than Scuds had made Israel more vulnerable than ever, its expanded borders notwithstanding.

The Palestinians, poorly led for decades, had to settle for a good deal less cake than they could have had in 1936, 1947, or

1978; that and the iffy promise of a second, bigger helping within three years, providing their behaved themselves. Some argued that they had been snookered by the clever Israelis, who, in their test of the PLO's ability to govern, had divested themselves of little more than the poisoned pill of the Gaza Strip. In fact, both sides were at risk.

Possibly, as Israeli right-wingers outraged by the deal were quick to allege, the cunning PLO was still surreptitiously committed to the piecemeal destruction of Israel, and would eventually convert its precarious foothold into a base from which it could revert to terrorism or even launch another war.

Writing in *Commentary*, before anything was known about the negotiations in Norway, David Bar-Illan dismissed the Israeli peacemakers as the country's new Pollyannas: "Whatever some Israeli doves may imagine, it is a given that the Palestinians will not budge from the demand that autonomy — and later sovereignty — include half of Jerusalem. And it can be taken for granted that they will not agree to any substantial compromises on the territorial definition of autonomy: it will have to extend to all of Judea, Samaria, and Gaza. Nor will they give up on officially including the PLO in the talks."[1]

Immediately the deal was done, Likud MK Binyamin Begin, son of the prime minister who had made peace with Egypt at Camp David, denounced Rabin for taking a giant leap backward. "What Prime Minister Rabin did on the White House lawn, with that handshake and with that agreement...catapulted us forty-six years back, to 1947," he said.

The newly elected Likud leader, Binyamin Netanyahu, declared, "The impetuous rush to embrace an enemy who uses the language of peace for the purposes of war...will be seen as an historic blunder.[2]"

After *The Jerusalem Post* came out against the deal, Conrad Black, principal shareholder of Hollinger, which owns the newspaper, took space in it to run a dissenting opinion. He was proud, he wrote, that since he had purchased the *Post* in 1989, its editorial policy had ceased to be "pro-PLO." He pronounced the settlement with Arafat not perfect, but without a practical alternative. "I understand the Arab view that Israel was created by the West out of guilt at the unspeakable barbarities inflicted on the Jews (and others) by the Nazis and the quislings who collaborated with them, and that the comparatively defenseless Arabs were made to pay for them by yielding the territory to Israel. There is some, though less than complete truth to this."[3]

In another article, Yehuda Levy, publisher of the *Post*, responded that the Arab view was not only less than the complete truth, it was "one of the biggest lies of the effective Arab propaganda."[4] Furthermore, he wrote, the real enemy of Israel was not the Palestinians, but the surrounding Arab states who merely used the Palestinians as a tool to pressure Israel by terror.

Certainly Israel, the only democracy in the Middle East, is still no more than a threatened little Jewish raft — albeit a heavily armed one — bobbing in an unpredictable Arab sea of military dictatorships and corrupt sheikhdoms. Menacing Muslim fundamentalists have already been triumphant in Iran and Sudan, and were denied office in Algeria only after the military intervened following their election victory. Should they succeed in toppling Egypt's notoriously inefficient, bribe-ridden government, then their first item of business would be the cancellation of the peace treaty with Israel, and the second a Holy War.

The Palestinians are at risk because, if the Likud is returned to office within the next couple of years, they will get no more than the Gaza Strip and Jericho, and can forget about statehood.

During one of his American television appearances during the Gulf War, Binyamin Netanyahu displayed a map of Arabia, an immense territory, and demonstrated how it took no more than his thumb to blot out Israel. It was a clever ploy, but also an evasion of the real issue. However teeny the land of Israel, it was, and remains, the legitimate home of two peoples.

After the peace treaty was signed, Amos Oz recalled in a *Time* essay how, as a teenager at Kibbutz Hulda, he stood guard one night with an elderly ideologue. "What do you expect from those Palestinians?" asked the old man. "From their point of view, aliens have landed in their country and gradually taken some of it away, claiming that in return they will shower the natives with loving-kindness, and Palestinians simply said no thanks, and took to arms in order to repel the Zionist invaders."[5]

Being the product of a conventional Zionist home, wrote Oz, he was shocked by the old man's use of the word Palestinians, as well as by the treacherous revelation that the enemy had not only a point of view, but a fairly convincing one at that.

However, in the eyes of Ruth Wisse, one of the Likud's most impassioned advocates, Jewish American friends of Israel who are also critical (say Seymour Martin Lipset and Nathan Glazer, among others), as well as Israel's most highly regarded writers, are compromised by two sins: a hunger for profit and an unacknowledged need to win approval from the gentiles. In a deplorable polemic, *If I Am Not for Myself—: The Liberal Betrayal of the Jews*, Wisse, gathering all virtue unto herself and attributing only base motives to anybody who disagreed with her, wrote, "The rewards that [left-liberal Jews] get from overseas readers and publishers for delivering up the image of the ugly Israeli cannot obscure the ugliness of the cultural trend that this image represents."[6] Such people, to her mind, have sympathy for the Palestinians only because they are craven, and compelled to advertise their goodness.

AFTER ALL these years I can still recall the excitement we felt on November 29, 1947, after the U.N. General Assembly voted to create a Jewish state. That night, Jerry, Hershey, Myer, and I linked arms with our other *chaverim* and trooped downtown, singing "Am Yisrael Hai." At the time, the four of us were pledged to make *aliyah*. But Ezra Lifshitz, our group leader, did make *aliyah*, and told me that he felt a part of something in Eretz Yisrael. "The day I arrived I already felt at home." I too continue to feel a part of something, and at home, right here in Canada. Even so, today I take my stand with Ezra — forty years on the desert, a veteran of two wars, and still with that endearing smile, without guile, that I remember from our days together in Habonim. Ezra, who says, "I will tell you openly, they have a right to a homeland as much as we do. I am for a Palestinian state. The only way to solve the problem."

GLOSSARY

Agudat Yisrael "Union of Israel"; world organization of Orthodox Jews

Aliyah literally, "ascent"; emigration to Israel; original usage is religious: each person called up to the reading of the Torah at services has received an *aliyah*

Alter kocker an old fart

Alte zachen old things; secondhand goods

Americanishe gonovim American thieves

Am Yisrael Hai "the people of Israel lives"

Apikoros an agnostic, an atheist

Ashkenazi (pl. *Ashkenazim*) a Jew of North, Central, or East European descent

Ba'al Shem a master of the Holy Name

Ba'al teshuvah (pl. *ba'alei teshuvah*) a non-observant Jew who has returned to the faith

Bar "son of" in Aramaic

Beigele diminutive for bagel; a doughnut-shaped bread roll

Ben "son of" in Hebrew

Betar ultra-nationalist Zionist youth movement founded by Vladimir Jabotinsky

Bobbe-myseh literally, a "grandmother's tale"; an old wives' tale, a tall tale, a fabrication

Bonim literally, "builders"; high-school-age members of Habonim

Bucher a young man

Bupkes nothing, trifling, worthless

Chag sameach happy holiday

Chai life

Chalitzah religious ceremony that excuses a widow from marrying her brother-in-law

Chalutz (fem. *chalutza*, pl. *chalutzim*) a (Zionist) pioneer

Chanukah an eight-day holiday that commemorates the victory of Judah the Maccabee and his followers over the Syrian Antiochus Epiphanes, and the rededication of the Temple in Jerusalem

Chaver (fem. *chaverta*, pl. *chaverim*) comrade, friend

Choleria literally, "plague"; "To hell with..."

Chutzpah insolence, audacity

Dunam 1,000 square meters (about one-quarter acre)

Dybbuk a demon who takes possession of someone and renders him or her mad, corrupt, vicious

Emmes the truth

Fatah Hawk Palestinian guerrilla, or terrorist, depending on where you pay your dues

Faygeleh literally, "little bird"; vernacular for homosexual

Fedayeen armed Arab infiltrators into Israel, or terrorists

Flanken brisket

Fusgeyer hikers

Gaon (pl. *geonim*) title held by the head of Babylonian Talmudic academy; a genius

Garin literally, "a seed"; a group of *chaverim* who make *aliyah* together

Gedilim twisted cords

Genizah depository of sacred writings

Geshmat a Jew who has converted to the Christian faith

Golem a mechanical man who has been raised to life by magic

Goy (pl. *goyim*, male adj. *goyisher*, neuter adj. *goyish*) a gentile

Guten neshuma a good soul

Gut gezukt well said

Habonim "The Builders": world organization of Socialist Zionist youth

Haggadah the narrative that is read aloud at the Passover seder

Haimish homelike, informal, cozy

Hakhsharah (pl. *hakhsharot*) training camp

Halakhah (pl. *halakhot*, adj. *halakhic*) rabbinical laws; also, the corpus of Jewish law collectively

Hamas Muslim zealots pledged to the destruction of Israel

Hamotzi "who brings forth": the blessing said over bread, before meals

Haredim ultra-Orthodox Jews

Hashomer Hatza'ir "The Young Guard," the youth organization of the more left-wing Socialist Zionists

Hatikvah literally, "The Hope"; Zionist, then Israeli, national anthem

Havdala end-of-Sabbath ceremony

Histadrut Israel's labor federation

Hizbullah extremist Muslim guerrillas, or terrorists, pledged to the destruction of Israel

Hok nit kain tchynik stop talking nonsense

Illuy an outstanding scholar or genius, especially a young prodigy; usually applied to Talmudic scholars

Intifada the Palestinian uprising on the West Bank

Irgun Zvai Leumi "National Military Organization": underground Palestinian Jewish military organization which fought against British and Arabs during the Mandate

Judenrein "cleansed of Jews"

Kasha buckwheat

Kesilim poltergeists; fools

Kibitz proffer unasked-for advice; tease; socialize aimlessly

Kiddush blessing over wine, preceding Sabbath or festival meal

Kipa skullcap

Kishka stuffed derma

Knish little dumpling filled with groats, grated potatoes, onions, chopped liver, or cheese

Knospen buds

Kreplach a form of Jewish ravioli, stuffed with meat or potatoes

Kugel potato or noodle pudding

Kvetchy a *kvetch* is a complainer, and a persistent complainer will be adjudged *kvetchy*

Kvutza group, collective

Landsman (pl. *landsleit*) fellow countryman

Langer loksh literally, "long noodle"; a tall, thin person

Lohame Herut Yisrael "Fighters for the Freedom of Israel"

Lokshen kugel noodle and raisin pie

Maharal acronym for "our leader, Rabbi Loewy"; Judah Lev ben Bezalel, Talmudic scholar of Prague, known in scholarship as the Maharal, creator of the legend of the Golem

Mamzer (pl. *mamzerim*) bastard

Maven expert

Mechaieh a pleasure, a joy

Menahel a group leader in Habonim

Mensh a gentleman; honorable, decent person

Meshugge (*meshuggener*: crazy man, *meshuggeneh*: crazy woman) crazy

Mezuma vernacular for money

Minyan the quorum of ten adult Jewish males required for a religious service

Mishnah codified version of Jewish oral law

Moshav a co-operative smallholders' farming village in Israel

Mossad Israeli secret service

Noar youth

Olim (sing. *oleh*) those who make *aliyah*

Oy vay iz mir literally, "oh, pain that is to me!"; an omnibus phrase for everything from personal pain to emphatic condolences

Oysvorf trash, a bum

Pamyat profoundly anti-Semitic, right-wing Russian nationalist movement

Poale Zion "Workers of Zion"

Pushke little charity collection can

Putz prick, jerk

Rebbe rabbi

Sabra Israeli-born Jew

Schnorrerville panhandler's heaven

Seder literally, "order of the service" or "program"; applied to the gathering round the table for a festive meal and religious ceremony on the first two nights of Passover

Shabbat "Sabbath" in Hebrew

Shabbes "Sabbath" in Yiddish

Shabbes goy a gentile who is designated to perform certain duties on the Sabbath that are forbidden to religious Jews

Shaliach (pl. *shlichim*) an emissary from Israel to Jewish communities abroad for the purpose of fund-raising, education, etc.

Shammes synagogue sexton

Shekhinah "Divine Presence": another way of referring to God without using His Name

Shiksa non-Jewish woman

Shivah seven days of mourning for the dead, immediately following the funeral

Shmatte rag

Shmock a dope, jerk, bumbling person; son of a bitch

Shmutz filth

Shnoz large, unattractive nose

Shochet ritual slaughterer

Shofar liturgical ram's horn

Shtetl Jewish village in Eastern Europe

Shtick a prank, a piece of clowning

Shtreimel black, broad-brimmed hat, trimmed with velvet and edged in fur, worn by *Hasidim*

Shtup push, press; vernacular: to fornicate, to screw

Shvitz sweat; steam-bath house

Shvartzers blacks; black-coats: used deprecatingly in reference to ultra-Orthodox Jews, who traditionally wear long black coats

Simcha literally, "rejoicing"; a celebration, a happy occasion

Sofer scribe

Sukkot Feast of Tabernacles

Tikkun healing, repair, transformation

Trayf unkosher food, ritually unclean

Tsemach Tsedek literally, "righteous plant"; an expression applied to a person of high morals, kind, pious, etc.

Tuchis-lecker ass-licker

Tzitzit the tassels or fringes of twined cord at the corners of the prayer shawl (*tallit*) and the *tallit katan* — the short jacket-like garment worn by Orthodox men under the coat or vest

Tzofim scouts

Tzofiut scouting

Yarmulke skullcap

Yeshiva (pl. *yeshivot*) rabbinical college

Yiddishe tochter (pl. *tekhter*) Jewish daughter

Yishuv literally, "settlement"; Jewish community in Israel, especially before 1948

Yordim "those who go down": a term for Israelis who have opted out, preferring the life abroad

Young Judaea U.S. Zionist youth movement

Zayde grandfather

SELECTED BIBLIOGRAPHY

Abella, Irving, and Harold Troper. *None Is Too Many: Canada and the Jews of Europe, 1933–1948.* Toronto: Lester & Orpen Dennys, 1982.

Avnery, Uri. *Israel Without Zionists: A Plea for Peace in the Middle East.* New York: Macmillan, 1968.

Bar-Illan, David. *Eye on the Media.* Jerusalem: The Jerusalem Post, 1993.

Ben-Dov, Meir. *In the Shadow of the Temple: The Discovery of Ancient Jerusalem.* New York: Harper & Row; Jerusalem: Kates, 1985.

Central Conference of American Rabbis. *Gates of Mitzvah: A Guide to the Jewish Life Cycle.* Ed. Simeon J. Maslin. New York: Central Conference of American Rabbis, 1979.

———. *Gates of the Seasons: A Guide to the Jewish Year.* Ed. Peter S. Knobel. New York: Central Conference of American Rabbis, 1983.

Churchill, Randolph S., and Winston S. Churchill. *The Six Day War.* London: Heinemann Ltd., 1967.

Cohen, Rev. Dr. A. *Everyman's Talmud.* London: J. M. Dent & Sons, 1932.

Elon, Amos. *Jerusalem, City of Mirrors.* Boston: Little, Brown, 1989.

Emerson, Gloria. *Gaza, A Year in the Intifada: A Personal Account from an Occupied Land.* New York: Atlantic Monthly Press, 1991.

Friedman, Robert I. *Zealots for Zion: Inside Israel's West Bank Settlement Movement.* New York: Random House, 1992.

Gilbert, Martin. *Jerusalem: Rebirth of a City*. New York: Viking, 1985.

Golan, Matti. *With Friends Like You: What Israelis Really Think About American Jews*. Trans. Hillel Halkin. New York: Free Press, 1992.

Goldberg, J. J., and Elliot King, eds. *Builders and Dreamers: Habonim Labor Zionist Youth in North America*. New York: Herzl Press, 1993.

Grossman, David. *Sleeping on a Wire: Conversations with Palestinians in Israel*. Trans. Haim Watzman. New York: Farrar, Straus & Giroux, 1993.

Herzog, Chaim. *Heroes of Israel: Profiles of Jewish Courage*. Boston: Little, Brown, 1989.

Hilberg, Raul. *The Destruction of the European Jews*. Chicago: Quadrangle Books, 1961. Reprint. 3 vols. Holmes & Meier Publ. Inc., 1985.

Howe, Irving. *World of Our Fathers: The Journey of the East European Jews to America and the Life They Found and Made*. New York: Harcourt Brace Jovanovich, 1976.

Johnson, Paul. *A History of the Jews*. New York: Harper & Row, 1987.

Joseph, Dov. *The Faithful City: The Siege of Jerusalem, 1948*. London: The Hogarth Press, 1961.

Kedourie, Elie. *Spain and the Jews: The Sephardi Experience, 1492 and After*. London: Thames and Hudson, 1992.

Koestler, Arthur. *Thieves in the Night*. London: Macmillan, 1946.

Kollek, Teddy, and Shulamith Eisner. *My Jerusalem*. New York: Summit Books, 1990.

Kramnick, Isaac, and Barry Sheerman. *Harold Laski: A Life on the Left*. London: Allen Lane, 1993.

Landau, David. *Piety and Power: The World of Jewish Fundamentalism*. New York: Hill and Wang, 1993.

Nolan, Brian. *Hero: The Buzz Beurling Story*. Toronto: Lester & Orpen Dennys, 1981.

O'Brien, Conor Cruise. *The Siege: The Saga of Israel and Zionism*. New York: Simon and Schuster, 1986.

Pawel, Ernst. *The Labyrinth of Exile: A Life of Theodor Herzl*. New York: Farrar, Straus & Giroux, 1989.

Rabinowicz, Harry M. *The World of Hasidism*. Hartford: Hartmore House, 1970.

Richler, Binyamin. *Hebrew Manuscripts: A Treasured Legacy.* Jerusalem: Ofeg Institute, 1990.

Rose, Norman. *Chaim Weizmann: A Biography.* New York: Viking, 1986.

Segev, Tom. *1949: The First Israelis.* New York: Free Press, 1986.

Silberman, Charles E. *A Certain People: American Jews and Their Lives Today.* New York: Summit Books, 1985.

Silver, Eric. *Begin: The Haunted Prophet.* New York: Random House, 1984.

Wisse, Ruth R. *If I Am Not for Myself —: The Liberal Betrayal of the Jews.* New York: Free Press, 1992.

SOURCE NOTES

Chapter One

1. Marion Magid, *Midstream*, September, 1962, p. 34.
2. J. J. Goldberg and Elliot King, eds., *Builders and Dreamers: Habonim Labor Zionist Youth in North America*, p. 33.
3. Ibid., p. 55.
4. Rev. Dr. A. Cohen, *Everyman's Talmud*, p. 136.

Chapter Two

1. Rev. Dr. A. Cohen, *Everyman's Talmud*, p. 137.
2. Chaim Herzog, *Heroes of Israel: Profiles of Jewish Courage*, p. 95.
3. Leo Rosten, *The Joys of Yiddish*, p. 17.
4. Raul Hilberg, *The Destruction of the European Jews*, 1-vol. ed., p. 312.
5. Goldberg and King, *Builders and Dreamers*, p. 124.
6. Ibid., p. 106.

Chapter Three

1. Goldberg and King, *Builders and Dreamers*, p. 7.
2. Martyn Green, *Treasury of Gilbert and Sullivan*, p. 132.
3. Isaac Kramnick and Barry Sheerman, *Harold Laski: A Life on the Left*, p. 207.

4. Ibid., p. 219.
5. Conor Cruise O'Brien, *The Siege: The Saga of Israel and Zionism*, p. 261.
6. Eric Silver, *Begin: The Haunted Prophet*, p. 61.
7. Ibid., p. 76.
8. Ibid.
9. *The New York Times*, May 15, 1947.

Chapter Four

1. Lester B. Pearson, *Mike: The Memoirs of the Right Honourable Lester B. Pearson*, vol. 2, p. 213.
2. Brian Nolan, *Hero: The Buzz Beurling Story*, p. xi.
3. Ibid., p. 143.
4. Ibid., p. 147.
5. Paul Johnson, *A History of the Jews*, pp. 434-435.
6. Ibid., p. 446.

Chapter Five

1. Magid, *Midstream*, September, 1962, p. 38.
2. George Orwell, *The Collected Essays, Journalism and Letters*, vol. 2, p. 377.
3. F. M. Dostoievsky, *The Diary of a Writer*, trans. Boris Brasol, p. 647.
4. Randolph S. Churchill and Winston S. Churchill, *The Six Day War*, p. 229.
5. Ibid., p. 231.

Chapter Seven

1. Dov Joseph, *The Faithful City: The Siege of Jerusalem, 1948*, p. 73.

Chapter Eight

1. Matti Golan, *With Friends Like You: What Israelis Really Think About American Jews*, pp. 8, 11.
2. Ibid., p. 9.
3. David Landau, *Piety and Power: The World of Jewish Fundamentalism*, pp. 91–92.
4. *The Jerusalem Post*, December 26, 1990.

5. Ibid.

6. Ibid., June 26, 1985.

7. *The Jerusalem Report*, November 5, 1992.

8. *The Jerusalem Post*, January 3, 1991.

9. Martin Gilbert, *Jerusalem: Rebirth of a City*, p. 22.

Chapter Nine

1. Christopher Sykes, *Orde Wingate*, p. 122.

Chapter Ten

1. Karen Alkalay-Gut, *Recipes: Love Soup and Other Poems*, Tel Aviv: Golan, 1994, pp. 55–56.

2. Tom Segev, *1949: The First Israelis*, p. 131.

3. Ibid., p. 138.

4. Ibid., p. 160.

Chapter Eleven

1. George Eliot, *Daniel Deronda*, pp. 594–595.

2. Ibid., p. 875.

3. Ernst Pawel, *The Labyrinth of Exile: A Life of Theodor Herzl*, p. 227.

4. Ibid., p. 229.

5. Ibid., p. 227.

6. Ibid., p. 230.

7. Ibid., p. 228.

8. Ibid., p. 231.

9. Norman Rose, *Chaim Weizmann: A Biography*, p. 48.

10. Pawel, *The Labyrinth of Exile*, p. 23.

11. Ibid., pp. 387–388.

12. Ibid., p. 385.

13. Ibid., p. 382.

14. Irving Howe, *World of Our Fathers*, p. 490.

Chapter Twelve

1. David Bar-Illan, *Eye on the Media*, p. IX.

2. Ibid., p. 78.

3. Ibid., p. x.
4. Ibid., p. 172.
5. Ibid., p. 16.
6. Ibid., p. 372.
7. Ibid., p. 4.
8. Ibid., p. 345.
9. Ibid., p. 312.
10. Ibid., p. 336.
11. Ibid., p. 277.
12. Ibid., p. 21.
13. Ibid., p. 45.
14. Ibid., p. 299.
15. Ibid., p. 250.
16. Ibid., p. 54.
17. Ibid., p. 197.
18. Ibid., p. 56.
19. Ibid., pp. 61–62.
20. Ibid., pp. 239–240.
21. Ibid., p. 141.
22. Ibid., pp. 141–142.
23. Ibid., p. 207.
24. Ibid., p. 167.
25. Segev, *1949*, p. 51.
26. Ibid., p. 49.
27. Ibid., p. 50.

Chapter Thirteen

1. Golan, *With Friends Like You*, pp. 6, 7, 12, 13.
2. Ibid., p. 13.
3. Ibid., pp. 51–52.
4. Ibid., pp. 52–53.

Chapter Fourteen

1. *The Globe and Mail*, April 17, 1993.
2. Menachem Begin, *The Revolt*, p. 52.

Chapter Sixteen

1. Segev, *1949*, p. 298.
2. *The Jerusalem Post*, July 3, 1992.

Chapter Seventeen

1. *The Jerusalem Post*, June 13, 1992.

Chapter Eighteen

1. O'Brien, *The Siege*, p. 226.
2. Ibid., p. 227.
3. Goldberg and King, *Builders and Dreamers*, pp. 42, 43.
4. Ibid., pp. 129-130.
5. Ibid., p. 130.

Chapter Nineteen

1. Goldberg and King, *Builders and Dreamers*, p. 185.
2. Ibid., p. 196.
3. Ibid., p. 219.
4. Ibid., p. 203.
5. Irving Abella and Harold Troper, *None is Too Many: Canada and the Jews of Europe, 1933-1948*, p. 9.
6. O'Brien, *The Siege*, p. 266.
7. Silver, *Begin*, p. 61.
8. Gilbert, *Jerusalem*, p. 49.
9. Pawel, *The Labyrinth of Exile*, pp. 40–41.
10. Johnson, *A History of the Jews*, p. 364.
11. Norman Rose, *Chaim Weizmann: A Biography*, p.254.
12. Ibid., p. 276.
13. Ibid., p. 149.
14. Silver, *Begin*, p. 166.

Chapter Twenty

1. *The Jerusalem Post*, October 18, 1992.
2. *The New York Review of Books*, May 14, 1992.
3. Ibid.
4. Arthur Koestler, *Thieves in the Night*, pp. 307–308.

5. Silver, *Begin*, p. 10.
6. Ibid., p. 20.
7. Binyamin Richler, *Hebrew Manuscripts: A Treasured Legacy*, p. 21.
8. Ibid., p. 24.
9. Ibid., p. 87.

Chapter Twenty-One

1. Rabbi Yudel Rosenberg, *The Golem of Prague and Other Tales of Wonder*, trans. Sonny Iddelson, Mosad Bialik, 1991.

Chapter Twenty-Two

1. *The New York Times Magazine*, March 15, 1992.
2. Ibid.
3. Robert I. Friedman, *Zealots for Zion: Inside Israel's West Bank Settlement Movement*, p. 7.
4. Ibid., p. 10.
5. Ibid., p. 40.
6. Amos Elon, *Jerusalem, City of Mirrors*, pp. 99–100.
7. Ibid., p. 102.

Chapter Twenty-Three

1. Howe, *World of Our Fathers*, p. 33.
2. Johnson, *A History of the Jews*, pp. 3–4.
3. *The Jerusalem Post*, August 3, 1992.
4. Ibid., August 7, 1992.
5. Ibid.
6. Ibid., August 26, 1992.

Chapter Twenty-Four

1. Koestler, *Thieves in the Night*, p. 75.
2. Ibid.
3. Ibid., p. 76.
4. Ibid.
5. Ibid., p. 153.
6. Ibid., p. 32.
7. Ibid., p. 40.

8. *The Jerusalem Report*, January 30, 1992.
9. Ibid., October 8, 1992.
10. Ibid.

Chapter Twenty-Five

1. *The Jerusalem Report*, January 30, 1992.
2. Ibid.
3. Golan, *With Friends Like You*, p. 20.
4. Ibid., p. 37.
5. Ibid., p. 60.
6. *The New Republic*, May 17, 1993.
7. Ibid.
8. Ibid.
9. Golan, *With Friends Like You*, pp. 21–22.

Chapter Twenty-Six

1. *Tikkun*, July/August 1993.
2. Ibid.
3. Koestler, *Thieves in the Night*, p. 152.
4. Charles Silberman, *A Certain People: American Jews and Their Lives Today*, p. 24.
5. Ibid.
6. Ibid., p. 25.
7. Landau, *Piety and Power*, pp. 292, 293.

Afterword

1. *Commentary*, September 1993.
2. *The Jerusalem Post*, International Edition, September 25, 1993.
3. *The Jerusalem Post*, September 18, 1993.
4. Ibid., September 25, 1993.
5. *Time*, September 20, 1993.
6. Ruth R. Wisse, *If I Am Not for Myself —: The Liberal Betrayal of the Jews*, p. 172.

ACKNOWLEDGEMENTS

I wish to thank all those whose works are quoted in the text (with references provided in the Source Notes) and who have kindly granted permission to reproduce copyrighted extracts, including the following:

Excerpts from *Thieves in the Night* by Arthur Koestler reprinted by permission of Sterling Lord Literistic, Inc. Copyright ©1967 by Arthur Koestler.

Excerpts from *Piety and Power: The World of Jewish Fundamentalism* by David Landau reprinted by permission of Hill and Wang, a division of Farrar, Straus & Giroux, Inc. and Toby Eady Associates Ltd., England. Copyright ©1993 by David Landau.

Excerpts from *With Friends Like You: What Israelis Really Think about American Jews* abridged and adapted with the permission of The Free Press, an imprint of Simon & Schuster. Copyright ©1992 by Matti Golan.

I also wish to thank my cousin Sam Orbaum whom I drafted as my researcher in Jerusalem.

M.R.

A NOTE ON THE TYPE

The text of this book was set in a digitized version of Bembo,
a well-known Monotype face. Named for Pietro Bembo, the celebrated
Renaissance writer and humanist scholar who was made a cardinal
and served as secretary to Pope Leo X, the original cutting of
Bembo was made by Francesco Griffo of Bologna only a few
years after Columbus discovered America.

Sturdy, well-balanced, and finely proportioned, Bembo is a face
of rare beauty, extremely legible in all of its sizes.

Composed by Sharon Foster Design, Toronto, Canada

Printed and bound by The Haddon Craftsmen,
Scranton, Pennsylvania